P9-CJX-237

INTRODUCTION TO
COMPETENCE-BASED
SOCIAL WORK

Advisory Editor
Thomas M. Meenaghan, *New York University*

Related books of interest

Social Work and Social Development: Perspectives from India and the United States
Shweta Singh

Social Service Workplace Bullying: A Betrayal of Good Intentions
Kathryn Brohl

Navigating Human Service Organizations, Third Edition
Rich Furman and Margaret Gibelman

The Recovery Philosophy and Direct Social Work Practice
Joseph Walsh

Best Practices in Community Mental Health: A Pocket Guide
Vikki L. Vandiver

Child and Family Practice: A Relational Approach
Shelly Cohen Konrad

Social Work Practice with Families: A Resiliency-Based Approach, Second Edition
Mary Patricia Van Hook

Getting Your MSW: How to Survive and Thrive in a Social Work Program
Karen M. Sowers and Bruce A. Thyer

Social Work with HIV and AIDS: A Case-Based Guide
Diana Rowan and Contributors

Civic Youth Work: Cocreating Democratic Youth Spaces
Ross VeLure Roholt, Michael Baizerman, and R. W. Hildreth

Introduction to Competence-Based Social Work

The Profession of Caring, Knowing, and Serving

Michael E. Sherr
University of Tennessee Chattanooga

Johnny M. Jones
Baylor University

LYCEUM
BOOKS, INC.
Chicago, IL 60637

© 2014 by Lyceum Books, Inc.

Published by

LYCEUM BOOKS, INC.
5758 S. Blackstone Avenue
Chicago, Illinois 60637
773-643-1903 fax
773-643-1902 phone
lyceum@lyceumbooks.com
www.lyceumbooks.com

All rights reserved under International and Pan-American Copyright Conventions. No part of this publication may be reproduced, stored in a retrieval system, copied, or transmitted, in any form or by any means without written permission from the publisher.

6 5 4 3 2 1   14 15 16 17 18

Printed in the United States of America.

Library of Congress Cataloging-in-Publication Data

Sherr, Michael E.
    Introduction to competence-based social work : the profession of caring, knowing, and serving / Michael E. Sherr, University of Tennesee Chattanooga, Johnny M. Jones, Baylor University.
    pages cm
    Includes bibliographical references.
    ISBN 978-1-935871-39-2 (alk. paper)
    1. Social service—Practice. 2. Social workers. 3. Social case work. I. Jones, Johnny M. II. Title.
    HV10.5.S46   2014
    361.3—dc23

                                                                      2013038297

To Stacey, Stacy, Brandon, Noah, and Grace and to every prospective social work student.

Contents

CONTENTS

List of Case Vignettes

What Is Social Work and What Do Social Workers Do?

Introduction

Textbooks are written for specific audiences. This book introduces the social work profession to two different groups of people. First, students considering social work will find this text engaging as they learn about the exciting career options available. Social work is a dynamic, international profession that offers nearly unlimited opportunities to make a tangible difference in the lives of people all over the world. This book provides the foundation for students embarking on the profession. Second, students from other majors taking an introductory social work course as an elective will also find the book useful. Regardless of academic or future professional interests, it is quite possible that students will interact with social workers at some point in their lives. The book provides such students an overview of what they can expect from competently prepared social workers.

Understanding the flow of content in the book is central to getting the most out of the information. This chapter presents an overview of the central purposes of the book, introduces students to the case-based learning (CBL) method of instruction, lays out the organization of the chapters, and describes the contents included in the accompanying Web site made available with the text.

WHY THIS BOOK?

A career in social work offers a broad spectrum of possibilities. Working to improve the lives of children, adolescents, adults, and older adults is all possible with a social work degree. Serving in government, nonprofit, private, domestic, and international settings are all possible with a social work degree. Working directly with individuals and families, or in administration, or to influence policy, are all possible with a social work degree. If you're interested in making a positive contribution or difference in the world, becoming a social worker gives you the knowledge, values, and skills needed to be successful. Social work is one of the most rewarding and challenging professions; in social work our identity and purpose—*why we do*—always informs the methods of practice—*what we do*. If students finish the book feeling welcomed to the profession and encouraged by what lies ahead, it will have fulfilled its purpose.

The profession has evolved significantly in the past decade. One change in particular has sparked a paradigm shift in how educators prepare students to become social workers. Instead of calling attention to what students learn through their courses, social work education now emphasizes what students should be able to do upon graduation. This shift in focusing on what students should be able to do upon graduation is called competence-based education. From the initial pre-cognate courses to the last year of study, the social work curriculum focuses on preparing students for competent practice. A main purpose of the book is to provide students with a vision of what competently prepared social workers are capable of doing. By the end of the book, students will have a comprehensive grasp of the core competences and practice behaviors of professional social work. They also will have developed and will be able to demonstrate the foundation for their own competent practice.

The transition to competence-based social work changes what needs to be addressed in an introductory course. Introductory social work texts geared simply toward presenting students with a lot of content are no longer relevant for social work education. Our review of the current texts available to educators and students is what led us to write this book. We discovered that current intro books tend to be anthologies of general, summarized material. While they offer a lot of content, they do little to help students prepare for competence-based social work. The purpose of our book goes beyond transmitting a lot of material to students: the book provides students with a conceptual framework for thinking about competence-based social work, and helps them develop a foundation for their professional identities. The framework will help students organize the competences and subsequent practice behaviors of social work into two meaningful and overlapping categories—professional identity—*why we do*—and method of social work—*what we do*. The themes of most chapters and use of the CBL method throughout the text will help students begin to develop their professional identities as social workers.

CASE-BASED LEARNING

CBL serves as the instructional method for the text. CBL dates back to the early 1900s when the Harvard Law School began experimenting with cases. In a similar fashion, early social work education programs (predating the university-based programs at the turn of the twentieth century) used CBL (Cossom, 1991; Jones, 2003). Today, CBL is seen as a way to create a learner-centered educational environment. CBL incorporates a participatory and cooperative learning approach with the traditional, hybrid, or virtual classroom. Twenty-five case vignettes will help students take the content in the chapters and develop and demonstrate competence using the information. The case vignettes describe social workers in situations involving decisions, challenges, or issues where there is more than one right answer or direction. Students will use the information in the chapters and their analytic skills to address the cases and then discuss them with their peers and the instructor (Erskine, Leenders, & Mauffette-Leenders, 1998). The benefits of using CBL include significantly improving student retention, developing critical thinking skills, enhancing ability to make objective judgments, identifying relevant issues and multiple perspectives, and developing awareness for ethical issues in social work practice (Prince & Felder, 2007).

The objective of social work education is to equip students with the ability to use what they learn in their daily practice. Competent social workers are able to retrieve and apply their knowledge and values in a manner that is appropriate to diverse situations. CBL will help social work students apply their knowledge within diverse contexts that they will encounter in the future. Cognitive psychologists have identified the importance of integrating new knowledge into existing knowledge while creating frameworks to organize, retain, retrieve, and use information (Barrows, 1985). CBL draws on the existing knowledge and experiences of students while introducing new concepts, theories, and practices within a framework that can promote retention and retrieval (Jones, 2003).

This book uses CBL in a specific way to create an interactive introductory learning experience. Most of the information and knowledge specific to social work will be new to students taking their first social work course. Their existing knowledge will likely come from other courses, personal experiences with social workers, and perceptions developed and informed by peers, the media, and other sources. A central theme of all the case vignettes, therefore, is to expose students to social workers from diverse backgrounds. The cases describe social workers practicing at the micro, mezzo, and macro levels, in very different settings and locations. Stated differently, the case vignettes serve to present students with a window into all the career possibilities of social work. To emphasize this diversity, each case vignette is organized in the same way—

a section focusing on the background, preparation, and experience of the social worker; a section describing the context of practice; and a section presenting students with a practice situation.

Each chapter after this one ends with discussion questions. Most of the questions are on cases from the same chapter. A few chapters (chapters 6, 7, and 10), however, include questions that ask students to reengage cases from previous chapters, though emphasizing analysis and application of content from the new material. Additionally, a few chapters have cases at the end of chapters as part of the discussion questions.

The discussion questions use a framework of three different levels of questions designed to engage different case vignettes—factual, analysis, and action. *Factual* questions promote rote, recall, and comprehension: students will need to draw on specific content in the chapters to answer the questions. *Analysis* questions promote inductive and deductive thinking: students will need to break down and reorganize content, apply the content in different settings, and incorporate material from different sources beyond the text. *Action* questions promote synthesis and evaluation of material: students will need to develop pathways of action as if they were the social workers in each case. Analysis and action questions usually have no single correct answer.

OUTLINE OF THE BOOK

The chapters are organized into three parts. What follows are a few paragraphs describing the primary themes and a synopsis of the chapters within each part. This summary is intended as a guide for helping students understand how the chapters fit within each part and within the book as a whole.

Part I: What Is Social Work and What Do Social Workers Do?

The initial chapters set the context for developing a foundation for competent social work practice. A solid foundation begins with examining the key elements that define the professional endeavor of social work. Social work is a broad and dynamic field, making it difficult for scholars to agree on a single definition. Chapter 2 provides students with a summary of how social work has been defined in the past. We then give our own definition and use the remainder of the chapter to provide an in-depth explanation of each component of the definition.

Chapters 3 and 4 transition from defining social work to describing competent social work practice. Equipped with a comprehensive working description of social work, students are ready to think about what social workers are capable of doing. Chapter 3 gives students an overview of competence-based learning as opposed to content-based learning. We examine the political, evaluative, and scientific- and research-based influences that brought about competence-based learning for social work. We then introduce the *why we do, what we do* conceptual framework to help students grasp the competences of social work for practical learning and application. Social work is a profession where our professional identity (*why we do*) always informs the method of our practice (*what we do*). The first group of competences emphasizes professional identity, and the second group emphasizes the method of practice. The rest of chapter 3 provides an overview of the competences and subsequent practice behaviors that inform our professional identity. Chapter 4 provides an overview of the competences and subsequent practice behaviors that describe the primary method of social work.

Each chapter in part I includes three case vignettes, or a total of nine cases in part I. The case vignettes present students with examples of different core competences in action. The discussion questions at the end of the chapters give students an opportunity to reflect on how the competences are applied. The questions will also ask students to think about ways in which other competences and practice behaviors may be used by the nine different social workers described in the cases.

Part II: The Professional Identity of Social Workers

Part II is where an introduction to competence-based social work differs from a traditional introductory text in social work. Whereas introductory texts in the past presented students with a wide spectrum of information for rote and recall learning of material, the emphasis in this book shifts to helping students use the material to begin developing their professional identities. The eight chapters in part II provide in-depth content and multiple opportunities for application, analysis, and synthesis of the competences that contribute to the distinctive professional identities of social workers.

Chapters 5 and 6 work together to prepare students for the personal and professional reflection needed for social work. Chapter 5 calls students' attention to the importance of self-awareness. Students will explore how their personal experiences, motivations, and values may influence how they interpret what they learn. They will also examine how their personal experiences can influence how they eventually practice as social workers. A main theme of the chapter involves helping students understand the ongoing cycle of personal and professional assessment needed for competent social work. Chapter 6 familiarizes students with the four primary ways social workers develop their professional identities. The formal education, licensure and credentials, membership and participation in professional organizations, and practice wisdom are the key elements contributing to the professional identity of social workers. Three new case vignettes in chapter 5 and subsequent discussion questions assist students in personal self-reflection and assessment of their own professional aspirations.

The characteristics contributing to the identity and methods of social work emerge from the history of the profession. Chapter 7 examines the history of social work from the perspective of helping students connect what they are studying and doing with the significant developments of social welfare from the past. A primary emphasis focuses on preparing students to understand the external challenges and internal tensions unique to social work. Our purpose or mission (*why we do*) often places social work in difficult positions that sometimes lead to critiques of the profession. As they read and discuss the content from the chapter, students will learn to recognize, embrace, and learn from the challenges and tensions. On the one hand, the critiques and challenges represent opportunities to learn and adapt to current conditions. On the other hand, critiques and challenges give social workers opportunities to rearticulate who we are and what we do for ourselves and for the broader society.

Building on the material from chapter 7, chapter 8 explores the historical set of values and ethical principles unifying social work practice. The main themes of chapter 8 are viewing the values as universal principles that make social work such a dynamic international profession; continuing to reflect on the relationship between personal and professional values; learning and applying the Code of Ethics from the National Association of Social Workers (NASW) and, as applicable, the Code of Ethics from the Canadian Association of Social Workers, the British Association of Social Workers, the Japanese Association of Social Work, the International Federation of Social Workers, and Codes of Ethics promulgated by other distinguished associations of social work; and tolerating the complexity and ambiguity often inherent in ethical social work practice. A section describing a few models of ethical reasoning includes two case vignettes. The end of the chapter includes two additional cases for students to apply the models and continue reflecting on the intersection of their personal values and the professional values of social work.

The next three chapters delve deeper into important professional values of social work. Advancing human rights, advocating for social and economic justice, and appreciating diversity and differences in practice underlie the core of what social workers value and do. The values are so important to social work that students have to do more than learn what they mean: they have to develop and demonstrate competence incorporating these values in all they do as social workers. Along with the content of the chapters, six cases are included (three in chapter 9 and three in chapter 11) that emphasize advancing social justice and engaging diversity at the micro, mezzo, and macro levels of practice. The combination of serving people at different levels of practice, while advancing human rights and engaging diversity, means that competent social workers must appraise and integrate multiple sources of knowledge. Social workers draw on logic, scientific inquiry, creativity, and curiosity to make sound judgments in practice. They then have to discern how to convert those judgments into effective actions. Chapter 12 examines the significant role of critical thinking in social work. We introduce students to the steps of evidence-based practice (EBP), a primary method for using critical thinking skills to make informed practice decisions. Showing students how to critically appraise sources of information is also a primary emphasis of chapter 12.

Part III: Method of Practice and Where We Work

The last two chapters in the book prepare students for what is ahead if they choose social work as a career. Students in social work will likely take courses that focus on research in practice, human behavior theory and development, the role of policy in practice, the contexts of practice, and specific practices with different populations. Students also may take specific courses focusing on advancing human rights, on advocating for social justice, or on diversity in practice. These and other courses will continue to help students develop their professional identities—*why we do*—while emphasizing the methods of social work—*what we do*. Chapter 13 provides students with an initial look at the generalist practice method—the foundation of social work practice. We introduce students to the core operational practice behaviors of engagement, assessment, intervention, and evaluation. We emphasize application of the generalist method at the micro, mezzo, and macro levels of practice. The chapter begins with two cases and concludes with the last case in the book.

Chapter 14 encourages students to think about what they could be doing someday as competent social workers. We describe a framework of factors that will help students understand where social workers practice. Pursuing a career in social work is an exciting and rewarding endeavor. We believe it is important for students to kindle their passion to serve others as they engage in the rigorous coursework ahead of them. Our hope is that students will allow themselves to envision working with different populations, in various fields and settings, making a difference in the lives of the people they serve.

ADDITIONAL RESOURCES TO SUPPORT STUDENT LEARNING

Students often benefit from learning information through different methods. The Web site available with the text (http://Lyceumbooks .com/1392) provides two additional ways of engaging with the material. Students can review PowerPoint slides providing a summary of the key points from each chapter. They can also access a series of ten- to fifteen-minute mini-podcast lecture files. Students can listen to the files with their computers. They also can upload the files to their phones or other mobile electronic devices to listen to the material at their convenience. Students can use the slides and the mini-podcast lectures separately or together. We recommend that students use the resources to supplement and reinforce their learning. An effective strategy would be to read a chapter, then to listen to the mini-podcast lectures while looking at the slides. Students can then come to class prepared to learn and discuss the material with their peers and instructors.

REFERENCES

Barrows, H. (1985). *How to design a problem-based curriculum for the preclinical years.* New York: Springer.

Cossom, J. (1991). Teaching from cases: Education for critical thinking. *Journal of Teaching Social Work, 5*(1), 139–155.

Erskine, J. A., Leenders, M. R., & Mauffette-Leenders, L. A. (1998). *Teaching with cases.* Ontario, Canada: Ivey.

Jones, K. (2003). Making the case for the case method in graduate social work education. *Journal of Teaching Social Work, 23*(1/2), 183–197.

Prince, M., & Felder, R. (2007). The many faces of inductive teaching and learning. *Journal of College Science Teaching, 36,* 14–20.

CHAPTER TWO

What Is Social Work?

CASE VIGNETTE 2.1. IAN HAWTHORNE

Background

Ian Hawthorne's journey from an oil and gas engineer to a social worker was anything but typical. Four years ago, Ian designed equipment for oil rigs. Although he earned a good living, he traveled at least eight months a year and rarely saw his wife, Ilene, and their three children. On one of his few weekends at home, when he was thirty-one years old, Ian's family had dinner with Brian, his roommate and best friend from college. At dinner, Brian and Ian talked about their childhoods.

Ian's father had left him and his older brother when he was thirteen. They lived with their mother. After twelve years of staying home to care for the boys, their mother had to work to support the family. She found work as a shipping and receiving clerk at a food processing plant on the outskirts of Calgary. The transition was not easy for any of them, but they eventually adapted—at least they did until Ian turned sixteen. A month after his sixteenth birthday, Ian's mother died in a car accident just three blocks from their apartment building. At the time, his brother had already left home to work as a park ranger in Waterloo, Ontario, more than 2,200 miles away from Alberta. Ian was halfway through his senior year of high school. After several extended conversations with a guidance counselor at his school, the counselor helped him apply for and achieve emancipated minor status. At age sixteen, Ian finished high school and took care of himself. He then went on to college to earn his degree in engineering.

Ian never had told Brian about his childhood before. Now, as he shared his story, it left him thinking about the relationships he had with Ilene and the three kids. Later that evening, Ian and Ilene talked about wanting him to be home more often. Ian told Ilene how he always thought about working with at-risk teenagers. Engineering served its purpose. It allowed him to support himself and his family. He wondered if it would be possible to work with teenagers and make enough to support Ilene and the children. Ilene encouraged Ian to look into going back to school.

Ian looked for programs that would allow him to work with teenagers. He thought he might be interested in counseling teens, but was also interested in other ways to help them. He met with an admissions coordinator at the University of Calgary who recommended social work. Four years later, after completing his bachelor in social work (BSW) degree and the advanced-standing master in social work (MSW) degree program at the university, he accepted a position working with the mentorship program at Alberta Children and Youth Services, the same agency where he did his field internship.

The Context

Ian lived in the Canadian province of Alberta, located north of Montana, between the provinces of Saskatchewan and British Columbia. Alberta is a large mountainous region with a population of more than 3 million. Edmonton is the capital of Alberta, though Calgary is the largest city. Agriculture, forestry, telecommunications, and oil and gas are the primary industries. Alberta Province has the largest crude oil reserve in Canada; Canada's reserves rank second in the world behind Saudi Arabia's reserves.

Alberta Children and Youth Services is a large government-supported social service agency. The agency offers a range of services organized into fifteen categories, from children with disabilities and victims of family violence, to family and community support, to women's issues. Ian works with the youth program division of the agency as the mentorship coordinator. He serves as a liaison between the children and the Alberta Mentorship Partnership—a group of thirty different government agency and business representatives linking teenagers with positive adult role models. Ian spends his time at work engaging and assessing youth, developing a network of relationships with potential mentors, and following up with mentor relationships every three months. He also cofacilitates the monthly partnership meeting.

The Situation

While Ian was sitting at his desk reviewing one of the kids' files, he received a phone call from Mr. Dougherty, Logan's mentor. Logan and Mr. Dougherty meet for at least an hour every Friday afternoon. They had started meeting when Logan's caseworker referred him to the mentorship program two years ago, when he was twelve. Logan has received services from the agency since he was seven. Since Logan and Mr. Dougherty started meeting, they have developed a good relationship. Mr. Dougherty helps Logan with his homework. They also do fun activities together almost every month. When they first met, Logan acted withdrawn from the rest of the kids at school. He also had difficulty getting all his work done. Now Logan has a few friends and usually gets his homework done on time.

On the phone, Mr. Dougherty explained to Ian that he was planning to take Logan to see an Edmonton Oilers hockey game that weekend. When he had met with Logan the past Friday, however, his foster mother told him one of his teachers had called her to check on Logan after he missed two days of school. Logan attends school regularly. The only time he is absent is when he is home sick. He was not sick last week and had no reason to miss school. Mr. Dougherty did not know if he should take Logan to the game. More important, he was concerned about Logan and not sure what to do. This type of situation had never happened before with Logan and he did not want to overstep his boundaries as his mentor. He had called Ian on Monday morning to ask for help. Ian replied that he would look into it and call him back by Wednesday afternoon. After Ian put down the phone, he stared at his computer screen thinking about Logan. He then opened Logan's file to document the phone conversation. Now he had to decide what to write and what to do next.

CASE VIGNETTE 2.2. SARAH ORMSBY

Background

Arriving at college in Tennessee, Sarah was going to pursue a degree in finance. She changed her major to social work after taking an economics and poverty course her sophomore year. There were seventy students in the class from different majors. Most of the students were planning to major in business, public affairs, anthropology, and social work. The course is a pre-cognate for students intending to pursue their BSW. One of the assignments for the course involved a group project. The instructor randomly assigned students to groups of seven. There were two students intending to major in social work in the group with Sarah. After hearing the two students talk about other classes and where they wanted to do their field internships, she began thinking about changing her major.

Although she wasn't exactly sure what she wanted to do when she graduated, she realized she wanted to do something to help people.

Sarah excelled in her social work courses. The combination of theory and practice courses helped her connect what she was learning to real-life application. Two courses in particular influenced what she wanted to do upon graduation: The spring semester of her junior year, Sarah enrolled in a macro practice course focused on administration, communities, and organizations. She also took an elective focused on international social work. Sarah knew she wanted to do macro practice as a social worker in another country. Sarah shared her desire to do international social work with her field director, who then placed Sarah in an agency in Nashville that provided services for Kurdish refugees. Six weeks after graduation, she traveled to Tamil Nadu, India, to begin working as a social service director for a children's home located in the Tirunelveli district.

The Context

Tamil Nadu is a fairly large state located at the southernmost point of India. It is the most urbanized and developed state in India, home to a majority of the country's businesses; it employs the highest percentage of the population throughout the country. In addition to the urban metropolitan regions, several regions of Tamil Nadu are filled with hills and abundant vegetation, producing onions, tomatoes, tapioca, bananas, and mangos. Tamil Nadu also has a long tradition of a rich culture. Literature, music, and dancing created and practiced in the region influence the culture of the whole country. The state consists of thirty-two districts that include ten large municipalities.

The Tirunelveli district is a unique area in Tamil Nadu. It is the only district in the state that has five different typologies—mountains, forests, paddy fields, coastlines, and desert. The city of Tirunelveli, one of the ten large municipalities, is located in the district. Two-thirds of the people living in the district are well educated and have gainful employment. In fact, Tirunelveli is known throughout the country as the Oxford of South India, as it is home to twenty-two colleges and universities. Unfortunately, not everyone gets to participate in the district's apparent prosperity. One-third of the population lives in poverty. Of those living in poverty, most are Dalits, a group known as the "untouchables" that falls below the strict caste system in India. Understanding and respecting the societal order of the Indian caste system is part of life in the district.

The children's home where Sarah works provides a stable and thriving environment for children in the district, most of them Dalits. Judges place children in the home after they have been abandoned by their families and are found by the police. Shortly after they arrive, staff members complete a thorough assessment of the children and assign them to live in family groups. Staff members create and assign these family groups based on the sex, age, and interests of the children. At least two adult volunteers or interns live with and help raise the children in each family group. As social service director, Sarah works with staff members, volunteers, and interns, and arranges for the children to attend school and participate in religious, sporting, and cultural activities. On Thursday mornings at 8:30, Sarah also participates in a weekly leadership meeting with the administrator, the director of development, and the volunteer coordinator.

The Situation

Sarah spent the first few months meeting with people working, volunteering, and affiliating with the children's home. Her plan was to learn about the home and the services from multiple perspectives. Part of her assessment included examining monthly financial statements so she could compare actual expenditures with the annual budget. After reviewing several statements, Sarah noticed what she thought was a disturbing pattern in the financials. It seemed to her that a significant disparity existed between the amount allocated for services, the amount recorded in the financial statements, and the actual amount spent on services as indicated by the receipts.

The actual expenditures for services totaled less than 30 percent of the amount recorded in the statements.

Sarah shared her concerns about the budget at the leadership meeting. She explained how she noticed a significant discrepancy between actual purchases for services and the amount reflected in the financial statements. After hearing her concerns, the administrator asked Sarah for her records so he could check her findings. Later that afternoon, the administrator emailed Sarah asking her to stop by his office before leaving that evening. When she met with the administrator, he closed the door, sat down at his desk, dropped his head in his hands, and sighed. A moment later, the administrator looked up and thanked Sarah for discovering the discrepancy in the budget. Then he asked her to figure out where the missing funds for services were going and propose a strategy at the next leadership meeting for making sure the allocated resources were being used appropriately. He also asked her not to share what she was doing with anyone else at the home until after they had agreed on a plan of action. Sarah left his office wondering where to begin.

CASE VIGNETTE 2.3. DUSTIN JORDAN

Background

Coming from a family where his father, grandfather, and great grandfather were decorated Army veterans, Dustin always expected that his life would involve the military. From fourth grade to high school, his family moved three times and he attended five different schools. His family spent years stationed in Germany, South Korea, and Hawaii. During his junior year, his family made one final move to Fort Sill, Oklahoma, where his father retired from the Army as an artillery instructor. After high school, Dustin enlisted in the Army and spent four years on active duty as an M1A2 Abrams tank operator. As he approached the end of his enlistment, Dustin decided he did not want to pursue a lifelong career in the military. After he finished his enlistment in the Army, he moved home with his parents and returned to college to study social work.

Dustin returned to school with the help of the GI Bill. He took advantage of the five-year program offered at his university in social work. If he completed his courses with at least a 3.0 grade point average and received positive feedback on his field internship evaluation, Dustin could continue into the MSW program as an advanced-standing student. The advanced-standing program allows students graduating with a BSW to enter directly into the second year of graduate school (often called the advanced or concentration year) and complete their MSW in an additional twelve months. Two weeks after graduating in May with his BSW, Dustin started the summer courses offered to advanced-standing students to prepare them for graduate school. The following May he earned his MSW with a health and mental health concentration. After graduation, Dustin was hired as a social worker in the homeless program at the Veterans Affairs (VA) Medical Center in Oklahoma City.

The Context

The VA Center is a large facility offering a multitude of services to former members of the military and their families. The center is organized into several divisions, including women's health, diabetes, food and nutrition, research, family services, and mental health and psychological services. The main campus also houses a large teaching hospital. Nine smaller clinics located throughout the state are also affiliated with the VA Center. The homeless program is administered under the mental health and psychological services division. In addition to the homeless program, the division offers a day treatment center, intensive case management, a program for veterans with posttraumatic stress disorder, a community residential care program, and a psychiatric inpatient unit.

The homeless program is staffed by a multidisciplinary team of six members. The team includes a psychiatrist, a psychologist, a nurse, a vocational rehabilitation counselor, a substance abuse counselor, and a social worker. As the social worker, Dustin spends most of his time out in the community trying to help veterans in three ways. First, he travels around Oklahoma City looking to engage and develop rapport with veterans who are homeless. He visits homeless shelters, food banks, social service agencies, public libraries, parks, and anywhere else he thinks he may find people needing assistance. Next, he assesses the veterans' needs, develops an intervention plan with them, and connects them to services they are eligible to receive. Finally, once he develops a plan, he continues meeting with veterans, providing transportation when needed, and following up to evaluate progress toward individualized goals. In some instances, Dustin meets veterans who do not want anything to do with him or the VA. He also encounters veterans who want and need services from the VA but are ineligible because they received a dishonorable discharge from the military. On other occasions, he develops working relationships with veterans that can last several weeks or, depending on the circumstances, up to a few years.

The Situation

As he does every Monday morning, Dustin arrived at the VA Center at 7:00, signed out a vehicle, and headed to the City Rescue Mission. The mission is a faith-based, private, nonprofit organization that provides room and board for more than four hundred men, women, and children, in hopes of helping them find a stable living environment. At the mission, Dustin met with the director to see if any of the new residents were veterans that wanted and were eligible to receive assistance from the VA. The director picked up the roster, flipped through a few pages, and pointed at a name. He looked up at Dustin and said, "Here is someone new who came to us Friday afternoon. His name is Terry Esherhut. He apparently served twelve years in the Air Force—at least that is what he told Steven, our weekend admissions volunteer." He continued, "We don't know anything else about him at this point. He is in room 47, the last room downstairs on the left. I will take you to see him before he leaves for the day."

When they got to room 47, the director introduced Terry to Dustin and left them to talk alone. Terry was packing a backpack with his belongings because he had to be out of the mission by 8:30. He would be able to return to the mission at 5:30 in the afternoon. Dustin shared with Terry that he worked with the VA and was interested in learning more about him. Terry responded that he was about to eat breakfast at the cafeteria. He invited Dustin to sit and eat with him.

After they sat down with their food, Terry told Dustin he had loved being in the Air Force. During his enlistment, he served as an aircrew flight equipment specialist. In just twelve years, he had earned the rank of tech sergeant. His relationship with Jan, his ex-wife, however, was difficult. A few months before he was about to reenlist, Jan wanted to get divorced. She was tired of him being gone all the time and wanted him home more if they were going to start a family. Terry decided not to reenlist so he could save his marriage. They moved in with Jan's parents after he left the Air Force and he looked for work. After eight weeks, he still had not found a job. He and Jan continued to struggle, getting into increasingly heated arguments. He explained to Dustin that living with her parents didn't make it any easier. They had very little room and no privacy. As the situation continued, Terry tried to find reasons not to stay at the house. He started drinking and eventually met a woman who introduced him to cocaine. At that point, Terry shared, things spiraled downward fast. He had left town six years ago and has been on his own and homeless ever since. When he finished talking, Dustin asked him if he was comfortable signing a release of information. Dustin explained that he needed to verify his discharge status and years of service. Once verified, Dustin told Terry that he might be eligible for support from the VA. Terry signed the form and left to see if he could find temporary labor work for the day. Dustin made plans to come back to the mission the following morning to see him again at the same time.

Dustin went back to his office and verified Terry's discharge status and years of service. The following morning he returned to the mission to have breakfast again with Terry. At breakfast, he asked him if he wanted help putting his life back together. Terry looked Dustin in the eyes, choked up as if he were about to cry, paused, and said, "Man, I sure do, but I don't even know where to begin." Dustin responded, "You already began the process by agreeing to meet with me. Now we work together to assess your needs and develop a plan." Dustin took out a few forms from his folder, ready to begin.

THE BLIND AND THE CAROUSEL

A group of blind men and women went to an amusement park where they encountered a big beautiful carousel. An employee of the amusement park asked the people to examine and describe what was before them. After exploring on their own, the group came together to share what they examined. Everyone described what they experienced in great detail. Some shared how they had touched something shaped like horses. Others described feeling a bunch of smooth poles. Some had stumbled on places to sit. Others had found the fence on the outside of the carousel. A few had found the swinging gates where people entered and exited the ride. Still others had decided to kneel down and so felt the brick walkway. They described feeling bricks that were engraved with different emblems symbolic of the theme of the park. All of them heard loud jovial music. In all of their descriptions, however, none of them could agree on what they were all examining. None of them could describe the carousel as a whole. In the same way, this metaphor aptly portrays attempts to define social work as a whole.

Ask a group of social workers or social work scholars to define social work as a whole and they are likely to respond with different answers. The case vignettes of Ian Hawthorne, Sarah Ormsby, and Dustin Jordan portrayed practitioners working with different populations in different settings. The other case vignettes throughout the book present other people practicing in a variety of ways. Still, amidst the diversity, all of the cases describe social workers engaged in competent practice. But what exactly is social work? What unifies professionals working all over the world doing very different things?

This chapter briefly examines how scholars and practitioners have worked to define social work up to this point. Reviewing previous efforts will help students appreciate the amount of energy that has gone into describing social work as a whole, and will help them grasp the continued ambiguity inherent in the profession. It will also provide the context for the working definition we set forth that is helpful for becoming competent social workers. A central thesis for the chapter is that the purposes of the profession, inherent in our definition, makes it possible to describe social work as a whole, while accounting for the variety of roles, settings, and populations in practice.

EFFORTS TO DEFINE SOCIAL WORK

There have been several deliberate efforts to bring social work practitioners and scholars together to define social work as a whole over the last century. The majority of the work ended in similar ways: The groups identified lists of practice settings and areas of knowledge, values, and skills needed of social workers. They determined they could not agree on a concise definition. Then they reconfirmed their commitment to continue working toward articulating a definition in the future.

The Milford Conference

The first effort occurred at the Milford Conference in 1929 when groups of agency leaders and scholars gathered for a series of meetings to define social work. The conference ended with a ninety-two-page report describing the details of social work (NASW, 1974). The report acknowledged there seemed to be commonalities among social workers practicing in different settings. The report confirmed the importance of trying to articulate these common areas, rather than creating definitions of the work performed in specific fields of practice. Eight areas of commonalities were listed:

1. Knowledge of typical deviations from accepted standards of social life;
2. The use of norms of human life and human relationships;
3. The significance of social history as the basis of particularizing the human being in need;
4. Established methods of study and treatment of human beings in need;
5. The use of established community resources in social treatment;
6. The adaptation of scientific knowledge and formulations of experience to the requirements of social work;
7. The consciousness of a philosophy which determines the purposes, ethics, and obligations of social work; and
8. The blending of the foregoing into social treatment. (p. 15)

The report listed commonalities, and also emphasized characteristics that distinguished social work from other professions. A distinguishing focus of social work was to deal with human beings' capacity for independent social functioning. The group writing the report posited that the greatest contribution social work could make to society was to work with people so they could eventually develop the capacity to care for themselves without continued assistance. A related distinguishing feature was that social work was a profession where the effectiveness of the work was often difficult to measure objectively. The report listed a number of methods and potential areas of knowledge used within the context of relationships between social workers and clients. There was agreement that improved confidence, a sense of mastery to cope with life, and holistic improvement in social functioning were intangible outcomes for clients that were unique to social work. The report ended, as did the conference, with the stipulation that a concise definition of social work was not possible at that point. The hope of those participating was that future efforts could make progress toward a definition.

The Hollis-Taylor Report

More than twenty years after the Milford Conference, another group of social workers was brought together to articulate what social work was and what it was not. By the 1950s, internal and external influences made it necessary to revisit defining social work. Internally, developing a definition became an issue of professional status and identity. Practitioners wanted to be able to describe what they do as social work. They also were concerned with preserving roles in social service agencies that could only be executed by trained social workers. Externally, there was the issue of public sanction and assurance. Without being able to define social work, there was no way to describe what professional social work involved. There was no way to assure the public of the quality and professionalism of receiving services from those calling themselves social workers. What resulted was an even longer document of 422 pages, *Social Work Education in the United States*, commonly known in social work as the 1951 Hollis-Taylor Report.

The Hollis-Taylor report (Hollis & Taylor, 1951) contributed toward a definition of social work in three ways. First, the report identified the levels of social work practice. Individuals, families, small groups, organizations, and communities were all potential recipients of social work services. Second, the report identified the target of social work practice. Whereas physicians, psychologists, and counselors provided care to individuals, and sociologists, economists, and political scientists focused on the functioning of large groups, social workers emphasized the interactions between individuals and groups they belonged to, from families and small groups, to schools, social institutions, and entire communities. Third, the report introduced the concept of well-being as the purpose of social work practice. Social workers trained with the knowledge, values, and skills needed for competent practice sought to promote and maintain the well-being of individuals and their communities.

The one element missing from the report was a concise definition of social work as a whole. An elaboration of what was meant by promoting and maintaining well-being was also needed, especially if the concept was going to serve as the unifying purpose of the profession. Seven years later, a committee sponsored by NASW built on the work of the Hollis-Taylor report (Hollis & Taylor, 1951) to provide the first of a series of working definitions of social work that would appear over the next half century.

The Working Definition

Developing a concise definition of social work was one of the first tasks of NASW. In 1955, NASW emerged as the unifying professional organization for social work practitioners. The membership formed after the leaders of seven separate organizations agreed to join together as one association. The seven organizations included the American Association of Social Work, the American Association of Medical Social Workers, the American Association of Psychiatric Social Work, the Association for the Study of Community Organization, the National Association of School Social Workers, the Association of Group Workers, and the Social Work Research Group. For NASW, at the time a nascent organization, taking up the necessary challenge of developing a concise definition served to build cohesion for the members of the seven subsumed organizations, each with its own history and perception for describing social work. The committee working on the definition, therefore, consisted of representative leaders from the seven groups. Their efforts resulted in the briefest statement of social work up to that point.

Compared to the previous reports, the document produced by NASW was indeed concise. The chairperson leading the committee developed a six-page article that included the committee's attempt at disseminating a definition of social work (Bartlett, 1958). Other than the brevity of the document, however, the content of the work was quite similar to the previous reports. Commonly known as the Working Definition of Social Work Practice, the document begins by essentially describing social work as beyond a concise definition: "Social Work practice, like the practice of all professions, is recognized by a constellation of value, purpose, sanction, knowledge, and method. No part alone is characteristic of social work practice nor is any part described here unique to social work. It is the particular content and configuration of this constellation which makes it social work practice and distinguishes it from the practice of other professions" (p. 6).

The rest of the definition listed statements describing the characteristics of each constellation designed to clarify the essence of the profession. For example, values included six statements intended to describe the philosophical foundation of social work. Nine statements spelled out the eclectic knowledge base that informed social work practice. The descriptions for the purpose, sanction, and method constellations were also similar to the previous reports. The one description missing from the article was a concise definition of social work as a whole.

Reactions and Revisions to the Working Definition of 1958

Shortly after dissemination of the Working Definition, two social work scholars suggested actual definitions. Boehm (1958, 1959) conducted a comprehensive study of social work that empirically supported the Working Definition's goals and values of social work. His study added to the definition by describing the various levels of social work as involving practice with individuals, groups, and communities. Boehm also asserted that social work involved five specializations:

casework, group work, community organization, policy, and research. Perhaps most significant, his research led him to posit enhancement of social functioning as the potential outcome of social work. He categorized enhancement of social functioning to include restoration of impaired capacity, provision of resources, and prevention of social dysfunction. Boehm then suggested a synthesis of his statements could serve as a concise definition of social work as a whole. He stated, "Social work seeks to enhance the social functioning of individuals, singly and in groups, by activities focused upon their social relationships which constitute the interaction between man and his environment. These activities can be grouped into three functions: restoration of impaired capacity, provision of individual and social resources, and prevention of social dysfunction" (1958, p. 18).

Three years later, Gordon (1962) critiqued the Working Definition and suggested a concise description of social work. Although the Working Definition helped characterize social work practice, Gordon believed it did not define what social work was as a whole. He also pointed out that while the characteristics of the components were adequately described, there was no effort to explain how the components held together. As presented, he asserted that the different components appeared to exist separate and equal to each other, making it nearly impossible to examine social work as a whole any further. He attempted to resolve the limitations by suggesting a definition that pulled together the separate components. Notice how he listed each one in his definition. He stated, "Social work practice is interventive action directed to purposes and guided by the values, knowledge, and techniques which are collectively unique, acknowledged by and identified with the social work profession" (p. 11). He then tried to explain the implications of his definition for social work practice. Though rather confusing, we share his statement here so readers can appreciate the depth of his work and his implicit call to refine his work further:

> The definitive element of social work practice remains in the combination or constellation of those elements which control the interventive action. When the profession can make explicit its shared values and specific purposes and its knowledge and techniques, it has defined its practice. Action not controlled by the definitive constellation of value, knowledge, purpose, and techniques of a profession may be interventive but is not professional practice. This clearly removes the definitive element from action or activities, an eminently desirable outcome, since any attempt to define professional practice by characteristics of action alone has been singularly unfruitful. It also makes more urgent the question of what combination of value, knowledge, techniques, and purposes the profession acknowledges and causes to be identified with it. (p. 11)

It is clear that Gordon thought additional work was needed to describe the combination of purpose and method unique to social work.

Additional Efforts from 1970 to the Present

Scholars and practitioners heeded the need for additional work. Beginning in 1970, a few concerted efforts eventually led to tentative agreement on *definitions* of social work. Notice the use of the plural "definitions" in the last sentence, meaning that a unified definition still does not exist, though the elements mentioned in the various definitions seem to overlap.

Bartlett (1970) again provided a starting place for the modern working definitions of social work. After the many critiques on the Working Definition of 1958, Bartlett could have become defensive and ignored the feedback. Thankfully, she did the opposite. She integrated the work of others into her final writing on the subject, perhaps her greatest contribution to the profession, *The Common Base of Social Work Practice*. In this book, she operationalized social work as involving three main components: direct and indirect practice, emphasis on enhancing and restoring social functioning, and the use of professional interventions. She also identified the domain of social work as the interactions between person and environment, thus beginning the person-in-environment model as the foundation of social work. For social workers, Bartlett explained, "people and environment are encompassed in a single concept, which requires that they be constantly viewed together" (p. 116).

A few years later, NASW called another meeting to again search for a common definition. The 1976 Madison meeting sought to examine if a common conceptual framework could be articulated for the profession. However, other than continuing the definitional debate, very little of their work advanced beyond the themes espoused by past efforts. Instead, the scholars at the meeting produced a report reiterating the complexities of the activities of social work, the primacy of the person-in-environment model, the enhancement and restoration of social functioning at the outcome, and the use of professional interventions with individuals, groups, and communities (NASW, 1977).

In 1982, the search for a unified definition for the profession continued internationally. Members of the International Federation of Social Workers (IFSW) met in Brighton, England, to develop a definition that could encapsulate the nature of the profession as it existed in different countries. The meeting ended with a definition approved by the membership representing forty-four countries. A revised version of that definition now serves as the international definition of social work adopted by the IFSW and endorsed by NASW. The definition states, "The social work profession promotes social change, problem solving in human relationships and the empowerment and liberation of people to enhance well-being. Utilising theories of human behaviour and social systems, social work intervenes at the points where people interact with their environments. Principles of human rights and social justice are fundamental to social work" (IFSW, 2000).

The same page of the definition on the IFSW Web site ends with the following sentence: "It is understood that social work in the 21st century is dynamic and evolving, and therefore no definition should be regarded as exhaustive" (IFSW, 2000). The sentence suggests the continuing need to revisit and refine what is meant by social work.

As we discussed in chapter 1, the profession has evolved significantly in the past decade, further reinforcing the continuing need to revisit and refine what is meant by social work. Two overlapping shifts, in particular, make revisiting our definition and purpose especially important. The importance of outcomes in social work practice represents a significant shift in the profession. Although social workers have always valued the incorporation of systematic research to evaluate the efficacy of their practice, they also acknowledge that searching, developing, and using the best available evidence to guide practice are now central components of the profession. Just ten years ago, it was rare to hear students, social workers, and social work educators even mentioning evidence-based practice (EBP) or evidence-informed practice (EIP). Now, in almost every field of practice and every setting, social workers use, debate, and/or discuss the role of evidence. We want to know if what we are doing produces valued outcomes. We also want to demonstrate that the practices used are grounded and supported by the best available knowledge and skills.

A corollary to this renewed emphasis on outcomes is the historic paradigm shift in how educators develop the curriculum to prepare students to become social workers. The development and implementation of the 2008 Educational Policy and Accreditation Standards (EPAS; Council on Social Work Education [CSWE], 2008) changed the foundation of social work education from objectives and intentions to competences and outcomes. Stated differently, in concrete language, social work educators no longer design the curriculum asking, "What do students need to know and learn to become social workers?" Instead they ask, "What should students be capable of doing upon graduation with a degree in social work?" The definition and purpose of social work, therefore, needs to be considered in light of these influential changes to the profession.

A DEFINITION OF SOCIAL WORK FOR THE FUTURE

We submit that a definition of social work needs to combine the essential attributes articulated from the past with an appreciation for current trends that we think will remain permanent in the future. Central elements that need to be incorporated from the past include

- multiple levels of practice often described as practice with individuals, groups, and communities (also referred to as micro, mezzo, and macro levels of practice);
- person-in-environment interactions as the target of practice; and
- the enhancement and restoration of social functioning or well-being as the intended outcome of practice.

In addition to the elements that remain relevant from the past, the definition needs to

- account for the renewed emphasis on the use and development of best available evidence; and
- communicate the fundamental principles that underscore the professional identity and purpose of competent social work practice.

Considering the five elements, we posit the following definition of social work:

Social work is the profession of caring and intervening in the interactions between individuals, groups, and communities to enhance or restore well-being, and to create societal conditions that help individuals, groups, and communities enhance their own well-being. Social workers select, use, and develop interventions based on the best available evidence.

As with any effort to define social work, we agree with the sentiment of the IFSW. Social work is and will remain a dynamic profession that precludes arriving at a single universal definition. We encourage students, practitioners, and educators to continue contemplating, now and in the future, what is meant by social work. For now, however, let us briefly examine the components of the definition we use for the text.

A Profession of Caring

Our inclusion of *caring* in the definition helps describe the unique professional identity of social workers. When we use the verb "to care," we mean to be affected by and to have concern for another person. Social work practice occurs through helping relationships. Social workers use a combination of knowledge, values, and skills in the form of interventions within the context of helping relationships. The reason social workers enter into helping relationships is because of their concern for improving the lives of individuals, groups, and communities. Caring implies that social work is more than a scientific field of study or an objective method of practice. Social work is rooted in the values of service, social justice, dignity and worth of the person, the importance of human relationships, integrity, and competence. Those values mean that social workers do not remain aloof or indifferent when practicing; rather, we are invested in and affected by the people we engage. Stated differently, the purpose of social work—*why we do*—always supersedes the methods of social work—*what we do*. Competent social work practice then involves the combination of knowledge, values, and skills used by persons with the professional identity and judgment akin to the purposes of social work.

Intervening with Individuals, Groups, and Communities

A characteristic that distinguishes social work from other helping professions is the preparation and expertise to intervene at the micro, mezzo, and macro levels of practice. Micro practice usually involves interventions directed toward individuals on a case-by-case basis. Mezzo practice involves interventions with families and small groups. Macro practice involves interventions aimed at larger communities and organizations to create conditions where individuals and groups can enhance their own well-being (Barker, 2003).

Whereas other helping professions emphasize one primary level of intervention, social workers consider the most appropriate levels of intervention given the unique circumstances presented to them in practice. Social work students complete courses that train them to practice effectively with individuals, groups, families, communities, and organizations. Students learn to view their knowledge, values, and skills as being transferable to each level of practice. A part of the professional identity of social workers is that we learn to assess our work with individuals in the context of the families, small groups, and the communities in which they belong. In the same way, when practice involves working primarily with communities and organizations, social workers consider the implications of interventions for individuals and small groups. Likewise, social workers attend to the individual needs of each member of families and small groups as well as community and organizational influences.

Using and Developing Interventions Based on the Best Available Evidence

When social workers engage in helping relationships, they do so with the capacity to synthesize multiple sources of knowledge with professional values and specific interpersonal practice skills. The complex issues and diverse settings that social workers encounter require knowledge from several fields in addition to social work, such as psychology, sociology, economics, anthropology, political science, and biology. Social workers use this broad range of knowledge to inform their practice. A distinctive part of becoming competent social workers is learning to assess and select the best available evidence to guide interventions. Selecting the best available evidence involves using the best available scientific knowledge as one basis for guiding professional interventions, combined with professional ethical standards, clinical judgment, and practice wisdom (Barker, 2003). When adequate information is not available for particular situations, competent social workers are able to conduct the necessary research to assess the effectiveness of newer strategies and communicate those findings to helping professionals.

To Enhance or Restore Well-Being

The purpose of social work practice has been described using two concepts: to enhance or restore social functioning, and to enhance or restore well-being. While at first glance the phrases seem interchangeable, examining the concepts further reveals significant differences in how social workers think about and communicate their purpose. Enhancing or restoring social functioning implies that the intended outcome of social work practice can be reduced to helping people improve their interactions with other individuals, groups, and communities. There are at least two advantages to thinking about the purpose of social work in this way. First, social functioning connotes a purpose that is measurable. The effectiveness of whatever interventions social workers use can be easily examined using behavioral indicators of social functioning. For instance, social workers providing family counseling can evaluate the effectiveness of interventions by recording the number of times the family eats together, the number of times the family sits together to have a fifteen-minute conversation, or the number of times the parents report that their children followed through on assigned chores. In the same way, school social workers can assess the effectiveness of their interventions by counting the number of days students attend school, the number of days teachers report that students completed their homework, and students' overall academic performance.

Second, a corollary advantage to social functioning is that the phrase connotes an objective separation between social workers as professionals and clients as the targets of practice. A consistent challenge and theme influencing the development of social work has been a historic insecurity about being considered a profession. At the 1915 convention of the National Conference of Charities and Corrections (NCCC)—a precursor to NASW—Dr. Abraham Flexner, an accepted authority on the study of professions, was invited by the organizers of the conference to present an analysis of whether social work was a profession. Flexner described social workers as intelligent, kindhearted, and resourceful people who performed an important mediating function. Nevertheless, he concluded that social work was not a profession (Flexner, 1915). What happened thereafter was an all-out attempt to demonstrate to colleagues, clients, society, and most important to ourselves that social work was and is a profession. Framing social functioning as the purpose of social work helped align the field with the scientific method of knowing and learning and with fields that already had gained professional status, such as psychiatry, psychology, and other areas of behavior and physical medicine. Almost a century after Flexner's speech, with the professional status of social work secure, we agree with the IFSW (2000) definition that describes the purpose of social work as enhancing well-being.

Enhancing and restoring well-being is a concept involving total human thriving or flourishing in multiple areas of life. The physical, emotional, intellectual, social, environmental, and spiritual parts of living all influence the well-being of people. Social workers engage in helping relationships to assess and intervene in all aspects of human living to enhance the well-being of individuals, groups, and communities. Social functioning is one component of well-being. Social workers do indeed measure the behavioral outcomes of their interventions. Helping people improve their interactions with other people is an important part of human flourishing. The scope of social work assessments, interventions, and evaluations, however, are more holistic. The outcomes of social work practice are not always as easy to measure as are observable behaviors. In some instances, observable behavioral measurements can even be misleading or be misinterpreted as a continuation of social and economic injustice instead of as improvement or effectiveness.

Consider the example of the school social worker. Simply measuring school attendance and performance may seemingly suggest effectiveness of interventions. But what if the social workers engage with students and families who are struggling day to day to have enough food to eat? What if the social worker learns that many of the families believe that the school does not involve them enough in their children's education? What if some of the children skip school because they are afraid of some of their peers? What if some of the children missing school believe they have to work to help support the family, or need to stay home to care for younger siblings while their parents work? Will measuring the number of days at school or their school performance indicate enhancement of well-being? Can we say that the social workers' intervention efforts are effective if school attendance is up, without also intervening and evaluating other concurrent issues? The answer is, "Of course not." The physical, emotional, and environmental issues could all influence the reasons why children are unable to get to the school or perform well. Enhancing, or, in this case, restoring their well-being involves attending to all the aspects of life preventing the children from flourishing in and out of school.

Enhancement of well-being is also consistent with the care and concern social workers have for the people we engage in practice. Social workers enter into helping relationships with people because they have a vested interest in seeing them thrive. Social workers are more than mechanistic objective robots choosing the right interventions based on completely systematic algorithms designed to predict effective outcomes. They are human beings who enter into reciprocal relationships where they appreciate the dignity and worthiness of other human beings and partner with them to enhance or restore their own well-being. The foremost distinguishable attribute of competent social work is the use of knowledge, values, and skills tailored to and used within the context of authentic caring relationships.

CARING AND SERVING ROOTED IN SPIRITUAL AND RELIGIOUS BEGINNINGS

The emphasis on caring relationships and a sincere desire to enhance well-being is grounded in the religious and spiritual roots of the profession. Social work emerged from religiously instilled beliefs about the importance of helping fellow human beings. Alan Keith-Lucas (1994), one of the leading scholars in the area of social work and religion, suggests that the desire to help others develops as a part of religion. He points out that almost all major religions converge on stressing responsibility for all humanity, kindness and justice for the needy, and self-fulfillment through service. In fact, in all five of the world's major religions (Buddhism, Christianity, Hinduism, Islam, and Judaism), caring and serving others in need is a part of worship. For example, Muslims are supposed to perform *sadaga*, which means to freely give of their time, money, and resources to help others in need (Stillman, 1975). In order for people to be considered Muslims they have to dedicate themselves to following God's laws and make a daily commitment to act on their beliefs. Caring for and serving people in need, therefore, are conceived as acts that all Muslims should perform, whereby services rendered to others become evidence of their dedication to God. In Judaism and Christianity, providing service to others represents an outward expression of their love for God. Furthermore, when Jews and Christians offer support, they are to remember that they are no different from the people receiving help, because they too were in a position of needing assistance. It is noteworthy to point out that the word "love" connotes affection and concern for others, similar to the care and concern social workers have for enhancing the well-being of those they engage in helping relationships.

The religious and spiritual influences to care for others is also fundamentally connected to the Charity Organization Societies (COS) movement and the Settlement House movement—the beginning of the social work profession. For instance, the COS movement involved women from churches giving of their time to help people in need. These women would volunteer their time to offer encouragement and provide tangible assistance to poor families. As Amato-von Hemert (2002) describes, these women's efforts were intended "to reform and uplift the poor, not merely to mitigate their sufferings" (p. 48).

Religion also played an important role in the Settlement House movement. In her analysis, Crocker (1992) summarized the Settlement House movement as elaborate partnerships between volunteers, religious groups, and businesses. For example, although not mentioned in most textbooks, it was Jane Addams' consistent attendance at worship services and Bible studies at Fourth Presbyterian Church that allowed her to eventually network with the business leaders that helped her establish the Hull House. Moreover, England's Toynbee Hall (the model for settlement houses in America) was founded by the Anglican Church as an effort to fulfill the church's obligation to provide outreach and social justice to those in need.

SUMMARY

Social work is distinct from other helping professions. While the knowledge and skills have expanded and become more systematic since the COS and Settlement House movements, caring about the well-being of individuals, groups, and communities is still the unifying purpose that underscores all social work practice. Synthesizing a sincere desire to help other human beings flourish with the knowledge, values, and skills needed for professional practice is the hallmark of competence-based social work. As we move ahead to the following chapters, remember that the purpose of social work—*why we do*—is the distinct foundation for the methods of social work—*what we do*. Continually reflecting on the relationship between our purpose and our methods is essential to developing the professional identity of a social worker.

DISCUSSION QUESTIONS

The discussion questions at the end of chapters 2 through 4 will be in the following format: The first two or three questions are designed to spark interest and/or group discussion about significant topics raised in the chapter. Following those, a series of questions designed to engage the reader and instructor in meaningful discussion around the case vignettes will be presented by addressing (1) fact-based questions about the case and/or topics related to the chapter; (2) analysis-based questions that call students to make sense of the facts presented and come to some conclusions; and (3) action-based questions that call for some plan of action based on the facts obtained and conclusions made.

The questions are designed to increase in complexity throughout the remaining chapters.

1. How would you define social work to an interested family member?
2. What are some of the essential elements of social work practice that distinguish it from other professions?
3. The case vignettes of Ian, Sarah, and Dustin illustrate the variety of backgrounds, strengths, abilities, and motivations that individuals bring to the social work profession. What significant aspects of your background have led to your interests in social work? What are the strengths and abilities that you possess that could aid you in helping others?

Facts: Fact gathering and gaining as full an understanding of a situation as possible is essential to good social work practice.

4. In each of the three case vignettes presented in this chapter, what are the relevant facts that should be considered in resolving their respective issues? List each fact and assert why it is important.

5. In social work practice, contextual issues are very important in determining the appropriate course of action in any given situation. What are the relevant contextual aspects in each of the three case vignettes described in this chapter?

Analysis: After identifying the facts available in a given situation, social workers make judgments about those facts in order to determine how to intervene.

6. In each of the vignettes presented in this chapter, what are the resources that the social worker has readily at his or her disposal that might help in each situation?

7. What additional resources might be needed in each of the three vignettes to ensure effective action?

Actions: After fact gathering and analysis of those facts, social workers decide on a plan of action that involves clear action steps designed to address any given situation.

8. What action steps would you engage in to address the issues presented in the case vignettes of Ian, Sarah, and Dustin?

REFERENCES

Amato-von Hemert, K. (2002). Battle between sin and love in social work history. In B. Hugen & T. L. Scales (Eds.), *Christianity and social work: Readings on the integration of Christian faith and social work practice* (2nd ed., pp. 45–58). Botsford, CT: North American Association of Christians in Social Work.

Barker, R. L. (2003). *The social work dictionary.* Washington, DC: National Association of Social Workers (NASW).

Bartlett, H. (1958). Working definition of social work practice. *Social Work, 3*(2), 5–8.

Bartlett, H. (1970). *The common base of social work practice.* New York: National Association of Social Workers (NASW).

Boehm, W. (1958). The nature of social work. *Social Work, 12,* 10–18.

Boehm, W. (1959). *Objectives of the social work curriculum of the future* (Vol. 1). New York: Council on Social Work Education (CSWE).

Council on Social Work Education (CSWE). (2008). *Educational policy and accreditation standards.* Alexandria, VA: Author.

Crocker, R. H. (1992). *Social work and social order: The settlement movement in two industrial cities, 1889–1930.* Urbana-Champaign, IL: University of Illinois Press.

Flexner, A. (1915). Is social work a profession? In National Conference of Charities and Corrections, *Proceedings of the National Conference of Charities and Corrections at the Forty-second annual session held in Baltimore, Maryland, May 12–19, 1915.* Chicago: Hildmann.

Gordon, W. E. (1962). A critique of the working definition. *Social Work, 7*(4), 3–13.

Hollis, E. V., & Taylor, A. L. (1951). *Social work education in the United States: A report of a study made for the National Council on Social Work Education.* New York: Columbia University Press.

International Federation of Social Workers (IFSW). (2000). *Definition of social work.* Retrieved from www.ifsw.org/f38000138.html

Keith-Lucas, A. (1994). *Giving and taking help* (Rev. ed.). Botsford, CT: North American Association of Christians in Social Work.

National Association of Social Workers (NASW). (1974). *Social case work: Generic and specific: A report on the Milford conference.* Washington, DC: Author. (Original work published 1929).

National Association of Social Workers (NASW). (1977). Special issue on conceptual frameworks. *Social Work, 22*(5), 338–444.

Stillman, N. A. (1975). Charity and social services in medieval Islam. *Societas: A Review of Social History, 5,* 105–116.

What Is Competence-
Based Social Work?

CASE VIGNETTE 3.1. STACY LYNN

Background

In her sophomore year, Stacy entered her first social work course thinking she was interested in working with older adults. She envisioned herself working as a social worker in a nursing home or as a social worker practicing with the local Area Agency on Aging. A few semesters later, it was time for her to fill out her field internship application and interview with the field director. On her application, she listed three preferred internships, all of them at agencies that worked with older adults. When it was time for her interview, Stacy entered the field director's office expecting to hear that she had been placed in one of the agencies listed on her application. During the interview, the field director reminded Stacy that the knowledge and skills of social work were transferable to many different practice settings. She encouraged Stacy to use her BSW placement as an opportunity to become a generalist social work practitioner. She could expose herself to an area of social work that was different from what she expected and still develop the practice skills and experience to work with older adults. She reminded Stacy that if she continued on to her MSW degree, she could then do a placement with older adults as part of her area of specialization. Stacy heeded the field director's advice and ended up completing her placement with the local juvenile probation office as a forensic social work intern. Her decision changed the course of her professional career.

Stacy worked with an experienced probation officer as her field instructor. The probation officer had earned an MSW and a certificate in criminology. She also had completed a basic probation officer training program that made her eligible for hire as a probation officer. At first, Stacy spent her time at the internship observing. Eventually she worked with a small caseload of adolescents under the direct supervision of the field instructor. During her internship, Stacy learned how prevalent issues of loss and grief were for many of the adolescents that ended up on their caseload. She also learned how important relationships with parents and grandparents were in helping teens make better decisions about their future and stay out of the criminal justice system. Most significantly, the internship changed what Stacy wanted to do with her life. She wanted to pursue a career as a juvenile probation officer. After finishing her BSW, Stacy earned her MSW in an advanced-standing program. An advanced-standing program allowed Stacy to earn her MSW in just one year. She then earned her basic probation officer training certificate, passed the Juvenile Probation Officer State Exam, and was hired as a juvenile probation officer at the same office of her field instructor, who was now the chief juvenile probation officer in Fayette County, Georgia.

The Context

Fayette County is in the northwestern part of Georgia, just fifteen miles south of the city limits of Atlanta. The juvenile probation office is located in the city of Fayetteville, the county seat. The juvenile probation officers assigned to Fayette County are part of the state Department of Juvenile Justice (DJJ), which employs more than four thousand staff members organized into four regional and twelve district offices. Stacy works in the District 3a office of the northwest region for the DJJ. Her basic responsibilities include conducting intake assessments; developing predisposition or presentence assessments; and supervising youth who are placed on probation, sentenced to short-term incarceration, or committed to the DJJ's custody of juvenile courts.

The Situation

As she does every Tuesday morning, Stacy heads to the regional youth detention center to meet with teens assigned to her caseload. Shane Young, the first teen she meets with that morning, is scheduled for release from the detention center by Friday. Stacy needs to develop a release plan for Shane that will help him transition back into the community and remain out of detention in the future. In preparation for meeting with Shane, Stacy had met with his parents, the school principal, and representatives from a few human service agencies. In talking with Shane's parents, Stacy had learned that they were fearful for him to return home after his latest altercation. At age fifteen, Shane is six foot three inches tall and weighs 290 pounds. He is bigger than his mother and stepfather. The police arrested him two months ago in the middle of the night after he assaulted his eleven-year-old stepbrother while in the midst of a drunken rage. This was the second assault incident for Shane in the past year, prompting the judge to sentence him to thirty days in detention and six months of probation.

In the few weeks that Stacy has met with Shane, she has found him to be a likable young man. He also seemed to benefit from his time in detention. He attended school, participated in an alcohol and drug support group, and was a model inmate, avoiding altercations with any of the other juveniles. Shane also expressed remorse about hurting his stepbrother. Despite her update and assessment to his parents, they remained fearful of how Shane would behave after he returned home. Stacy has to develop her report for the judge by Wednesday at the end of the day so the judge can approve his release and rehabilitation plan. She also had to talk to Shane about his parents' fear and unwillingness to have him come home. She is concerned about how Shane would respond to his parents' fear. She hopes she can eventually intervene with his parents to make a plan for him to return home and for them to feel safe. As she sat down to meet with Shane, Stacy wondered what to say and what to recommend to the judge.

CASE VIGNETTE 3.2. STAN HARRIS

Background

Stan knew since high school that he wanted to become a social worker. It always seemed as if his friends came to him whenever they needed someone to help them deal with their struggles. Stan also spent a lot of time talking with Jake, his older brother, before Jake left for college. At the age of fourteen, Jake confided in his brother that he was more attracted to other boys than to girls. For two years, Jake talked with Stan about his desire to fit in at school and maintain his relationships with his friends and parents. A few weeks into his first year at college, Jake met a romantic partner and finally worked up the courage to tell his parents about his orientation. Though at first their parents were shocked, they eventually accepted Jake's lifestyle. They were also supportive of Stan studying social work.

Stan continued to be very close to Jake. In college, he also developed a large network of friends from the lesbian and gay community. In his social work courses, he appreciated the emphasis on diversity, the dignity and worth of all human beings, the right to self-determination, and the emphasis on social and economic justice.

When Stan learned that his assigned field internship agency was the Victorian AIDS Council, he was thrilled.

The Context

Stan's family lived in Somerville, a city located in the southwest part of Melbourne, Australia. The Victorian AIDS Council is located in South Yarra, Victoria, a suburb on the opposite side of Melbourne. The agency exists as a resource for the community dealing with the HIV/AIDS epidemic. Another important function of the agency is to provide counseling and referral services to support the overall health and well-being of the lesbian, gay, bisexual, transgender, questioning, and intersex (LGBTQI) community. Stan's field instructor works in the counseling services program. The program provides individual and group counseling services focused on helping individuals and couples through common issues faced by members of the LGBTQI community. Some of the common issues addressed in counseling include anxiety and depression, self-esteem, grief and loss, same-sex domestic violence, making informed safe sex decisions in relationships, and dealing with a new or recent HIV diagnosis.

Stan spent most of the fall semester in field observing his field instructor during individual counseling sessions. He also observed two therapeutic groups. One was a six-week anxiety group, and the other was a negative partners group for persons in a relationship with someone diagnosed with HIV. Stan also attended a weekly clinical supervision meeting and met alone with his field instructor for an hour each week. In the spring semester, the field instructor assigned Stan a limited group of clients to work with under his direct supervision. He also gave Stan the opportunity to cofacilitate a therapeutic group.

The Situation

During the fifth week of an eight-week negative partner group, Michael, a thirty-seven-year-old investment banker, showed up to group with several bruises on his face. His left hand also had a few abrasions and cuts. The six other men in the group stared at him as he walked into the group therapy room. After Michael sat down, Calvin, another member of the group, asked abruptly, "Shit, man, what happened to you?" Although not a typical way to start a therapeutic group session, Stan, the field instructor, and the other men were all drawn, out of concern and curiosity, to focus on Michael. Appropriately, Stan reframed Calvin's question: "Michael, I think the group is shocked to see you like this and is concerned about you. You don't have to say anything. Just know the group is here as a place of support if you want to share what happened."

Michael began rubbing the abrasions on his knuckles. Then he touched one of the bruises and said, "Patrick and I had a terrible fight last night. I know we agreed to a nonmonogamous relationship, but we also agreed to make sure we practice safe sex when we are with other people. I wanted to understand what happened, so I confronted him. Patrick became very defensive. He started yelling out of control. I tried to comfort and calm him down. I told him I loved him, I just wanted to understand. Then he started punching me." Another member asked "Did you hit him back?" Michael quickly answered, "Oh no no . . . I would never hit Patrick. I just used my hands to try and block him." He continued, "I am just so confused. One day everything is fine. All of sudden Patrick has HIV and he is having unprotected sex with someone else. I feel so embarrassed. What do I tell my friends and family?" When Michael finished, Stan noticed his field instructor and the other group members looking at him. He wondered what he should say or do next.

CASE VIGNETTE 3.3. DORIS LIEBERMAN

Background

Sitting at her desk and staring at the schedule for the Spring Community Banquet, one of the annual fundraisers for Jewish Family Services (JFS) in Milwaukee, Doris thought back to what her professor in community and organizational practice shared with her class seven years ago: "The longer social workers practice, the more likely they are to have opportunities to move into leadership. As social workers move into leadership, their work often shifts from direct practice with clients to indirect practice that supports the work of frontline professionals. The comprehensive training for social workers as generalists prepares them to be successful practitioners in both capacities. Still, when practitioners move into leadership, they have to cope with the transition."

Coping with the transition is exactly what Doris was experiencing. After graduating with her social work degree, Doris accepted a position as an adult case manager at JFS. She worked with a caseload of sixty-five clients and their families as they dealt with the transitions associated with aging. Her position put her in contact with a large network of community professionals as she developed and implemented service plans with her clients. She stayed in the position for three years, becoming a respected professional with a diverse network of relationships with community leaders. When the development director of the agency retired, the executive director of the agency received an informal recommendation from her friend, a nursing home administrator, about considering Doris for the position. The executive director approached Doris, encouraged her to apply, and eventually hired her as the director of development.

The Context

JFS is one of the oldest and most active human service organizations in Milwaukee. Since the 1860s, JFS has offered services to support and nurture healthy families, children, and individuals. Two religious values guide the work of JFS. Staff members view the service they provide as opportunities to live out the Jewish values of *chesed* and *tzedekah*. When considered together, the two Jewish values mean to show love and kindness to others (*chesed*) and to promote justice and righteousness in their relationship with God (*tzedekah*). Consistent with the agency values, JFS provides services to people living in the Milwaukee community regardless of race, religion, or lifestyle. JFS uses a life-cycle approach to organizing services, offering counseling and case management to children and youth, teenagers, families, adults and couples, and older adults. There is also a separate program that provides case management services to immigrants and survivors of the Holocaust.

Providing comprehensive services to the community is expensive. Even though JFS is a nonprofit organization, the agency must generate enough revenue to pay for the services. A significant portion of the revenue comes from foundations, grants, and government contracts as well as individual and corporate contributions, endowments, and special fundraising events. Similar to other nonprofit service organizations, client fees account for only a fraction of the revenue. Client fees are determined with a sliding scale fee, and most of the people needing services from JFS usually pay the lowest level of the fee scale. The agency simply could not provide services to the community without the financial support generated from development.

For the past four years, Doris has shifted her time and efforts to raising support for the agency. Her networking and communication skills were part of what made her an effective case manager. In that direct micro practice role, the networking relationships developed made advocating and coordinating services for clients possible. As director of development, Doris cultivates relationships with people representing various stakeholders (e.g., individual donors, foundation staff, government employees, religious leaders) to develop collaborative partnerships that lead to financial support. She also works closely with the executive director, the chief financial officer (CFO), and members of the board of directors to prepare fiscal budgets, annual reports, and strategic plans for the agency.

The Situation

The Spring Community Banquet is one of the annual fundraisers for JFS, usually clearing $90,000 to $110,000 after expenses. Each of the other three fundraisers usually generates similar levels of support. The support raised from the banquet and other fundraisers help offset some of the costs of the intensive one-on-one counseling services that are more expensive to provide. Planning for the spring banquet is an ongoing endeavor. Doris personally meets with and invites nearly all of the guests each year. She also works with her development assistant to plan the evening.

This year, the preliminary figures indicate the banquet will be a success. A week before the dinner, 355 of the 400 people invited had replied that they would attend. Another twenty guests reported they could not attend, but enclosed checks to cover the cost of the evening. Altogether, Doris estimated that the banquet could potentially raise the most support for JFS in a single event. Guests pay $360 to attend the banquet. The evening includes a five-course meal, a live band, ballroom dancing, and a guest speaker.

In planning the banquet, Doris contacted a colleague at the mayor's office who had connections with the vice president (VP) of marketing for the Milwaukee Brewers. The colleague arranged for Doris to meet the VP where she would have the opportunity to arrange for one of the baseball players to be the guest speaker. Doris quickly developed a rapport with the VP, shared her vision for the banquet, and invited him to attend. The VP accepted, and also agreed to talk with some of the players to see if any were interested in attending as a guest speaker. Within a few weeks, the VP sent Doris an email telling her that one of the players had agreed to speak at the event. Two days before the event, Doris finds out from her development assistant that the VP had called to let her know that the player had a family emergency come up and had to fly home. Therefore, he would not be coming to the event. Doris had 355 guests paying a lot of money expecting to hear from this baseball player. She sat down at her desk, looked at the schedule for the evening, and wondered what she could do.

THE DIVERSITY AND UNITY OF SOCIAL WORK

After reading the case vignettes from this and the previous chapter, we hope the tension between the diversity and unity of the social work profession is apparent. Social work is a diverse profession where people practice in national and international settings. Social workers practice directly with clients in one-on-one relationships, in group settings, and in family interactions. Social workers are also prepared for leadership and other indirect practices. Social workers help draft and implement policy, develop budgets, write grants, organize fundraising, administer programs and human resources, coordinate volunteers, organize social movements, or even run for public office. Consider Stacy Lynn, Stan Harris, and Doris Lieberman: Stacy practices as a juvenile probation officer. Her work involves microlevel work with adolescents, mezzolevel work with families, and macrolevel work with the court system. Stan is completing his internship where he practices as a clinician. He works individually with a limited number of clients and cofacilitates groups, but also looks for opportunities to advocate for his clients at mezzo and macro levels by lobbying politicians and service providers regarding pertinent policy issues. Doris used to work directly with clients as a case manager, and now she is a development director.

Amidst the diverse populations and practice settings, social work is also a unified profession. Social workers share a genuine concern for others, especially for the most vulnerable and disenfranchised. Social workers also practice for the same purpose—to enhance or restore well-being. Consider again the three cases: Stacy Lynn, Stan Harris, and Doris Lieberman are all social workers. They all work within the context of caring professional relationships to contribute to social work's overarching purpose of enhancing or restoring well-being. They also share a common set of core competences and practice behaviors that serve as a foundation of their work. As we introduce the core competences and subsequent practice behaviors of social work, we encourage students to think about how competent social work occurs in all the cases provided in the book.

WHAT IS COMPETENCE-BASED LEARNING?

The purpose of a college education is at the center of understanding the difference between content-based and competence-based learning. On the one hand, college exposes students to a broad range of knowledge from different academic disciplines to prepare them to be well-rounded and well-educated citizens. On the other hand, college exists to prepare students with the knowledge and skills needed to enter and thrive in the workplace. As an applied professional discipline, social work, as well as many other professions (e.g., medicine, law, accounting, teacher education), are held accountable for providing effective services by properly trained professionals. The purpose of higher education for social work (as well as other professional disciplines) is twofold: to prepare people to enter the field, and to serve a gatekeeping function by making sure people attempting to enter the field are capable of practicing as professional social workers. Consistent with the purpose of social work education, competence-based learning is educational preparation of students toward agreed-on knowledge, values, and skills needed to enter and thrive in the workforce as professional social workers.

Although social work has emphasized competences to some degree in the past, the 2008 EPAS shifted the entire emphasis of social work education to competence-based learning. The EPAS is the document used by the Council on Social Work Education (CSWE) to assess social work programs for accreditation. Accreditation is important because most employers of social workers will hire only graduates of programs accredited by CSWE. Before 2008, social work programs showed how they offered courses that fit into five traditional curricular areas of social work education (practice, policy, research, human behavior in the social environment, and field). They also documented all the content they were teaching their students in those five curriculum areas. Under the new EPAS, however, accreditation decisions by CSWE moved away from assessing content to assessing how programs demonstrated what their students would be able to do after graduation with a BSW or an MSW degree. Specifically, social work programs now must document evidence of student proficiency in the core competences and practice behaviors outlined in the new EPAS. Programs also have the flexibility to design their curriculum to fit their context, providing they can document how students demonstrate competence. They do not have to (though many still do) offer courses in the five traditional curricular areas.

THE *WHY WE DO, WHAT WE DO* FRAMEWORK

Social work education is an active and engaging field of study. Becoming competent in social work requires more than listening to lectures, taking notes, studying, and taking exams. Students must be able to take what they are learning and actually use it in the context of helping relationships addressing real social problems. Stated differently, students need to understand the bigger picture. When they are in one class, they need to incorporate what they are learning with information from other classes and use it in their field internships, and eventually their professional practice. Therefore, students need to have a solid grasp of the necessary knowledge, values, and skills they will be learning and developing as they complete their social work educations. The core competences serve as a unifying guide for educators to develop social work programs that adequately prepare students for careers in social work. As outlined in the EPAS, however, students may find the list of competences and practice behaviors overwhelming and unwieldy. The *why we do, what we do* framework can help students understand how all the competences fit together to encapsulate what they will be learning in their social work courses.

The *why we do, what we do* framework (see figure 3.1) organizes the core competences into two groups. As we discussed in chapter 2, the combined purpose of social work (caring to enhance or restore well-being) and the practices of social work make our profession unique. Becoming competent social workers involves developing the professional identity and the methods to enter into helping relationships at the micro, mezzo, and macro levels of practice. The core competences of social work summarize both parts of professional practice. Looking at figure 3.1, students can see that the

Figure 3.1. The *Why We Do, What We Do* Framework

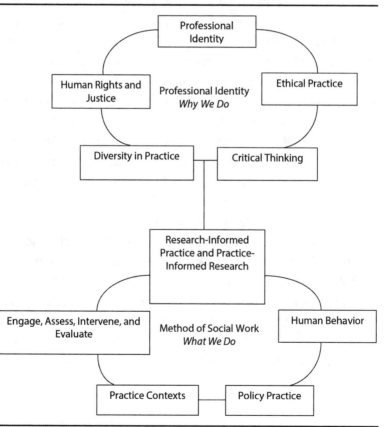

first group of competences describes the professional identity (*why we do*) of social work. The second group of competences describes the method (*what we do*) of social work. We use the rest of the chapter to provide a brief overview of the first group of competences that describes our professional identity. In chapter 4, we provide a brief overview of the second group of competences that describes our method. Then we transition to part II of the book, where students will have the opportunity to begin developing their own professional identity as social workers, the foundation for competent practice.

THE COMPETENCES THAT DESCRIBE *WHY WE DO*

Social workers share a foundation of knowledge, values, and skills that make up our unique professional identity. Considered together, the first group of competences describes what it means to be a social worker. The competences also reinforce the central principle of social work so eloquently stated by the former president of CSWE: "The purpose of social work should always supersede the methods of social work" (Mildred C. Joyner, personal communication, October 14, 2010). Stated differently for students just entering their first course in social work, becoming competent social workers involves learning and understanding *why we do* before learning *what we do*. To be clear, the methods of social work are important. Students will need to learn and demonstrate proficiency using the methods of social work. But they will learn and use the methods within the context of their developing professional identities.

We encourage students to think about the professional identities of the social workers described in the case vignettes as we outline the competences learned and demonstrated by people ready to enter the field (CSWE, 2008). We will consider the professional identity of Stacy Lynn (case vignette 3.1) as an example at the end of the chapter.

Competence: Professional Identity

Students ready to enter the field identify themselves as professional social workers and conduct themselves accordingly. They realize they represent the profession, its mission, and its core values. They know the history of the profession, are ready to contribute to the future of the profession, and are committed to enhancing their own professional conduct and growth throughout their careers. Students show they are ready to identify as social workers by advocating for client access to services, engaging in personal reflection and continual professional development, staying attuned to professional roles and boundaries, demonstrating professional demeanor in behavior, appearance, and communication, and using supervision and consultation to enhance their work with clients.

Competence: Ethical Practice

Competent social workers apply ethical principles to guide their practice. When students enter the field, they are ready to conduct themselves ethically and to engage in ethical decision making. They have a sound knowledge of the value base of the profession, the ethical standards, and relevant laws guiding their practice. Students demonstrate ethical practice by managing personal values in a way that allows professional values to guide practice, by applying the standards of the NASW's Code of Ethics and, as applicable, of the IFSW and the International Association of Schools of Social Work (IASSW) Ethics in Social Work Statement of Principles. Furthermore, students must show they are capable of tolerating ambiguity in resolving ethical conflicts and applying strategies of ethical reasoning to arrive at principled decisions.

Competence: Critical Thinking

Social workers have to apply critical thinking to inform and communicate professional judgments in their practice. Social work involves incorporating logic, scientific inquiry, and other sources of the best available information with creativity and innovation into the helping relationship. Competent social workers are capable of synthesizing multiple sources of knowledge to fulfill the purpose of the profession to enhance or restore the well-being of people. Throughout their course work, students need to learn and demonstrate an ability to distinguish, appraise, and integrate multiple sources of knowledge, including research; and eventually to practice wisdom. Students must develop the analytic and research skills needed to analyze models of assessment, prevention, intervention, and evaluation in their practice. They also must effectively communicate their analyses with different client groups, including individuals, families, groups, organizations, communities, and colleagues in social work and other helping professions.

Competence: Diversity in Practice

Engaging diversity and differences in practice is a central part of the profession. Social workers are knowledgeable and aware of the multiple dimensions of diversity to include age, class, color, culture, disability, ethnicity, gender, gender identity and expression, immigration status, political ideology, race, religion, sex, and sexual orientation. They understand how diversity influences and shapes human experience and is critical to the formation of identity for individuals, groups, and communities. As a consequence of differences, social workers appreciate that life experiences may include oppression, poverty, marginalization, and alienation, as well as privilege, power, and acclaim. In the process of completing the social work curriculum, students will learn to recognize cultural structures and values that may marginalize and alienate certain groups, while creating or enhancing privilege and power in other groups. Within the context of helping relationships, students also learn to gain sufficient self-awareness to eliminate the influences of personal biases and values as they work with diverse groups. They must demonstrate to faculty they are capable of communicating an understanding of the importance of difference in shaping life experiences and are willing to continue learning and engaging those with whom they work as informants about such differences.

Competence: Human Rights and Justice

Social workers practice to advance human rights and advocate for social and economic justice. Inherent in our purpose of enhancing or restoring well-being, social workers perceive every person in society as having basic human rights, including the rights to freedom, safety, privacy, an adequate standard of living, health care, and education. Social workers recognize the global influences of oppression and are knowledgeable about theories of justice and strategies to promote human and civil rights. They incorporate social justice practices at the micro, mezzo, and macro levels of social work. When students graduate from accredited social work programs, they should be capable of demonstrating understanding of the forms and mechanisms of oppression and discrimination. They should also be prepared to advocate for human rights and engage in practices that advance social and economic justice.

EXPLORING THE PROFESSIONAL IDENTITY OF STACY LYNN AS A SOCIAL WORKER

Consider the case vignette of Stacy Lynn (case vignette 3.1) through the lens of the first group of competences. In addition to earning a degree in social work, people can become juvenile probation officers by completing a degree in criminology, psychology, or other helping professions. What is it about Stacy that makes her more than a juvenile probation officer? What is it that makes Stacy a competent social worker practicing as a juvenile probation officer?

Perhaps the simplest place to begin is with her education. Stacy completed her BSW and MSW degrees. Though not stated specifically in the case, we can infer or assume that she earned both of her degrees in social work programs accredited by CSWE. If that is true, she took courses that prepared her to represent and contribute to the profession. In order to graduate, she must have at least demonstrated a satisfactory level of proficiency of the competences and subsequent practice behaviors outlined in the EPAS (CSWE, 2008). Stacy also demonstrates her professional identity as a social worker in other ways. For instance, her journey to juvenile probation is evidence of her engaging in personal reflection and continued professional development. Although she entered her first social work course thinking she wanted to work with older adults, she embraced the notion of social workers as generalists, and applied her acquired knowledge, values, and skills in a field placement working with adolescents. As she completed field, her personal reflections guided her to develop her professional identity as a social worker practicing in juvenile probation. She then demonstrated a commitment to continued professional development by completing the basic probation officer training. In her interactions with Shane, Stacy maintained professional boundaries, finding him to be a likable young man that she wanted to help, while simultaneously fulfilling her rehabilitation and correctional responsibilities. In her preparation for talking with Shane, she demonstrates appropriate use of consultation, meeting first with his parents, the school principal, and representatives from a few human service agencies.

Stacy applies ethical principles of social work practice in her work as a juvenile probation officer. First, her decision to become a juvenile probation officer is consistent with the purpose of social work outlined in the preamble of the Code of Ethics (NASW, 2008). The first paragraph of the Code of Ethics states, "The primary mission of the social work profession is to enhance human well-being and help meet the basic human needs of all people, with particular attention to the needs and empowerment of people who are vulnerable, oppressed, and living in poverty. A historic and defining feature of social work is the profession's focus on individual well-being in a social context and the wellbeing of society. Fundamental to social work is attention to the environmental forces that create, contribute to, and address problems in living" (NASW, 2008, p. 1).

As a social worker practicing in juvenile probation, Stacy uses her knowledge, values, and skills to enhance the well-being of the adolescents who, by their age and situation with the courts, are likely to be in vulnerable predicaments and may be members of oppressed groups and/or living in poverty. Her focus is also consistent with the profession, as she must consider the individual well-being of the kids on her caseload in the context of the well-being of the community. In the same way, she manages personal values allowing professional values to guide practice. For instance, when she learns of the fear Shane's parents have about him coming home, she balances her personal hope and desire to help him with his parents' concerns for themselves and the well-being of his stepbrother.

Stacy also embraces and fulfills the core values of the profession. (Chapter 8 provides in-depth coverage of the core values of ethical social work practice.) When she interacts with Shane and others involved in his case, she elevates her service to others above her self-interest. She sees her role as an advocate for social justice to the kids, the families, and the community. She respects the dignity and worth of the people she engages in practice—Shane, the parents, the school principal, her supervisor, and representatives of other human service agencies. Her reliance on the importance of human relationships is evident in the time she spends getting to know Shane as well as all the people she includes in consultation. She practices with integrity as she keeps in mind her responsibilities to the court, the client, the family, and the community in developing and recommending a plan to the judge. She also practices within her area of competence, working as a juvenile probation officer only after completing her field internship, her undergraduate and graduate degrees, and her specific training (NASW, 2008).

Stacy uses critical thinking to inform her practice. Her knowledge of relationship skills, the laws, and available resources influences her work as juvenile probation officer. For instance, in developing her plan for Shane, she will have to synthesize her understanding of family dynamics and theory, her knowledge of available resources, the needs of the court, and her assessment of Shane to put together a creative plan. She will also have to communicate the situation to different client groups to enlist their participation and support for the plan. She needs to explain the parameters and expectations of probation to Shane. She needs to share with him the reality of his parents' concerns, help him empathize with their concerns, and help him work toward earning their trust. She has to share her plan with his parents, acknowledge their concerns, and enlist their support and openness to Shane eventually returning home. She also has to describe the plan to the judge in such a way that he or she feels comfortable ordering Shane to comply with the plan.

As a social worker, Stacy brings her understanding and appreciation of diversity to her work. When working with individuals, groups, and families, she has to be mindful of how their unique dimensions of diversity influence their experiences. She is aware and mindful of the disproportionate numbers of certain groups on her client roster and the difficulty in keeping some of her kids out of trouble. She has to continue being willing to learn about the culture of the people she works with as it helps her develop rapport and trust with clients, families, and other people she consults with in fulfilling her responsibilities.

Stacy brings her focus on human rights and social justice to her work. She is a social worker practicing as a juvenile probation officer. Like any other competently trained social worker, her purpose is to enhance the well-being of different client groups—the kids, the families, and the community. She sees all people as human beings with the right to be treated with dignity and worth, even adolescents who have committed crimes and are in detention. She serves as both an officer of the court and an advocate for the clients. Helping kids become productive citizens is part of social justice practices. She also works to help others understand and appreciate some of the challenges her kids must overcome in becoming productive citizens.

SUMMARY

At the core of what makes Stacy Lynn a social worker is her professional identity and her practice methods. As a social worker practicing as a juvenile probation officer, she brings a commitment to representing the profession, engaging in ethical practice, using critical thinking, understanding and appreciating the dimensions of diversity, and advocating for human rights and social justice. The constellation of those competences represents *why* social workers do what they do. A primary theme of this book is to begin helping students develop their own professional identities. Our hope is that students will finish the book feeling excited about their futures and ready to embrace the challenge of becoming competent social workers. Before focusing on the competences that make up the *why* of social work, we use chapter 4 to introduce students to the competences that outline the foundational practice methods of the profession.

DISCUSSION QUESTIONS

1. Given the diversity of arenas for social work practice and the differing levels (i.e., micro, mezzo, and macro) of intervention, what distinguishes competent social workers and social work practice?

2. In your opinion, what are some ways that the recent shift to competence-based education will affect the social work profession? What are the implications for the vulnerable populations that social workers seek to help?

3. What are the factors from this chapter that help to define social workers as professional practitioners across areas and levels of practice?

Facts: Fact gathering and gaining as full an understanding of a situation as possible is essential to good social work practice.

4. Using your favorite Internet search engine, perform a search using the search terms "children's code" and "Georgia juvenile justice." Using results from your search, discuss the policies and resources that may affect case vignette 3.1's Stacy Lynn and her recommendation to the judge regarding Shane Young.

5. In case vignette 3.2, Stan Harris needs to understand a vulnerable population that is only somewhat familiar to him. Perform a search of the LGBTQI community online, and identify and discuss some of the current issues facing providers and professionals who address the mental health needs of this population.

6. In case vignette 3.3, Doris Lieberman is faced with a dilemma that could have a profound effect on the nature of her relationship with major donors to her agency. Visit the NASW Web site and access the Code of Ethics. Also, visit the Association of Fundraising Professionals' Web site and access the Donor's Bill of Rights. What ethical principles should be considered in Doris's dilemma?

Analysis: After identifying the facts available in a given situation, social workers make judgments about those facts in order to know how to intervene.

7. How do the policies and resources in the Georgia child welfare system limit or guide Stacy Lynn's recommendation to the judge regarding Shane Young?

8. What does culturally competent practice entail and/or dictate in the case of Stan Harris' current dilemma in case vignette 3.2?

9. Social workers should have a strong sense of their own biases when addressing ethical dilemmas. Using Doris Lieberman's dilemma in case vignette 3.3, discuss your personal biases with

regard to fundraising and Doris's current situation. Compare and contrast your biases with ethical considerations discovered from your consideration of Question 3 above.

Actions: After fact gathering and analysis of those facts, social workers decide on a plan of action that involves clear action steps designed to address any given situation.

10. For each of the case vignettes presented in this chapter, develop an action plan consisting of three or four action steps, listed in order of priority, that the social worker should take in his or her respective situations. Discuss these with your classmates and/or instructor.

REFERENCES

Council on Social Work Education (CSWE). (2008). *Educational policy and accreditation standards.* Retrieved from http://www .cswe.org/File.aspx?id=13780

National Association of Social Workers (NASW). (2008). Code of ethics. Retrieved from http://www.socialworkers.org/pubs/ code/code.asp

What Do Competent Social Workers Do?

CASE VIGNETTE 4.1. TERESA ROGERS

Background

Since turning thirteen, Teresa has spent every summer traveling with the youth group from her church to work on mission trips. One summer she traveled to Mexico to help build homes. Another summer she spent two weeks in Thailand volunteering in an orphanage. She also worked one summer in Charleston, South Carolina, helping a team of youth from different churches renovate three church buildings in need of repair. The summer mission trips shaped her interests in pursuing a career in social work. During her senior year of high school, Teresa applied and was accepted to four different universities to major in social work. She decided to attend Trinity Christian College, a small college located in Palos Heights, Illinois.

After completing the prerequisite courses, Teresa applied and was admitted into the social work program. She successfully completed her initial social work courses and then was interviewed by the field director. Teresa shared her interests in doing her field placement in a church setting. The field director sent her to meet with Shelly Stone, the youth pastor at a local church who had an MSW as well as a master's degree in divinity. During the meeting, Teresa and Shelly talked about what a social worker does as part of the pastoral staff at a church. They talked about meeting with families in need of counseling, linking church members with professional resources in the community, and conducting assessment interviews with people who come to the church in need of assistance. Shelly also explained that one of her roles involved facilitating the planning and implementation of Project Hope, a ministry of the church designed to provide support and assistance for single mothers. Shelly told Teresa that if she completed her field internship at her church, one of her primary responsibilities would be to work with the Project Hope planning committee as they make plans to build a long-term residential facility. The facility will give four single mothers and their children an opportunity to live in a safe environment with minimal cost long enough to find gainful employment and then save enough money to rent or purchase their own home.

The Context

Project Hope was one of several programs run by the church. The church operated a small private school, a day care, a morning-out program for parents and guardians with children, and a recovery program for persons struggling with addictions. There was also a senior adult ministry designed to link younger members of the church with older members needing assistance with transportation, grocery shopping, and minor home maintenance. Project Hope provided long-term support for a few single mothers. Support included temporary financial assistance with relocation expenses; reduced and, in some cases, free child care for mothers looking for employment; participation in a group of caring volunteers who were members of the church; and case management services. In addition to working as the youth pastor, Shelly provided the case management services and attended the meetings with the volunteers and the mothers.

Under supervision, Teresa worked with a caseload of two families. She also worked with Shelly in planning for the residential facility. During her first semester in field, Teresa observed the meetings. Eventually, however, Shelly gave Teresa the opportunity to lead the committee. Teresa currently spends most of her time leading the committee as they plan for the residential facility.

The Situation

The Project Hope planning committee meets every week. The meetings occur Thursdays at 6:00 a.m. at the church, before the members of the committee have to be at work. In addition to Teresa, the committee consists of six members: four men and two women. All the members work in professional occupations. Teresa is a social work intern, one member is a physician, one is a dentist, two are lawyers, one owns an accounting firm, and one is the chief loan officer of a credit union. As she does every Wednesday, Teresa had sent the members an email with the agenda for their Thursday morning meeting. This week the committee needed to focus on approving the contract for beginning the renovations needed to turn the second floor of the fellowship hall into four apartment units, reviewing the lease agreement contracts that will be issued to the residents, and reviewing the mission statement for the program.

As she does every week, Teresa asked someone to open the committee with a prayer. Next, she asked the group to review the minutes from the meeting last week. After a long pause, she asked if anyone was ready to make a motion to accept the minutes from their previous meeting. One member moved to accept the minutes, and another seconded the motion. Teresa asked the group if anyone had need for further discussion, then she asked for a vote to approve the minutes. The group unanimously voted to approve the minutes. Teresa then asked one of the members to give a report on the status of the renovation contract. Following the report, the group agreed to wait until receiving one final estimate before deciding on which contractor to hire. Another member, one of the lawyers, shared copies of a potential lease agreement she had developed. The committee reviewed the contract. After a few minutes, as she attended to the verbal and nonverbal communication of the group, Teresa determined there was a consensus. She asked if the group was ready to vote to accept the contract. She then led the group through the voting procedure to officially adopt the lease agreement.

The committee then discussed the proposed mission statement. Teresa walked over to the whiteboard and wrote the current iteration of the statement: "The Project Hope apartments exist to provide a supportive environment for residents to develop their independence." She then asked if the committee was ready to approve the mission statement. Again, someone motioned to accept the statement, another person seconded the motion, and then Teresa asked if the group needed further discussion. After a brief pause, one of the committee members expressed a concern; she wondered if the mission statement was sending the wrong message to the residents and the members of the church who are supporting the facility. She continued by asking the group if the mission of the facility may inadvertently encourage residents to choose not to remarry and to remain single. As soon as she asked her question, one of the other committee members reinforced her concern. Then the other members all agreed they needed to change the wording. Teresa was shocked and upset about their concerns. She thought their concerns undermined empowering these single mothers to enhance their well-being. She also, however, needed to think about the context of where she is practicing social work. She controlled her emotions and wondered what to say next.

CASE VIGNETTE 4.2. NICOLE TANBAUM

Background

Nicole entered her sophomore year at Long Island University wanting to major in psychology or social work. She wanted to do work as a clinician someday; she was unsure, however, of which major would provide her with the best opportunities in the future. She scheduled an appointment with the chair of the social work department to discuss her options. The chair shared some of the differences in training between psychology and social work. She also listed some of the potential areas of practice available in social work. The chair told Nicole that both degrees could eventually help her achieve her goals. The differences existed in the emphasis in preparation and the opportunity to work with people. She explained that psychologists emphasize work with individuals, especially intrapersonal aspects of functioning. Social work places emphasis on the person in the environment and focuses on the well-being of individuals and the community. She told Nicole that social work students learn to practice with individuals, groups, families, and communities, with emphasis on the intersection and interactions of the various systems. The chair also explained that an important part of social work education involves students completing hundreds of hours in field internship placements. If she chose social work, Nicole might have the opportunity to intern in a clinical setting. Finally, the chair talked about the possibility of Nicole earning an MSW in just twelve months after completing her BSW. If she did well in the BSW program, Nicole would have the option of entering an advanced-standing MSW program where she could specialize in clinical social work.

Nicole completed her BSW at Long Island University, then earned admission into the advanced-standing MSW program at New York University. The MSW program at New York University emphasizes teaching clinical social work skills. In addition to her coursework, the field director placed her at a private, nonprofit behavioral health-care center. The field internship provided the opportunity to practice under the supervision of her field instructor, a licensed clinical social worker with more than twenty years of direct practice experience.

The Context

The behavioral health-care center offered three services—time-limited counseling for individuals, couples, and families; an intensive outpatient substance abuse program; and a partial hospital program. Clients seeking counseling meet with a licensed clinical social worker for a predetermined number of sessions authorized by their insurance company. The substance abuse program offers nine weeks of group counseling. The groups meet five days a week. After nine weeks, clients participate in a maintenance group that meets once a week for twelve months. The center bundles the cost of the substance abuse program into a single charge. The insurance companies usually cover a percentage of the program, with clients paying the remainder of the cost. The partial hospital program provides group counseling services from 8:00 a.m. to 2:00 p.m. for up to twenty-five days. Clients attending the program are referred so they can transition from an inpatient psychiatric unit back into the community. Some clients attend the program as a preventive measure to avoid hospitalization. The center charges a set rate for each day clients attend the program. All clients initially meet with a licensed clinical social worker for an assessment. They also meet with the nurse and psychiatrist to determine and manage medications.

Nicole interns in the time-limited counseling program. Her field instructor provides five to six counseling sessions per day. She also keeps evening hours on Tuesdays to meet with clients who need services after work. Nicole spends three days a week at the center. After Nicole had spent the first few weeks observing, the field instructor assigned her a caseload of four clients. The five licensed social workers in the program work with an assigned caseload of twenty to twenty-five clients. Nicole also attends the weekly clinical supervision meetings with the rest of the social workers. On Thursdays, she spends an hour alone in supervision with her field instructor.

The Situation

As she has done the past three weeks, Nicole met with Ms. Sanders on Tuesday from 9:00 to 9:50 in the morning. A psychiatrist referred Ms. Sanders for counseling as part of her treatment with depression. She prescribed Ms. Sanders with imipramine, a tricyclic antidepressant, which she has been taking for the past six weeks. Although most of her symptoms had subsided, the psychiatrist remained concerned about Ms. Sanders' relationship with her boyfriend. The psychiatrist decided she would benefit from talking with a social worker.

At her first visit to the behavioral health center, Ms. Sanders met with the intake social worker for an assessment. In her assessment, Ms. Sanders described her boyfriend as "unpredictable." Sometimes things are fine and he treats her well. At other times, he becomes short-tempered and says very hurtful things. The intake social worker completed the necessary paperwork, contacted her insurance company to preauthorize the counseling services, and assigned her to Nicole, under the direct supervision of her field instructor. The insurance company authorized four counseling sessions, fifty minutes each.

Nicole's sessions with Ms. Sanders focused on helping her work through thoughts and feelings about her relationship with her boyfriend. As Ms. Sanders stated during their first session, she needed to decide if she wanted to remain in the relationship. She also needed support and encouragement if she were to decide to end the relationship. Ms. Sanders began the final session telling Nicole she had decided to leave her boyfriend. She attributed many of her depressive symptoms to her unhealthy relationship. Nicole and Ms. Sanders then rehearsed what, where, and how she was going to tell her boyfriend. Toward the end of the session, as things seemed to be ending well, Ms. Sanders shared with Nicole that she was still nervous. She was nervous about being alone, and about not being able to find another partner. She asked Nicole if she could continue with a few more sessions after she told her boyfriend. Nicole asked Ms. Sanders to wait while she checked with her supervisor. She then went and asked the intake social worker if Ms. Sanders could have two additional visits. The intake social worker contacted the insurance representative who denied Ms. Sanders the additional sessions. Nicole headed back to her office wondering what to say to Ms. Sanders.

CASE VIGNETTE 4.3. ARNOLD YOUNG

Background

Arnold arrived on campus as the first person in his family to go to college. Leaving home in Jacksonville, Florida, was difficult for him because he was the youngest of three brothers and the last to leave home. At sixteen, he and his mother had lived on their own. Both of his brothers had become involved in a gang and were in prison serving time for multiple charges of aggravated assault and drug trafficking charges. He did not see his mother often because she worked two jobs. With the help of a few caring teachers and a guidance counselor, Arnold managed to stay out of trouble. He also did very well in school. In fact, he did well enough to earn a scholarship to attend the University of West Florida, in Pensacola.

As he had in high school, Arnold excelled in the college classroom. Unsure of what to study, however, he began college as a general studies major. To earn extra money, he also found a job working every other weekend with children who were living in a group home. By the beginning of his second semester at school, Arnold realized that he wanted to major in a field that allowed him to work with children. He shared his interest with an advisor, who encouraged him to consider a course in social work. He completed an intro course and changed his major to social work halfway through the semester.

After taking the required social work courses his junior year, Arnold applied to and was selected to participate in the Title IV-E Child Welfare Education Stipend Program. This program provides selected students with stipends to assist with tuition and other expenses in college in return for working in child welfare after graduation. Arnold received two stipends—one each for the fall and spring semesters of his senior year. In accepting these stipends, he committed to working in public child welfare for at least two years—one year for each stipend. He completed his internship with the Florida Department of Children and Families (DCF), and then was hired as a social worker in the foster care program in the Duval County DCF office in Jacksonville.

The Context

The DCF organizes locations and services into six regional offices and four types of services. The Duval County office is one of four offices located in the northeast region of DCF. The four types of services provided are (1) assistance with food, health care, and emergency cash; (2) prevention services for adults, including prevention of domestic violence, adult protective services, and assistance for adults who are homeless; (3) mental health and substance abuse services; and (4) services for children, youth, and families, including adoption, child care, foster care, and services for refugees.

As a social worker in the foster care program, Arnold assists abused and neglected children. He spends a majority of his time at work with three activities: He recruits and trains a cadre of foster parents ready to offer children a place to live outside their family homes. He is one of four people in the office that rotates as the on-call social worker handling requests for emergency placements. He also completes initial and follow-up inspections for group homes to make sure the rights of the youth residents are protected.

The Situation

Tuesday evening after work, Arnold headed to the gym to work out. After the gym, he met his mother for dinner at her favorite restaurant. He then went home, watched some television, and went to bed. A few hours later, he received a phone call. After two rings, he reached over to the nightstand and picked up the phone. A nurse from Memorial Hospital was on the other end of the line. She told Arnold that Ms. Williams gave birth to a baby girl three hours ago. The baby was stable, but her initial blood tests indicated the presence of THC (the chief intoxicant found in marijuana) in her blood. When Ms. Williams had arrived to deliver twelve hours ago, she also tested positive for THC. Arnold has interacted with Ms. Williams in the past. This is her third child. Arnold helped place the other two children in foster care. Arnold hung up the phone, dressed, and headed to the hospital.

When he arrived at the hospital, he headed to labor and delivery on the fourth floor. As he walked through the halls, he phoned three different foster parents to see if they were interested in caring for the baby girl. All three of the couples said no for different reasons. One couple was leaving on vacation the next day. The wife of another couple was recovering from the flu. The third couple did not feel comfortable caring for a child that was of a different race. As he stepped off the elevator, the head nurse told him the baby was in the nursery and Ms. Williams was in the second room on the left. Arnold headed first to the nursery to see the baby. As he was looking in the window, the pediatrician on call noticed him and came out of the nursery to give him an update on the baby. Arnold then went to see Ms. Williams. As he walked in, Ms. Williams recognized him and began crying uncontrollably. As she cried, she kept screaming, "Not again!" Arnold needed Ms. Williams to calm down so he could talk with her. He had to talk to her about her rights and his initial plan for the baby girl. At this point, he had no idea where he was going to place the baby. He also could not get a word in with Ms. Williams because of her screaming. He paused for a moment, let out a sigh, and wondered what to do and say next.

THE FOUNDATION OF SOCIAL WORK PRACTICE

These three case vignettes provide another look at the diversity and unity inherent in social work practice. Remember, the three social workers presented share a genuine care and concern for others, especially the most vulnerable and disenfranchised. They also practice for the same purpose, to enhance or restore well-being. Still, the vignettes again demonstrate the broad professional options available to social workers. Teresa Rogers completed her field internship in a religious congregation. Her internship provided Teresa experiences with micro, mezzo, and macro social work practice. Nicole Tanbaum interned at a behavioral health-care center that offered different types of clinical services. Arnold Young worked for the Florida DCF, a large state agency that provided an array of different services. Beyond their unified purpose, even though they were working in three very different settings, their social work practice is rooted in the same foundation of specific competences.

This chapter presents students with an initial overview of the foundation of social work practice. As in the previous chapter, we introduce the second group of competences that describe the method of social work. Then we provide an in-depth look at how one of the social workers in the case vignettes uses the methods to practice social work. The chapter concludes with discussion questions that provide students with opportunities to explore the use of the competences in the other cases. As we introduce the core competences and subsequent practice, we encourage students to think about how competent social work occurs in all the cases provided in the book.

THE COMPETENCES THAT DESCRIBE *WHAT WE DO*

Chapter 3 introduced the competences that describe what it means to be a social worker (*why we do*). Recall that the competences were professional identity, ethical practice, critical thinking, diversity in practice, and human rights and justice. In writing an introductory book for an introductory course, our intention is to emphasize the first group of competences to help students begin developing their own identities as social workers before focusing too much on the methods of practice. The content covered in this chapter, therefore, simply offers students an initial exposure to the foundations of social work practice methods.

Competence: Research-Informed Practice and Practice-Informed Research

Competent social workers have the ability to incorporate research and evaluation in their practice. When students graduate with a degree in social work, they can evaluate their own practice and use the findings of their evaluations to improve their work. Moreover, students demonstrate that they are knowledgeable consumers of research able to use findings from the extant literature to inform their practice and to improve policy and service delivery. As they assess the literature, students can demonstrate their ability to appraise and select interventions with the best available evidence. A part of demonstrating competence for research-based practice involves understanding the scientific process for building knowledge. Students have to comprehend qualitative and quantitative research methods commonly used in social science research. As students graduate and gain experience, they are expected to use their practice experiences to inform research in the field. For instance, as they interact with clients, students may eventually adapt current practice strategies to work with specific circumstances or to try new and innovative ways to enhance their effectiveness. Competent social workers are able to document their experiences and help researchers develop research questions and hypotheses to examine the efficacy of their efforts so other social workers can use the findings to improve their own practice with clients.

Competence: Human Behavior

Social workers incorporate knowledge of human behavior and the social environment into their practice. They are able to apply theories and knowledge from the liberal arts to understand the biological, social, cultural, psychological, and spiritual development of people in practice. Students ready for competent practice must demonstrate that they are knowledgeable of human behavior development across the life course. They also must understand the range and interactions of social systems that influence how people live and grasp the ways in which social systems can promote or deter people from maintaining or achieving enhanced well-being. As social workers contemplate the use of different theories in practice, they must be able to critique and apply what they know with diverse persons and various levels of the social environment. Moreover, students ready for practice can demonstrate using knowledge of development and of human behavior to guide the engagement, assessment, intervention, and evaluation of practice.

Competence: Policy Practice

Understanding the role of policy is an important part of social work practice. Competent social work actually involves engaging in policy practice to advance social and economic justice and to improve the effectiveness of services. Being actively engaged in policy practice requires students to know the history and current structures of social policies and services. They must be aware of how policy influences service delivery as well as the role practice plays in policy development. Competent social workers are able to analyze and formulate policies that enhance well-being. They are also able to develop and participate in collaborative efforts to advocate for policies that enhance the effectiveness of services for clients.

Competence: Practice Contexts

Social work practice occurs in many different settings. The combination of policies, personnel, fields of practice, and populations served creates a context for practice. Competent social workers can recognize and describe their context of practice. They also can recognize that the context of practice can change. Competent social workers remain informed, resourceful, and proactive in responding to the changing organizational, community, and societal contexts at the micro, mezzo, and macro levels of practice. Upon graduation, students must demonstrate the ability to continuously assess and attend to the changing locales, populations, scientific and technological developments, and emerging social trends relevant to providing effective services. Similar to policy practice, they should also be able to lead and participate in efforts to promote sustainable changes that affect the context of practice to improve the quality of services.

Competence: Engage, Assess, Intervene, and Evaluate

Amidst the different practice contexts, competent social work involves using a systematic helping process, commonly referred to as the generalist intervention model (Gibbs, Locke, & Lohman, 1990; Kirst-Ashman & Hull, 2008; Pincus & Minahan, 1973; Schatz, Jenkins, & Sheafor, 1990). The generalist intervention model is a dynamic and interactive process that includes four steps: (1) engagement, (2) assessment, (3) intervention, and (4) evaluation. Social workers combine their knowledge of individuals, groups, families, organizations, and communities with their skills in using the helping process to work with clients at the micro, mezzo, and macro levels of practice. As social workers use the generalist intervention model, they incorporate their professional identity, ethical practice, and critical thinking, as well as their knowledge and appreciation for diversity in practice and human rights and justice. They also incorporate their knowledge of research, human behavior, policy, and context to identify, analyze, and implement interventions based on the best available evidence to achieve client goals at all three levels of practice.

EXPLORING THE METHODS OF ARNOLD YOUNG AS A COMPETENT SOCIAL WORKER

Consider the case vignette of Arnold Young (case vignette 4.3) through the lens of the second group of competences. As a social worker in the foster care program, Arnold needs more than a desire to help children and families: He needs knowledge about human development, effective parenting, and family dynamics. He has to know how to access different sources of information, including research findings, to develop intervention strategies based on the best available evidence. He must know the formal state and agency policies that guide his practice. He must also be able to assess and work effectively within the informal policies and practices of his office. His practice also takes place in many different contexts. Arnold needs to understand how the various contexts may influence his work with clients. In some instances, he needs to be prepared to collaborate with other professionals to advocate for sustained changes in policies and contexts that can improve the quality of services. Finally, Arnold needs to be proficient at using the four-step helping process to intervene with children, families, foster families, and organizations in the community.

Let us now consider the competences as he fulfills the three primary functions in the foster care program. Recall that Arnold spends the majority of his time recruiting and training a cadre of foster parents, handling requests for emergency placements when he is the on-call social worker, and completing initial and follow-up inspections for group homes.

Arnold will need to use all the competences to successfully recruit and train foster parents. He will need a working knowledge of different theories of motivation to help him communicate effectively with potential foster parents. He also may need a working knowledge of different theories of learning so he can implement effective training materials. Deciding on actual methods also involves research-based practice. Arnold needs to know how to search for and examine relevant research to implement the best available strategies for recruiting and training foster parents. Knowing the agency and state policies for foster parents is also important: He must know the policies well enough to help people navigate the process of becoming licensed foster parents. He also needs to know the policies well enough to screen out people who are ineligible to become foster parents. The context may also influence his efforts. Arnold works for a large public agency where his practice involves matching foster parents with children served by the state. The way he recruits and trains foster parents may be different from another social worker working for a private agency. Moreover, the children served by the state, as opposed to a private agency, may face unique circumstances that require special consideration when placing them with foster parents.

Arnold will also need to use the four-step helping process to successfully recruit and train foster parents. In fact, he will likely have to engage, assess, intervene, and evaluate his work at two levels of practice. On the one hand, Arnold will use the four-step process with individuals and families: Arnold needs to engage, assess, intervene, and evaluate his work with individuals and families as he decides whether they are prepared to be foster parents. On the other hand, Arnold will use the four-step process with the whole program: Arnold will need to engage, assess, intervene, and evaluate the effectiveness of the overall program from the perspectives of the children, families, colleagues, supervisors, and other stakeholders. He also will need to use the process to initiate and advocate for changes he determines will improve the process of recruiting and training foster parents.

Conducting inspections for group homes also requires the knowledge and skills of a competent social worker. Using the four-step process, when Arnold engages owners and employees of group homes, he incorporates all of his knowledge from human behavior theory and research to ensure that children have safe and supportive living environments. His inspections involve collecting, organizing, and interpreting different types of data to make assessments about the suitability of the group homes. Arnold must examine the credentials and availability of the staff, the amount of space, the rules and activities, and the financial stability of the homes when making assessments. He also needs to consider the unique contexts of different group homes. The neighborhood, type of housing, proximity to schools, and the number and specific characteristics of the staff and children all influence the appropriateness of the environment. In addition, he needs to know the state and agency policies so he can interpret the information to determine whether to approve different group homes.

After assessment, Arnold will need to intervene with group homes. In his role of inspector, Arnold will serve as a negotiator and mediator between the children, the agency, and the group homes. If he discovers anything in his assessment that group homes need to address, he will have to initiate a plan of action with owners and employees to improve their facilities. When Arnold determines group homes are ready for approval or are deemed unfit, he will need to intervene by facilitating the transition of status of the group homes. Arnold will also critically analyze, monitor, and evaluate the changes made by group homes attempting to be in compliance. Macrolevel or program-level evaluation of the overall inspection process is also essential as he seeks to improve the quality of the living environments for children and the customer service interactions with representatives from the group homes.

Handling on-call emergency placements involves using the second group of competences, though perhaps targeted to time-limited situations. Before serving as an on-call social worker, Arnold needs knowledge of crisis intervention theories and strategies, the policies guiding the emergency removal of children, as well as an understanding of the research literature on best practices for working with clients in crises in general, and working with parents and children specifically. He also needs a vast knowledge of the emergency resources in the community, including members of families, foster parents, group homes, and other housing options.

As part of his knowledge of resources, Arnold needs to assess the contextual environments of different living situations to understand how they may potentially affect the children. He also needs to understand the contextual influences of the places where he handles emergency placement requests. The circumstances involved in going to a single residential home in a small community are probably different from those involved in going to a doctor's office, a school, or a large apartment complex with hundreds of tenants. Arnold may have to adjust how he engages people from different contexts as he fulfills his responsibility of protecting the safety of the children. He also will use the four-step process to work with people on a very short-term basis. In most cases, his direct practice with people seeking help with emergency placements may occur during the course of just a few hours or a single day.

Recall the situation described in case vignette 4.3. Arnold received a phone call from a nurse at a hospital telling him that Ms. Williams gave birth to a baby girl that tested positive for THC in her blood. The nurse also told him that when Ms. Williams arrived at the hospital, she too tested positive. We also learn that Arnold has worked with Ms. Williams before. This is her third child and Arnold helped place the other two children. Consider all of the things Arnold must think about and do as he seeks to serve those involved. Arnold must consider the safety and rights of the infant, the needs and rights of Ms. Williams, the needs and perspective of the hospital, the needs of the potential foster family or children's home, and even the needs and perspective of the agency. As a competent social worker, Arnold will have to call on his knowledge and skills to work effectively with everyone involved. His ability to use the four-step helping process informed by his knowledge of human behavior, research, policy, and context will help him make sound judgments in a short amount of time.

SUMMARY

Arnold Young is an effective social worker because of the unique combination of competences that define his professional identity and method of practice. He incorporates his knowledge and skill of research, human behavior, policy, and context with his ability to use the four-step helping process of engagement, assessment, intervention, and evaluation. Furthermore, his training and experience prepared him to represent his professional identity, engage in ethical practice, use critical thinking, understand and appreciate the dimensions of diversity in practice, and advocate for human rights and justice. Taken together, the competences represent *why* and *what* Arnold does as a social worker. As students contemplating or pursuing careers in social work, we recognize some may be excited about the many opportunities to care about and enhance the well-being of people. In the same way, we recognize some may be overwhelmed with all they need to learn, know, and do as competent social workers. The next eight chapters will empower students as they begin developing their own professional identities so they are ready to continue their journey of becoming competent social workers.

DISCUSSION QUESTIONS

1. In what ways has your liberal arts education prepared you for understanding developmental stages of human development? What areas do you need to continue to develop in regards to understanding human development?

2. What and where are the most appropriate resources for learning about policies that affect the vulnerable populations with whom social workers work?

3. Compare and contrast some of the contextual factors that you think might arise for a social worker who is working in a public, governmental organization versus one that works in the same role at a privately funded, not-for-profit agency providing similar services to clients.

Facts: Fact gathering and gaining as full an understanding of a situation as possible is essential to good social work practice.

4. In case vignette 4.1, Teresa Rogers is faced with a contextual issue in the church where she interns that involves a possible conflict with her perceived values and ideals as a social work intern. Review the latest edition of the NASW Code of Ethics and determine which portions are pertinent in guiding Teresa's next steps.

5. In case vignette 4.2, Nicole Tanbaum is faced with a dilemma that often is found with people with whom social workers practice. Her client's insurance company has refused to pay for services that the client needs. With your instructor and classmates, discuss what the responsibilities are for social workers who wish to continue providing services to clients in need.

Analysis: After having identified the facts available in a given situation, social workers make judgments about those facts in order to know how to intervene.

6. In addition to the NASW Code of Ethics, what additional resources are available to help Teresa address the concerns of the board regarding the mission statement of Project Hope? What priority should Teresa give each resource as she makes her decision about how to respond?

7. What are the systems and organizations that are restricting Ms. Sanders' access to needed services with Nicole Tanbaum in case vignette 4.2? What other resources might be available if this situation were to occur in your area?

Actions: After fact gathering and analysis of those facts, social workers decide on a plan of action that involves clear action steps designed to address any given situation.

8. For case vignettes 4.1 and 4.2 presented in this chapter, develop an action plan consisting of three or four action steps, listed in order of priority that the social worker or social work intern should take in their respective situations. Discuss these with your classmates and/or instructor.

REFERENCES

Gibbs, P., Locke, B. L., & Lohman, R. (1990). Paradigm for the generalist-advanced generalist continuum. *Journal of Social Work Education, 26*(3), 232–243.

Kirst-Ashman, K. K., & Hull, G. H. (2008). *Understanding generalist practice* (5th ed.). Pacific Grove, CA: Brooks/Cole.

Pincus, A., & Minahan, A. (1973). *Social work practice: Model and method.* Itasca, IL: Peacock.

Schatz, M., Jenkins, L., & Sheafor, B. (1990). Milford redefined: A model of initial and advanced generalist social work. *Journal of Social Work Education, 26*(3), 217–231.

PART II

The Professional Identity of Social Workers

CHAPTER FIVE

Developing the Personal Self-Awareness for Professional Social Work

As a profession with the broad, noble, and perhaps daunting purpose of caring about and enhancing the well-being of people, social work requires a unique approach to education. The social work curriculum has to prepare students to synthesize an understanding of *why* they practice, with an understanding of *what they do* in practice. Stated differently, social work education involves training students to incorporate specific knowledge and skills with awareness and appreciation for values that inform who they are becoming as professional social workers. It is not enough for students to learn the theories, techniques, and helping strategies that inform practice methods. Developing an identity and understanding of what it means to be a social worker is actually part of developing competence to practice as professionals. Again, the question of *why* social workers do what they do is inseparable from the question of *what* social workers do.

The next eight chapters focus on helping students begin the process of becoming competent social workers. The process starts here by giving students an opportunity to consider their personal self-awareness as a key element contributing to their professional identity as social workers. If students find what we have shared in the book thus far to be exciting or encouraging, or if they can envision themselves doing what has been described in the case vignettes from previous chapters, then they are ready to begin learning what it takes to develop the professional identity needed for competence-based social work. Consider the influence and interaction between personal self-awareness and professional identity of the social workers described in the next three cases.

CASE VIGNETTE 5.1. JEREMY WILLIAMS

Background

Jeremy took a circuitous route before finding social work. Growing up, he always seemed to get in trouble. His parents divorced when he was eleven, leaving him as the only male in his home living with his mother and three sisters. Because he was the oldest of the four children, his mother depended on him to help more. She especially needed him to watch after his sisters when she worked late or went out on the weekends. After his father left, however, Jeremy had other plans. With his father gone and his mother not around as often, he found himself with too much freedom for a teenager. Instead of helping out and being home, Jeremy spent a lot of time with friends, some of whom introduced him to drugs. Between tenth and twelfth grade his life revolved around using, selling, and buying drugs. Although he did enough to graduate on time with his high school diploma, his grades were so bad that he could not get into any four-year colleges. He spent the next four years living at home and going from job to job working for minimum wage. By this time, most of his friends had gone off to college, even many of the ones that had introduced him to drugs. While most of his peers were spending their late teens and early twenties preparing for careers and having fun at school, Jeremy found himself alone with very few options.

Things changed after his twenty-first birthday. In the spring of that year, Jeremy experienced two difficult losses that made him reevaluate his life and his future. Within the span of nine months, his grandfather and his mother were both diagnosed with cancer. His grandfather died in January, and his mother died just three months later. When his mother died, Jeremy faced having to live on his own and fend for himself for the first time in his life. His three sisters were all in college. He was the only one living at home with his mom. After her diagnosis, Jeremy watched his mother go through radiation and chemotherapy until her doctor determined that her health was not going to improve. He eventually referred Jeremy's mother to hospice services, where she received at-home palliative care until she died.

Jeremy learned about social work through his interactions with the hospice staff caring for him and his mother. Several weeks after his mother died, the social worker invited Jeremy to participate in a six-week bereavement support group she facilitated. It was during the group that he learned that one way of coping with grief is to complete something left undone as a living memorial for the person deceased. By the end of the support group, Jeremy decided to get his priorities straight, go back to school, and do something productive with his life in honor of his mother. He enrolled at a community college, completed a year of remedial course work, then applied to the local university where he earned his BSW. The following year, he earned his MSW. Now, at the age of thirty, Jeremy works as a medical social worker in the oncology unit of a large hospital.

The Context

As one of three social workers on the oncology unit, Jeremy is a member of a multidisciplinary medical team. The team consists of several oncologists, a pain management specialist, three nurses, a nutritionist, and a social worker. His primary responsibilities are to provide counseling, education, and community resource referrals to people with cancer and their families and friends. Jeremy also functions as a liaison and an advocate between patients and the rest of the medical team. He spends a lot of time gathering and organizing information for patients and families so they can make decisions about their treatment options. He then meets with patients and families to discuss their options, assess their concerns, determine their preferences, and make sure the rest of the medical team honors their wishes and rights.

As the social worker, he is also primarily responsible for discharge planning when patients receive treatment that requires overnight admission to the hospital. In a brief period, often less than twenty-four hours, Jeremy often has to assess the discharge orders from the physician, meet with patients and family to discuss their options, and make referrals for services. In some instances, after assessing the bio-psycho-social-spiritual and economic issues, Jeremy has to go back to the physicians to advocate on behalf of the patients to alter the discharge plan to fit the unique needs of patients and families.

The Situation

David and Heidi Elders arrived an hour early for treatment to meet with Jeremy. Six weeks ago, David had surgery to remove a malignant tumor in his left arm. He is almost finished with his postoperative chemotherapy treatment, after which he will have a follow-up appointment with the physician. Heidi usually takes David for treatment, then stays to take him home afterwards, because he usually feels too weak to drive.

The Elders are seeing Jeremy to talk about some of their day-to-day challenges in coping with David's cancer. David and Heidi have been married for eleven years. They have four children. Before surgery, David worked full time as the head butcher at a large supermarket. He started working for the supermarket at age fourteen, worked his way up behind the deli counter, and eventually became the head butcher. As head butcher, David earned enough so Heidi could stay home to raise the children. After their oldest child turned five, she took a job as a teaching assistant in the same school district where their kids attend school. It has been four months since David worked. Bills are mounting and they do not know what David will do for employment. Although the surgeon was able to remove the tumor without amputating his arm, he still is unable to use that arm for any extended period and has limited range of motion. He certainly cannot perform all the needed functions of a head butcher. Jeremy spent the first part of the session listening and empathizing with the Elders' situation. Now he wondered what to say and do to help them address their concerns. He needs to work with them to develop a plan.

CASE VIGNETTE 5.2. KRISTEN LANCASTER

Background

At an early age, Kristen learned to distinguish the two types of people in McCall, Idaho—tourists and residents. As a small town in central Idaho, most of the two thousand residents earned their livings working for places catering to tourists on vacation. People visit McCall to engage in an array of outdoor recreational activities such as skiing, fishing, and hunting. Don Lancaster, Kristen's father, worked as a wildlife parks and recreation officer. Cheryl, her mother, managed a motel located across the road from one of the large ski resorts. As one of the few families that have lived in McCall for more than three generations, they knew almost everyone in the community. As an officer, Don was friends with everyone in the police and fire departments. He also had gone to school with the mayor. Cheryl sings in the church choir. Every Wednesday for the past twenty-two years, she has had supper with the other choir members at church and then rehearsed with them. Until Kristen finished high school, she too went with her mother on Wednesday evenings. If there was anything going on in town, Kristen heard it discussed by her mom and the other people in the choir.

Kristen attended the only public school in the area. The school had only 250 students. Fewer than one-third of the students went to college after high school. Most students expected to learn a trade, get a job at one of the ski resorts, go to work in the lumber mill at the other end of the county, or enlist in the military. Kristen wanted to be the first person in her family to go to college. She also wanted to move back home after school and work in town or in the county. She attended Idaho State University and majored in social work. As a student, she was selected for the Title IV-E Idaho Child Welfare Scholars Program tuition assistance that helped cover her tuition and expenses. After earning her BSW and MSW, she worked with the Idaho Department of Health and Welfare (DHW) in the satellite office in McCall. She was the only social worker in the community.

The Context

As the only social worker in McCall, Kristen had to balance the unique context of working in her small town with being part of a large state agency. The DHW offices are organized into seven regions. Because the town is relatively close to Boise, the state capital, she was part of region four, which is the largest DHW office in the state. All of her colleagues and supervisors worked in Boise. Kristen spent most of her time screening and investigating the child protective and adult protective calls in the town. She also provided case management and supportive counseling to children and families seeking assistance, and participated in a staff supervision meeting in Boise every Thursday afternoon.

The Situation

A constant challenge in her position was trying to develop and coordinate access to needed services while respecting the rural culture of her clients. Residents of McCall referred to driving to Boise as "traveling over the hill." It was something they usually tried to avoid. Although separated by only one hundred miles, there was not much of the "big city" that folks from town appreciated. Even so, Kristen often had to make referrals for clients that involved multiple trips to Boise.

Recently, Kristen recognized that she made a significant number of referrals for young adults to attend parenting classes. The classes were important because she assessed that many of the young parents on her caseload needed to learn the necessary skills to care for their children. She also recognized, however, that she created tremendous strain for parents when she referred them for classes. The eight-week class was offered in Boise. In order to attend, parents had to arrange their work schedules so that they could block out the six hours needed to travel to Boise, attend the two-hour class, and return home. The weekly trip was expensive and difficult. Assuming they had transportation, it could take almost a whole tank of gas to make the round trip. In addition, the only road that connects McCall from Boise is a narrow, mountainous, two-lane highway that could be dangerous in inclement weather. Kristen decided to submit a proposal to her supervisor to allow her to facilitate the parenting classes for her clients in McCall.

A few weeks after submitting her proposal, Susan, her direct supervisor, asked Kristen to stick around after the Thursday staff meeting to talk about the parenting classes. In their meeting, Susan told Kristen she was impressed with the proposal. She also thought that she could convince the regional director to approve offering the parenting classes in McCall. Before taking it to the director, Susan asked Kristen to address two concerns she had about the proposal. Susan explained that she was concerned with the extent to which Kristen could protect the confidentiality of the clients in such a small community. She also was concerned about Kristen maintaining appropriate boundaries with clients she served in multiple capacities. Kristen performed all of the child investigations for the clients.

She also served as their case manager. Now she would be practicing as a direct provider. Kristen thought about her concerns. She appreciated Susan's perspective. She also knew Susan grew up in Los Angeles and has only been living in Idaho for four years. She lived in the biggest city in the state and did not really understand how different it is from living in McCall. She wondered how to respond.

CASE VIGNETTE 5.3. COURTNEY WHITT

Background

Until Courtney turned thirteen, she felt as if she lived two separate lives. She did very well in school, had a lot of friends, and teachers found her engaging, but her life at home was quite different: Courtney and her older brother never knew what to expect at home. Their mother suffered from depression and was critical of everything they did. She often yelled at them for even the smallest misbehavior. Their father was mostly disengaged from the family, except when he came home intoxicated, which happened a lot. Courtney knew to stay quiet and in her room whenever she suspected that her father was drunk. As critical as her mother was, at least she was not violent. When her father came home drunk, however, he became abusive.

A few days after her thirteenth birthday, Courtney walked into her house after school and found her parents in the kitchen having an intense argument. As she headed upstairs to her room, she heard her father hit her mother. Her mother screamed in pain. Courtney turned around and ran into the kitchen to plead with her dad to stop. He did not listen. Instead, he began yelling at her and eventually hit her several times in the face with a closed fist. The next day in school, the homeroom teacher noticed the bruises and cuts on her face. When the school bell rang at the end of homeroom, the teacher stopped Courtney to ask what happened. Courtney walked over to her teacher and broke down crying. She told her everything that happened. The teacher took Courtney to the front office, had her sit in the waiting area, and called the Department of Social Services (DSS) to report the abuse. After an investigation, the DSS moved Courtney and her brother to live with their grandparents.

Although Courtney loved her grandparents, at age thirteen she promised herself that as soon as she graduated high school she was going to make it on her own. A week after graduation, she enlisted in the Army and spent the next twenty-five years building a successful career. The year before she retired as a decorated master sergeant, she completed a course that helped prepare her for transitioning out of the military. As part of the course, Courtney met with a career counselor, took a career aptitude test, and learned that she would enjoy pursuing a career in the helping professions. Since she already had completed her undergraduate degree while in the Army, Courtney enrolled as a full-time student in an MSW program. Two years later, she was working as a civilian social worker in the Airman and Family Readiness unit at Wright-Patterson Air Force base (AFB) near Dayton, Ohio.

The Context

Wright-Patterson AFB is one of the largest military installations in the United States, with over 27,000 people working on base. The Airman and Family Readiness unit provides services to individuals, couples, and families with the primary purpose of ensuring the mission readiness of air personnel and supporting family adaptation to the Air Force way of life. Courtney works in the Exceptional Family Member Program (EFMP). The EFMP offers support to military families with members in need of special assistance. Social workers practicing in the EFMP can access a combination of local, state, and federal resources to address the medical, behavioral, and social needs of family members so that their military family members can remain mission ready. Courtney spends most of her time assessing and developing intervention plans for family members needing help from the EFMP that were recently assigned to Wright-Patterson AFB. She is also responsible for following up with family members receiving services every three months.

The Situation

As usual, Courtney had four assessments scheduled this morning. To prepare for the day, she arrived at work by 7:00 a.m. so she could review the files of the four people seeking assistance from the EFMP. Families receiving orders to the base that need help from the EFMP have to arrange for the program to receive all relevant records before they move to the installation. Her first appointment was at 7:30 a.m. with Captain Nelson and his wife Leslie, and their three children. When they arrived for their appointment, the person at the front desk called Courtney to let her know the Nelson family was in the waiting area.

Courtney walked to the waiting area to greet the Nelson family. When she saw that they had brought their children with them, she asked her colleague Taylor to come with her to meet the family. She introduced herself to everyone, showed the children where the playroom is for kids, and asked Captain Nelson and Leslie if it was okay for Taylor to stay with the children while they met in her office. They agreed and then followed Courtney to her office. Once in her office, Courtney sat down at her desk, opened up a large file, and asked how she could help them. Leslie responded by telling Courtney about her last two years and her concerns about being at Wright-Patterson AFB.

Leslie shared that two years ago, when she and her husband had been stationed at Patrick AFB in Florida, she began hearing voices. Although she had no prior history with mental illness, the voices became progressively worse and she ended up going into a hospital for three weeks. Living in Florida, Captain Nelson and his family had been close to Leslie's parents who were able to stay with the children when she went to the hospital. When the psychiatrist discharged Leslie, she referred her to a thirty-day partial hospital program to help her transition home. Again, her parents took care of the children. Since then, Leslie shared that she has been doing better. She said that for the next year, she sensed that everything was back in order in her life. Then Captain Nelson received orders to Wright-Patterson AFB. She shared that although she knew they were due to get orders, she dreaded having to move away from her parents. Now they lived over a thousand miles away from her family and anyone she knows. Moreover, her husband was about to head overseas on a short-term temporary duty assignment. She worried about being in a new place alone with just the children. She also worries about hearing voices again without her husband being close to home. Captain Nelson explained he, too, is concerned about his family. He leaves in two weeks and hopes that the EFMP can help Leslie develop a contingency plan in case she needs help while he is gone. Courtney looked over the file, thought about all the potential services Leslie may need, and then noticed the time. Her next appointment was in ten minutes. She wondered what to say and do next.

DEVELOPING A COMMITMENT TO PERSONAL SELF-AWARENESS

Competent social work involves attending to the interactions between personal and professional identity. Stated differently, social work is an applied profession that combines specific knowledge, values, and skills with an emphasis on personal self-awareness. On the one hand, Jeremy Williams, Kristen Lancaster, and Courtney Whitt earned degrees in social work where they learned core knowledge and skills that unify them as competent professionals. On the other hand, their unique backgrounds and experiences helped shape and continue to shape who they are as social workers. In fact, an important part of social work education involves learning to consider the integration of personal self-awareness with professional growth.

Throughout the curriculum, students must learn to give deliberate attention to how their personal beliefs and experiences influence their professional identities, and vice versa.

As part of considering potential careers in social work, we encourage students to consider how comfortable they are with engaging in self-reflection. Personal self-reflection is a key element of competent social work practice. Engaging in continual personal self-reflection is part of ensuring professional growth and development. It is one of the main ways social workers attend to professional boundaries. It is also part of engaging in career-long learning and recognizing the importance of supervision and consultation.

Attending to the interactions between personal and professional identity is often a primary focus of social work supervision. Recall that social work practice involves trained professionals using a combination of knowledge, values, and skills in the form of interventions within the context of helping relationships. As social workers enter into helping relationships, they are more than robots that calculate and assess situations in order to choose the correct intervention. They interact with clients (individuals, groups, communities) as caring human beings with their own personal histories, life trajectories, and experiences. As trained professionals, however, they can attend to their personal experiences by practicing self-reflection in combination with their use of knowledge, values, and skills to intervene with clients within the context of helping relationships. Supervision helps social workers remain deliberate in practicing self-reflection and self-correction to ensure continual professional development as they work with clients.

Consider the social workers described in the case vignettes. One quality that makes them competent professionals is their ability to engage in personal self-reflection and synthesize their personal and professional identities. Perhaps the most explicit example comes from Kristen Lancaster (case vignette 5.2). One factor that makes Kristen an effective social worker in McCall is that she knows the culture. Her personal history and life trajectory provide her with a unique perspective. The combination of her professional social work training with her being a resident of the town likely helps her work successfully in the community. In the same way, Susan, her supervisor, also has her own unique background. When Susan asks Kristen about her concerns, she understandably is asking Kristen to attend to the interactions between her personal identity and her professional identity. Susan probably appreciates the unique perspective Kristen brings to her work, and was impressed by the proposal. What she is doing is asking Kristen to be deliberate in practicing self-reflection so she can remain attentive to her professional roles and boundaries. In the same way, students must learn to practice deliberate self-reflection so they, too, can remain attentive to professional roles and boundaries as they become social workers.

Figure 5.1 illustrates the ongoing contemplative cycle needed for social work. Practicing deliberate self-reflection involves students learning to pay attention to how personal experiences, desires, values, and expectations influence their professional identities. It also involves synthesizing what they learn through education and practice with their personal identities. Deliberate self-reflection is a process of continual learning and assessment that leads to professional growth and development as social workers.

Figure 5.1. Contemplative Cycle Needed for Social Work

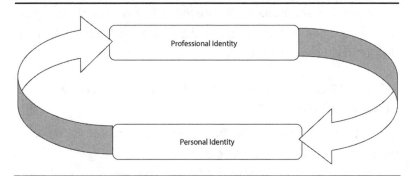

Professional Identity

Personal Identity

Three levels of personal reflection need to occur in social work: (1) Students need to develop a certain level of awareness of personal experiences, values, and expectations, then continually explore how their experiences, values, and expectations influence their interpretation of the knowledge, values, and skills they learn in their classes. (2) Students also need to reflect on how the knowledge, values, and skills they learn in their social work classes shape their future reflections of experiences, values, and expectations. (3) A third level of contemplation is needed when students enter field and then later accept positions as social workers. When students begin practicing, they need to continually examine how the knowledge, values, and skills learned in class and their personal experiences, values, and expectations influence their practice with clients (at the micro, mezzo, or macro levels of practice). Again, students also need to reflect on how their interactions with clients reinforce, challenge, or shape their knowledge, values, and skills, as well as their future personal experiences, values, and expectations.

Chapter 6 introduces students to the four ways social workers develop professional identity. The rest of chapter 5 provides students the opportunity to begin engaging in personal reflection on some of the major areas that warrant contemplation as social workers. We encourage students to consider the questions we provide as starting points for reflection. We also encourage students to practice engaging in ongoing personal reflection throughout their education and careers in social work. We provide a few contemplation questions at the end of the remaining chapters to support students as they practice engaging in ongoing personal reflection.

MAJOR AREAS THAT WARRANT CONTEMPLATION OF PERSONAL IDENTITY

We encourage students intending to become social workers to consider a few broad open-ended questions as they engage in personal reflection: What is your story? Why do you want to be a social worker? What do you want to do as a social worker?

What Is Your Story?

Social work is a diverse profession. People from different countries, cultures, and socioeconomic backgrounds become social workers. In the same way, people from different family backgrounds, with different beliefs and values, and different childhood experiences become social workers. Think about the social workers described in the case vignettes from the last few chapters. They all have unique stories. Their stories shape their personal identities, which subsequently intersect with and shape their professional identities. Understanding your story, therefore, is a good place to begin the process of engaging in personal reflection for competent social work. Use the following questions to begin thinking about your story.

Family
- Where did you grow up?
- How would you describe your childhood family?
- What were some of your family traditions?
- How did your family spend holidays?
- Were there times of joy and happiness in your family? Can you describe some of them?
- Were there times of hurt, loss, and sorrow in your family? Can you describe some of them?
- How would you describe your current family?
- How would you describe your relationships with different family members? Take time to consider as many as possible.
- How would family members describe you?
- How would they describe their relationships with you?

School and Peers
- What experiences from school do you remember?
- How would you describe yourself as a student?
- How would your teachers describe you as a student?
- How have you changed since high school?

• How would you describe your relationships with friends?

• What kind of exposure have you had with people who are different from you?

Interests, Strengths, and Areas of Growth

• What do you do for fun?

• How do you prefer to spend time on the weekends?

• What are your hobbies?

• What do you do well?

• What makes you a good person?

• What do you need to work on to become a better person?

Why Do You Want to Be a Social Worker?

Engaging in ongoing reflection about the reasons to become and remain a social worker is essential for competent practice. Social work is such a broad and dynamic profession that students, and even seasoned practitioners, sometimes discover that it can be overwhelming to find their place in the profession. Students will also find that entering into helping relationships to enhance the well-being of others and to create communities where people can enhance their own well-being is complex, challenging, and often emotionally draining work. It is important from the outset that students practice developing the self-awareness and introspection to remember why they are seeking to become social workers. Once they are practicing, it will be important for students to continually assess their reasons and motivations for remaining in the profession. Individuals, groups, families, organizations, and communities count on working with competently trained social workers. Other social workers count on their colleagues to advocate for client access to the most effective services, to be committed to continuous learning, and to represent the profession, its mission, and its core values. Use the following questions to begin reflecting on why you want to be a social worker.

- How did your interest in social work develop?
- What is it about social work that you find "fits" with what you want to do after college?
- What other fields of study have you explored?
- When thinking about the fields you have explored, why have you selected social work?
- How do you describe social work to your family?
- What do you tell your friends about social work?
- If family members or friends ask about your reasons for majoring in social work, what do you tell them?
- How has your interest in social work changed since the beginning of the course?
- What are all the ways you would finish the following sentence? "I am becoming a social worker because ..."

What Do You Want to Do as a Social Worker?

Students should begin thinking about what they want to do in the profession. There are a myriad of options available to competent social workers. There are different population groups, different types of organizations, different social issues to address, and different roles needing the unique blend of purpose, knowledge, values, and skills that only social workers can provide. Most of what students will learn in school is transferable across many areas of practice. Moreover, as students complete their field internships and begin working after graduation, they will gain experiences that are also transferable. In other words, you will have opportunities for professional growth and flexibility throughout your career. Based on our experience teaching and advising hundreds of students, we encourage you to practice reflecting on what you want to do in the profession in connection with your reasons for wanting to become a social worker. Thinking about both can help you gain a sense of cohesion necessary for developing and maintaining your professional identity. Use the following questions to begin reflecting on what you want to do as a social worker.

- What types of people can you envision working with in practice?
- What size agency do you envision working with in practice?
- Can you envision working directly with clients?
- Can you envision working with individuals, groups, and/or families?
- Can you envision working with organizations and/or community members?
- How important is professional autonomy in your practice as a social worker?
- How important is structure in your practice as a social worker?

SUMMARY

Personal self-awareness is a key component of professional identity. Competent social work involves developing the professional identity to serve as a representative of our field, our mission, and our core values. It also involves a commitment to personal and professional growth. Practicing personal reflection is an essential part of engaging the contemplative cycle of personal and professional identity needed for social work.

We encourage you to use the questions above to begin practicing deliberate personal reflection. Commit to continual personal reflection as you complete this course, take additional courses, and gain experience from field and professional practice. Use figure 5.1 as a visual representation and reminder to think about how your personal reflections shape what you learn and do in social work. Also, think about how what you learn and do in social work shapes your personal reflections. For instance, chapter 6 introduces the four primary ways social workers develop professional identity. As you read the chapter, continue thinking about your story, the reasons you want to become a social worker, and what you want to do as a social worker. You may discover that some of your thoughts and expectations about the profession change, while other thoughts and expectations stay the same. In addition, you may find it helpful to keep a journal or to share some of your reflections with one or two trusted colleagues. We recommend using whatever technique that keeps you invested in ongoing personal reflection.

DISCUSSION QUESTIONS

For the discussion questions in the remaining chapters, we ask that you consider the content provided in this and following chapters on self-reflection. Consider each question, keeping in mind what issues warrant self-reflection and consideration. Additionally, as you read the case vignettes, consider the self-reflection needed by the social workers, then consider how your own context might influence your actions in responding to the situation at hand.

1. What are some of the unique aspects of your personal story and journey that you believe warrant further exploration and reflection as you consider a career in social work?

2. Engage your fellow students in discussion about their unique stories and journeys that brought them to your class and inspired their curiosity about social work as a profession. What are some of the ways that your personal story and journey differ significantly from those of your classmates? What are some of the ways that they are similar? What strengths do you believe that you and your classmates would bring to a career in social work?

3. What are some populations and issues with which social workers engage in the helping relationship that you believe may pose some difficulty for you if you were to work with them as a professional social worker?

Facts: Fact gathering and gaining as full an understanding of a situation as possible is essential to good social work practice.

4. In case vignette 5.1, Jeremy Williams has a history of illicit (illegal) drug behavior. On the Web, explore the consequences of illicit drug behavior during adolescence on later life. What are some of the consequences that Jeremy needs to be constantly aware of as he engages clients in professional social work relationships?

5. In case vignette 5.2, Kristen Lancaster brings strength to her position because of her longtime knowledge of her birth community where she now practices. As discussed in the chapter, that strength might also be an area of concern when dealing with client confidentiality. What are some other potential areas of concern that Kristen should explore in self-reflection and in the context of supervision regarding her role as social worker where she grew up?

6. In case vignette 5.3, Courtney Whitt grew up in a home where her mother struggled with depression, which affected Courtney in subtle but significant ways. Now that she is in a situation where she will be working with a family with a mother dealing with a mental illness, what should she consider and do as she engages them in the helping relationship?

Analysis: After identifying the facts available in a given situation, social workers make judgments about those facts in order to know how to intervene.

7. In each of the vignettes presented in this chapter, what are the strengths (e.g., of the worker and the client) that you can identify that should be maximized in the helping relationship?

8. List as many factors as you can regarding each vignette, other than those you have already explored, that should be considered before developing action plans in each case.

Actions: After fact gathering and analysis of those facts, social workers decide on a plan of action that involves clear action steps designed to address any given situation.

9. For each of the vignettes presented in this chapter, develop an action plan consisting of three or four action steps, listed in order of priority that the social worker or social work intern should take in their respective situations. Discuss these with your classmates and/or instructor.

6

Developing the Professional Identity for Social Work

Becoming a competent social worker involves ongoing learning and self-assessment. Students need to practice personal self-reflection to develop the self-awareness needed to represent the profession and practice accordingly. Chapter 5 provided students an opportunity to consider their personal stories, why they want to become social workers, and what they want to do in the profession. Now students need to begin analyzing and incorporating what they learn in school with their personal self-awareness.

In this chapter, we introduce the four ways social workers develop and maintain professional identity: (1) formal education, (2) licensure and credentials, (3) membership and participation in professional organizations, and (4) practice wisdom. As students read the chapter and discuss the content in class, we encourage them to think about how what they are learning may reinforce, challenge, or inform their personal reflections. We provide a few contemplation questions at the end of the chapter to help students think deeply about the material.

FORMAL EDUCATION

Formal education is perhaps the primary pathway toward developing professional identity. For students considering the profession, it is useful to have a clear perception of social work education as compared to other social science fields. Whereas other social sciences emphasize the study of human phenomena, social work is an applied academic discipline and profession. For instance, psychology is the study of the human mind, sociology is the study of society, anthropology is the study of human kind, and economics is the study of the production, distribution, and consumption of goods and services. In social work, however, every course—even this introductory course—focuses on preparing students to engage people in helping relationships to enhance the well-being of individuals, groups, and communities, and/or to help individuals, groups, and communities enhance their own well-being. Students take courses from the other social sciences. Social work educators may also draw on information from several fields when teaching their courses. The critical distinction for students in social work is that they learn to incorporate and synthesize information from several areas of study into action or competent practice.

Information Needed for Competent Practice

Depending on when programs offer the introductory course in social work, undergraduate students considering careers in the profession have probably met with an advisor and have taken courses required for entry into the social work major. Before graduate students are admitted into an MSW program, an admissions committee probably assessed their undergraduate transcripts to make sure they had completed certain courses. In some instances, students may be admitted to an MSW program contingent on completion of a few additional courses before they start or before they graduate.

As part of developing professional identity, we believe it is helpful for students to understand and appreciate the relevance of their courses in helping them become social workers. Let us, therefore, briefly consider addressing two questions: (1) What do social workers need to know for competent practice? and (2) What courses help prepare students for what they will do as competent social workers?

Recall that social work involves engaging in helping relationships at micro (individuals), mezzo (groups), and macro (organizations and communities) levels of practice. Social workers need information for competent practice at each level. Micro practice requires a holistic understanding of human beings. Social workers need information to understand people as physical, emotional, social, and spiritual beings. Mezzo practice requires understanding how individuals interact and function with other individuals. Social workers need knowledge about families, about different cultures, and about the way individuals develop, access, and maintain relationships with different groups. Macro practice requires understanding how individuals and groups interact and function with and within organizations and communities. Macro practice also requires understanding how individuals and groups can shape organizations and communities. Social workers need knowledge of organizational theory, community change, community development, economics, and political science. At all three levels of practice, social workers also need knowledge of diversity and justice.

Based on years of experience and expertise, faculty members intentionally select courses to prepare students to enter into social work. The courses provide students with information for all three levels of practice. There are at least eight types of courses, also known as pre-cognates, students are often required to take as part of their admission into the field (see box 6.1). Given what social workers need to know for competent practice, students should

Box 6.1. List of Common Courses Required as Pre-Cognates for Social Work

- Biology (intro, human anatomy)
- Psychology (intro, abnormal, neuropsychology)
- Sociology (intro, human diversity)
- Economics (micro, macro, and/or economics of poverty)
- Political Science
- Philosophy (philosophy of ethics and/or philosophy of justice)
- Principles of Speech Communications
- Statistics

understand and appreciate why they take these eight types of courses.

Students usually complete courses in *biology* and *psychology* to provide them with knowledge they will need when working with individuals. Students complete courses in *sociology* so they can appreciate human diversity and understand how people tend to function in different groups. Courses in *economics* help students grasp the importance of having access to resources and services for well-being. In the same way, economic courses help students understand the financial dynamics of poverty. Courses in *political science* and *philosophy* provide students with a foundation for understanding policy and appreciating the social work emphasis on human rights and justice. Courses in *principles of speech communications* help students learn the principles of effectively preparing, presenting, and consuming messages in one-on-one, small group, and public speaking contexts. *Statistics* courses prepare students to assess and incorporate social work practices based on the best available evidence. Statistics courses also prepare students for research courses where they learn to analyze and evaluate their practice, as well as develop new knowledge to advance the profession.

Levels of Social Work Education for Competent Practice

Choosing a social work program is essential for developing professional identity. There are a few things students must consider when deciding where to complete their educations. Consequently, the decisions students make about their educations will strongly influence the extent to which they can identify themselves as professionally prepared competent social workers. Perhaps the most important consideration in the United States is choosing a social work program that is accredited by CSWE. Attending a CSWE-accredited program is crucial to being identified as a professional social worker. CSWE is the national social work organization that sets and oversees the educational standards for social work programs. As the national organization, the accreditation standards developed by CSWE are recognized all over the country. The public, therefore, recognizes that students graduating from an accredited program are indeed social workers. Consider, for example, Kristen Lancaster (case vignette 5.2) and Courtney Whitt (case vignette 5.3) from chapter 5. Kristen likely attended a social work program in Idaho. Courtney likely attended a program in Ohio. Still, they are both seen by the public as competent professional social workers because they attended and graduated from programs accredited by CSWE. As graduates of accredited programs, Kristen and Courtney can be hired anywhere in the United States because employers know they were prepared with similar content that was rigorously scrutinized and evaluated, and that was found to meet the educational standards necessary for competent practice. In the same way, graduating from accredited programs makes Kristen and Courtney eligible to seek further social work licensure and credentials anywhere in the country.

Students must also decide whether to pursue BSW, MSW, or doctoral education. Each level prepares students for different kinds of competent practice and subsequently shapes their professional identity as social workers.

Bachelor of Social Work

BSW education prepares students for basic professional practice. Basic professional practice means that graduates of BSW programs are ready to synthesize and apply theoretical knowledge, practice skills, and values in the service of clients, whether they are individuals, groups, families, communities, or organizations. CSWE characterizes basic practice as generalist practice. The definition of generalist practice, as given in the EPAS, highlights all the elements of basic competent social work. When reading the definition, notice how the terms and phrases make up the social work competences, and subsequently, the chapters of this textbook:

> Generalist practice is grounded in the liberal arts and the person and environment construct. To promote human and social well-being, generalist practitioners use a range of prevention and intervention methods in their practice with individuals, families, groups, organizations, and communities. The generalist practitioner identifies with the social work profession and applies ethical principles and critical thinking in practice. Generalist practitioners incorporate diversity in their practice and advocate for human rights and social and economic justice. They recognize, support, and build on the strengths and resiliency of all human beings. They engage in research-informed practice and are proactive in responding to the impact of context on professional practice. BSW practice incorporates all of the core competencies. (CSWE, 2008, pp. 7–8)

Master of Social Work

Social work education at the MSW level prepares students for advanced professional practice. In addition to incorporating the core competences necessary for basic practice, the MSW equips students with specific and demonstrated mastery of knowledge and skills in at least one specialized area of practice. An MSW program normally takes two years of academic course work to complete. The courses in the first year are commonly known in the profession as foundation courses. Similar to the BSW, the foundation courses in the

MSW program prepare students for basic competent practice. Because the first year of the MSW program is so similar to the BSW, students graduating with a BSW from a program accredited by CSWE are often eligible to apply for advanced standing in MSW programs. If admitted into an advanced-standing program, students can often complete their MSW degree in approximately one more year.

When students matriculate into the second year or are admitted into advanced standing of their MSW programs, they usually select a concentration area for specialized learning. Depending on the expertise of the faculty, MSW programs may offer concentration courses on practice with children and families, health and mental health practice, practice with communities and organizations, practice with older adults, specialized courses in clinical social work, forensic social work, international social work, or even advanced generalist practice for students working with rural populations. In each of the different concentrations, students learn to incorporate specific knowledge and skills with the core competences in nuanced ways when practicing in specific areas of social work. The CSWE EPAS states, "Advanced practitioners refine and advance the quality of social work practice and that of the larger social work profession. They synthesize and apply a broad range of interdisciplinary and multidisciplinary knowledge and skills. In areas of specialization, advanced practitioners assess, intervene, and evaluate to promote human and social well-being. To do so they suit each action to the circumstances at hand, using the discrimination learned through experience and self-improvement. Advanced practice incorporates all of the core competencies augmented by knowledge and practice behaviors specific to a concentration" (CSWE, 2008, p. 8).

Doctorate in Philosophy or Doctorate in Social Work

Beyond earning an MSW for advanced professional practice, a PhD or DSW prepares competent practitioners for teaching, research, or high levels of administration, supervision, and leadership in social work. CSWE does not accredit PhD or DSW programs, however. As a result, doctoral education varies greatly across different schools. Some programs emphasize advanced research training, while other programs emphasize doctoral-level clinical training and supervision. Many schools offer a balance between preparation for teaching, research, and administration.

Recognizing the inherent variation available in doctoral education, an organization called the Group for the Advancement of Doctoral Education in Social Work (GADE) developed a document to highlight guidelines for quality in social work doctoral programs (GADE, 2013). Briefly, students should consider the institutional context, the faculty, the students, the curriculum, the resources, and the presence of an active program review system when choosing a doctoral program in social work. An in-depth discussion of specific characteristics of quality in each dimension is beyond the scope and purpose of the book. We encourage students to visit the GADE website (www.gadephd.org) to learn more about doctoral education in social work and to read the *PhD Quality Guidelines and DSW Guidelines*.

LICENSURE AND CREDENTIALS

Along with formal education, licensure and credential options available in social work can help develop and maintain professional identity. Licensing in social work is mandatory in every state. In fact, according to state legislation in many states, licensure is required before students can refer to themselves as social workers. The purpose of licensure is to identify, uphold, and regulate standards of professional practice to protect citizens from malpractice or professional misconduct. States normally regulate four levels of licensure. The qualifications for licensure are entwined with completion of formal education from programs accredited by CSWE. (1) Upon earning a BSW from an accredited program, students planning to begin practicing are eligible to become licensed bachelor of social work professionals (LBSW). (2) Students earning their MSW from an accredited program are eligible to become licensed master of social work (LMSW) professionals. (3) After two years of post-master's experience practicing under the supervision of an experienced social worker, they are eligible to become licensed independent social workers (LISW). (4) When they have two years of post-master's clinical experience, they are eligible to become licensed clinical social workers (LCSW). We encourage students to learn more about licensure by visiting the state social work licensure board Web site for their state. We also encourage students to visit other state licensure boards' Web sites to compare the licensure options and requirements across different states.

In addition to licensure, social workers can choose to pursue a number of different credentials. Whereas licensure is mandatory in many states, seeking a certification or credential is a voluntary way of communicating advanced competence in specialized levels and areas of practice. Students can pursue credentials exclusive to social work as well as credentials offered to practitioners from multiple disciplines; describing all the options available to social workers is beyond the scope of the book. Instead, a brief review of some will provide students with examples of the kinds of options available to them after graduation.

Certifications and credentials are usually offered as an optional benefit of membership within professional organizations. To provide several examples, we review the professional and advanced professional credentials available through NASW (2012a). NASW offers certifications for BSWs, certifications for MSWs, and three different credentials. Notice how the eligibility criteria include completion of a social work degree from an accredited university as well as other criteria that build on completion of a social work degree.

Certifications and Credentials for BSWs

After completing their BSW, students can pursue four different certifications through NASW. They can become (1) certified social work case managers (C-SWCM), (2) certified children, youth, and family social workers (C-CYFSW), (3) certified social workers in gerontology (SW-G), or (4) certified hospice and palliative care social workers (CHP-SW).

Social workers with the certified social work case manager (C-SWCM) certification have training and experience working with clients to attain goals using specific knowledge, values, and skills. C-SWCMs are trained and committed to focusing on client strengths and client self-care strategies that account for individual bio-psycho-social-spiritual well-being and the strengths and challenges of the social systems that affect the well-being of individuals, groups, and families. The eligibility requirements for the C-SWCM include a BSW from an accredited university; evidence of at least three years and 4,500 hours of paid, supervised, and post-BSW experience as a case manager; current state BSW-level license or a passing Association of Social Work Boards (ASWB) BSW-level exam score; and evidence of adhering to the NASW Code of Ethics and the NASW Standards for Continuing Professional Education.

Students intending to focus their practice on children and youth may want to consider earning the certified children, youth, and family social workers (C-CYFSW) certification. NASW describes the C-CYFSW as a professional credential for a select group: social workers who have attained national distinction for their work with, or on behalf of, children, youth, and families. Social workers with this certification use their knowledge and experience of generalist practice to work in the areas of direct practice, advocacy, policy, program development, program evaluation, research, supervision, education, and administration, to enhance the well-being of children, youth, and families, in a variety of practice settings. The eligibility requirements for the C-CYFSW include a BSW from an accredited university; twenty hours of post-degree continuing education specific to practice with children, youth, and families; evidence of at least one year and 1,500 hours of paid, supervised, and post-BSW experience with children, youth, and families; current state BSW-level license or a passing ASWB BSW-level exam score; and evidence of adhering to the NASW Code of Ethics and the NASW Standards for Continuing Professional Education.

The social worker in gerontology (SW-G) credential is for social workers who practice primarily with older adults. Social workers with the SW-G have specialized skills including assessment of older adults' needs and functional capacity, expertise regarding physical and mental health issues, case and care management, long-term care, elder abuse, quality-of-life issues, service planning, and advance care planning. Work with older adults happens at the micro, mezzo, and macro levels of practice. Regardless of the practice level, the primary goal is to address the specific challenges of the aging process by promoting independence, autonomy, and dignity in later life. SW-Gs must be knowledgeable about unique legislation, policies, and social programs that affect older adults. In addition, they must be knowledgeable about the aging process and the issues facing older adults and their caregivers. They also must be adept at accessing resources for clients and becoming strong advocates who champion clients' rights. The eligibility requirements for the SW-G include a BSW from an accredited university; evidence of at least three years and 4,500 hours of paid, supervised, and post-BSW experience working with older adults under social work supervision; current state BSW-level license or a passing ASWB BSW-level exam score; and evidence of adhering to the NASW Code of Ethics and the NASW Standards for Continuing Professional Education.

The certified hospice and palliative care social worker (CHP-SW) credential is for social workers who practice primarily with clients and families facing a terminal illness. Social workers holding this certification focus on the bio-psycho-social-spiritual components of physical health and mental health from a strengths-based perspective. They also develop intervention plans of care in the context of, and contributing to, an interdisciplinary approach to comprehensive care of clients and their families. The eligibility requirements for the

CHP-SW include a BSW from an accredited university; at least twenty hours of continuing education related specifically to hospice and palliative care; evidence of at least three years of supervised experience working in hospice and palliative care; current state BSW-level licensure or a passing ASWB BSW-level exam score; and evidence of adhering to the NASW Code of Ethics and the NASW Standards for Continuing Professional Education.

Certifications and Credentials for MSWs

NASW offers students completing their MSWs even more certification options than it offers students completing their BSWs. Similar to the four credentials described for BSWs, there are certified advanced social work case manager (C-ASWCM); certified advanced children, youth, and families social worker (C-ACYFSW); advanced social worker in gerontology (ASW-G); and advanced certified hospice and palliative social worker (ACHP-SW). The primary difference in the eligibility criteria is completion of an MSW from an accredited university and additional years of post-MSW experience.

Social workers with MSWs have additional options. First is the academy of certified social workers (ACSW) certification for social work practice in schools and health-care settings, and certifications in clinical social work. The ACSW is perhaps the most common and respected credential in social work. Social workers holding the ACSW are recognized as qualified providers of social services across an array of different practice settings. The eligibility requirements for the ACSW include an MSW from an accredited university; at least twenty hours of continuing education; evidence of at least two years of post-MSW experience working under the supervision of an MSW-credentialed supervisor; professional evaluations that validate his or her knowledge, understanding, and application of social work principles and values from an MSW supervisor and two social work colleagues; and evidence of adhering to the NASW Code of Ethics, and the NASW Standards for Continuing Professional Education.

Certified school social work specialists (C-SSWSs) use theories of human behavior and development and methods of social work practice to support students within public and private school settings. They provide case management, conflict mediation and resolution, crisis intervention, group work, community organizing, advocacy, consultation, effective educational strategies, and documentation in their work with students and families. C-SSWSs recognize the rights of persons with disabilities, changes in the family unit, and the effects of increasing social, economic, and academic pressures on children that can significantly shape their experiences in schools. The eligibility requirements for the C-SSWS include an MSW from an accredited university; at least twenty hours of continuing education related specifically to school social work; evidence of at least two years of supervised experience working in a school setting; current state clinical licensure or a current exam-based school social work license, registration, or certification issued by a designated state office; and evidence of adhering to the NASW Code of Ethics, and the NASW Standards for Continuing Professional Education.

Students who want to practice in health-care settings may want to consider becoming a certified social worker in health care (C-SWHC). This credential signifies specialized experience and expertise helping clients, families, and groups to enhance or maintain their well-being in relation to their health. Social workers in health care respond to the ever-changing needs of those engaged in health-care services by modifying and expanding methods for providing services. Social work activities focus on the bio-psycho-social-spiritual components of health from a strengths perspective. Additionally, social workers with this certificate can use their knowledge to develop standards of practice, recommend health policy, improve health programs, and ensure that clients, families, and organizations receive high-quality and state-of-the-art services. The eligibility requirements for the C-SWHC include an MSW from an accredited university; at least twenty hours of continuing education related specifically to health-care social work; evidence of at least two years of supervised experience working in a health-care setting; current state clinical licensure; and evidence of adhering to the NASW Code of Ethics and the NASW Standards for Continuing Professional Education.

Clinical certification is another option for social workers with an MSW. After three years of clinical experience, social workers can seek certification as a qualified clinical social worker (QCSW). Social workers with the QCSW credential have expertise and experience engaging in clinical assessment, diagnosis, and treatment, including psychotherapy and counseling, with individuals, families, and small groups. They possess knowledge of theories of human development and practice the professional application of social work theory and methods to treat and prevent psychosocial dysfunction, disability, or impairment, including emotional and mental disorders. The eligibility requirements for the QCSW include an MSW from an accredited university; at least thirty hours of continuing education specific to clinical social work within the last two years; evidence of at least three years of supervised, post-MSW clinical social work employment in an agency or organization that provides mental health assessment and treatment; current state clinical licensure; and evidence of adhering to the NASW Code of Ethics and the NASW Standards for Continuing Professional Education.

The diplomate in clinical social work (DCSW) is for social workers that can demonstrate the highest level of expertise and experience in clinical settings. Similar to the eligibility requirements for the QCSW, the DCSW requires an MSW from an accredited university with at least twenty hours of clinical coursework; an additional three years of clinical practice experience that has occurred within the past ten years; and two satisfactory colleague references completed by clinical social workers.

MEMBERSHIP AND PARTICIPATION IN PROFESSIONAL ORGANIZATIONS

We strongly encourage students to join and actively participate in professional social work organizations. It is also important that students consider participating in other professional organizations specific to particular practice interests. Stated simply, interacting with colleagues from social work and other disciplines is essential for developing and maintaining professional identity. Professional organizations provide social workers with the opportunities for networking and collaboration necessary for professional development. Interacting with colleagues through social work organizations builds and maintains accountability to representing the profession, our core values, and our commitment to continuous learning. It also expands the network of relationships available to social workers to draw on for support when advocating for human rights and social and economic justice. There are many social work organizations. There are even more professional organizations potentially relevant to social workers practicing with specific populations or in specific settings. A comprehensive list and description of all the possibilities is beyond the scope of the text. Instead, we summarize the two organizations we consider central to students developing their professional identity: the National Association of Social Workers (NASW) and the Council on Social Work Education (CSWE).

National Association of Social Workers

Although not required, we encourage students to give special consideration to joining and becoming active members of NASW. NASW is the largest social work organization in the world. As a member of NASW, students will have opportunities for continuous professional growth and can network with other social workers to create and maintain professional standards and advance sound social policies (NASW, 2012b). A primary benefit of membership in NASW is the opportunity to become active in one of the state chapters of the organization. As described on the NASW Web site, the fifty-six chapters and the national organization are one unified group financially, legally, and programmatically. State chapters have units, branches, regions, and divisions where students can network with social workers in their communities. Students can visit the NASW

Web site at www.naswdc.org to learn more about the benefits of membership.

Council on Social Work Education

CSWE is another important organization for developing and maintaining professional identity. The organization consists of practitioners, educators, social service agencies, and undergraduate and graduate programs of social work education (CSWE, 2012). The organization fulfills three important functions for the profession: (1) It sets and maintains educational policy and program standards. (2) It credits BSW and MSW degree programs. (3) It develops and advocates for social work education throughout the United States.

We believe membership and participation of social work students and practitioners are essential for CSWE to fulfill its three functions. As an inherently applied profession, the effectiveness of social work education depends on policy and program standards producing curriculums that prepare students for practice. Social work educators need input from students and practitioners to ensure that the curriculum remains relevant so that future social workers are adequately prepared for competent practice. We encourage students to learn more about CSWE and consider becoming active members. Students can learn more about CSWE by visiting its Web site at www.cswe.org.

PRACTICE WISDOM

Developing and maintaining professional identity also occurs through practice experience. As social workers gain practice experience incorporating their knowledge, values, and skills, with continuous self-reflection, they develop practice wisdom. Practice wisdom refers to the ability of social workers to combine and translate empirical and theoretical knowledge and previous experience into current and future practice (Klein & Bloom, 1995). Dybicz (2004) describes practice wisdom as going beyond pure knowledge to the actualization of social work values. Stated simply, social workers develop and maintain their professional identities as they develop practice wisdom acquired from years of professional experience. For example, in working with children in institutional settings, social workers learn agency policy, evidence-based interventions, and the capacities and resources available, given their practice environment. Over time and with each new case, workers acquire and assimilate knowledge (e.g., about behavior patterns, worker characteristics, and community resources) that help them more readily assess and address new client issues in an increasingly more effective and efficient manner. As an applied field of study, social work education prepares students to acquire practice wisdom by creating opportunities for synthesizing their learning with deliberate self-reflection in practice situations. In fact, graduation from a CSWE-accredited social work program means a student has demonstrated competence as someone who simultaneously identifies with the profession and is capable of developing practice wisdom after years of experience.

SUMMARY

By this point in the book, students should understand two overarching points about social work: (1) Professional identity is a key social work competence that shapes and influences everything social workers do in practice. The expectation of competence in combining ongoing self-reflection with formal education, licensure and credentials, membership and participation in professional organizations, and practice wisdom together make social work unique among other helping professions. (2) In the same way, the social work curriculum is unique in that faculty expect students to do more than simply learn material and pass courses. In order to graduate, students must take what they learn, weave it in with their personal identity through self-reflection, and demonstrate the ability to synthesize and translate both into actions with different client systems. The expectation for practical application and mastery, therefore, means that students can approach all of their courses with the mindset that everything they learn is relevant and important for them as future social workers. It also means students should approach their formal education as merely the starting point for a lifetime of career-long learning. The contemplative cycle needed for competent social work practice (see figure 5.1) is a lifelong commitment. The interaction of personal self-reflection, continuing education, and experience that leads to practice wisdom should be ongoing throughout the career of every social worker. In the next chapter, we continue focusing on professional identity by helping students ground their emerging identities as social workers within the context of the history of the profession.

DISCUSSION QUESTIONS

As in discussion questions in chapter 5, we ask that you consider the content provided in this chapter on self-reflection. Please consider each question, keeping in mind your career goals.

Self-reflection questions regarding social work education:

1. What factors led to the selection of your current educational setting?
2. Have classes (pre-cognates) that you have taken in your studies this far prepared you for social work study and practice? Think about each of the eight areas discussed in this chapter (see box 6.1) when considering this question. How have these courses prepared you for social work education?
3. In which of the pre-cognates do you believe that you have particular strengths? In which do you believe you need to improve your skills?
4. Consider your long-term educational and career goals. Where would you like to be professionally five years from now? What level of social work education will help you obtain your goals? What factors should you consider when choosing a social work program? What level of education (BSW, MSW, DSW, or PhD) is required to meet your desired level of competence and practice?

Self-reflection questions regarding professional licensure and certification:

5. Locate and explore on the Internet your state or country's licensing board for social workers. What are the requirements and licensing levels for professional social work practice? What are the requirements for obtaining social work licensure? What can you do now to prepare for licensure upon graduation with a social work degree?

6. Review the various certification opportunities for social workers following graduation discussed in this chapter. What are the benefits of seeking certification by professional organizations such as NASW?

7. Why do you think that licensing and certification opportunities are offered to (and often are required of) social workers following graduation from accredited social work programs?

Self-reflection questions regarding membership in professional organizations:

8. Explore the Web sites for NASW and CSWE. What are the stated benefits of membership in these professional organizations for social workers? Consider and discuss the benefits of joining these organizations now, as a student in social work, with your instructor and your classmates.

9. Conduct an Internet search for other professional organizations for social work, especially using combinations of terms that include your particular areas of interests within social work (e.g., "social work professional organizations and child welfare" or "social work professional organizations and aging") in your favorite search engine. What options are available as resources to you? What factors should you consider in choosing membership in professional organizations?

REFERENCES

Council on Social Work Education (CSWE). (2008). *Educational policy and accreditation standards.* Retrieved from http://www .cswe.org/File.aspx?id=13780

Council on Social Work Education (CSWE). (2012). *About CSWE.* Retrieved from http://www.cswe.org/About.aspx

Dybicz, P. (2004). An inquiry into practice wisdom. *Families in Society, 85*(2), 197–203.

Group for the Advancement of Doctoral Education in Social Work (GADE). (2013). *Quality guidelines for PhD programs in social work* (rev.). Retrieved from http://www.gadephd.org/ Portals/0/docs/GADE%20quality%20guidelines%20approved% 204%2006%202013%20(2).pdf

Klein, W. C., & Bloom, M. (1995). Practice wisdom. *Social Work, 40*(6), 799–807.

National Association of Social Workers (NASW). (2012a). *NASW professional social work credentials and advanced practice specialty credentials.* Retrieved from http://www.naswdc.org/ credentials/default.asp

National Association of Social Workers (NASW). (2012b). *NASW membership benefits.* Retrieved from http://www.naswdc .org/join.asp

CHAPTER SEVEN

The Historical Emergence of Social Work as a Profession

Understanding the history of the profession is essential for competent social work practice. When engaging individuals, groups, or communities in practice, social workers act as representatives of the profession with knowledge of how the profession's past influences their work in the present and future. For instance, the historical emergence of the field informs professional identity and grounds the emphasis on ethics, diversity, human rights, and social justice, which are competences that shape the models, techniques, and approaches used when working with clients. Having knowledge of the history of the profession also helps students appreciate some of the current trends and develop well-articulated and informed views on the issues.

The emergence of social work and the history of social welfare in the United States are connected. Nevertheless, we make only a brief foray into social welfare history; a comprehensive examination is beyond the scope of the text and better left to social welfare historians (e.g., Axinn & Levin, 1982; Chambers, 1967; Jansson, 1988;

Katz, 1996; Trattner, 1999). We encourage students to read a few books that provide in-depth treatment of social welfare history. Here we focus material on events as they connect to the development of the profession.

We posit a key theme for students to contemplate as they think about social work's emergence. As the profession focused primarily on the well-being of the most vulnerable and disenfranchised, social work history is replete with inherent tensions and challenges. Tensions and challenges from our past remain and influence social work practice in the present, and will probably influence practice in the future. Part of developing professional identity as social workers is recognizing and appreciating these inherent tensions that are, in many ways, part of joining the profession. Some of the inherent tensions and challenges students need to understand and think about include

- critiques of the profession that never seem to go away;
- balancing the purpose of social work and the pursuit of professional status;
- appreciating the broad scope of the profession, while finding it difficult to articulate what social workers do and how they contribute to the public good; and
- our internal views and differences about types of practice (i.e., direct and indirect) and the role of the public, private, and volunteer sectors in providing social welfare.

We highlight some of the tensions and challenges that emerged and remain relevant to social work in each section of this chapter.

ELIZABETHAN POOR LAW OF 1601

Ask almost any social worker to identify some of the historical events that shaped the foundation of the profession and he or she will likely begin with the Elizabethan Poor Law of 1601. Colby and

Dziegielewski (2010), for instance, describe the year 1601 as the "watershed year for social welfare" (p. 47). Attempting to identify one event, however, as *the* defining moment for social welfare (and indirectly for social work) is one of the inherent tensions or challenges for the profession. There are more than seven thousand years of recorded human history. When thinking about the events that have shaped social welfare, recognize that decisions and efforts about caring for the most vulnerable occurred by every clan and tribe on Earth (Faherty, 2006). The foundation of what we construe as social welfare today was also organized and delivered long before 1601, "through the rich religious traditions of Buddhism, Christianity, Hinduism, Judaism, and thousands of other traditional religions and cultural practices embraced by humankind throughout the world" (p. 108).

Even in England, and again long before 1601, events occurred that informed the enactment of the Elizabethan Poor Law. For instance, although designed to prevent begging and to force laborers to remain working, Edward III issued the Statute of Laborers in 1349, the first of many poor laws that began the process of shifting some of the responsibility of the poor away from the church to the government (Kurzman, 1970). In 1530, seventy years before the Elizabethan Poor Law, Henry VIII enacted a statute whereby the poor were divided into two groups—the vagrants that were to be punished, and the impotent poor that were to be granted license to beg for assistance. A few years later, Henry VIII enacted a second statute that allowed volunteers to raise funds to care for the poor.

The enactment of the Elizabethan Poor Law of 1601 finally occurred after years of severe economic depression in the early 1590s in England. During the depression, the government was forced to recognize that there were many people willing and able to work, but who simply could not find employment. Confronted with rising inflation and unemployment, the English government molded a series of reforms and previous statutes into the first comprehensive uniform system of poor laws for the country. However, as Kurzman

(1970) points out, the Elizabethan Poor Law contained little that was new.

Although not necessarily new, the Elizabethan Poor Law of 1601 did several things that still contribute to the tensions and challenges of the social work profession. For instance, the Poor Law moved the burden of responsibility for the poor away from the church and private sector to the public sector. The Poor Law made local government the public entity most responsible for the poor (Katz, 1996). The Poor Law also divided people in need into two groups: the *unworthy poor* and the *worthy poor*. If local government officials determined that people seeking help were able bodied but not looking for work, they were deemed *unworthy* of public assistance. If, however, people seeking help were ill, disabled, orphaned, or elderly, they were seen as *worthy* of public assistance because they were experiencing poverty due to circumstances that were beyond their control (Cole, 1973; Katz, 1996).

Deciding who should receive services from social workers and determining the sector and location best suited to serve the most vulnerable is an ongoing debate in the profession. Social workers, who care equally about enhancing the well-being of individuals, groups, and communities, bring different perspectives about the role of the federal, state, and local governments; the role of volunteers; the role of private philanthropy; and the role of religion and spirituality (e.g., Cnaan, 1999, 2002; Sherr, 2008; Wineburg, 2001). The different perspectives manifest into tensions about the appropriate place and scope of competent practice. For example, should social workers practice primarily with government agencies? Should social workers be trained and licensed to practice as private clinicians serving people who have the resources to pay for services? Should social workers practice in churches, synagogues, mosques, or other religious entities? What role should social workers play in addressing poverty? Should they practice primarily in direct roles with people needing help or should they serve as organizers and facilitators of multiple professionals and volunteers who help people?

We wish we could provide clear and coherent answers for students to these kinds of questions. Similar to the rest of the profession, however, the two authors disagree about most of the answers. What we do agree about is that students need to embrace the complexity and diversity inherent in social work. We also agree that students need to contemplate their own answers to these kinds of questions as part of developing their professional identity as social workers.

FROM VOLUNTEERING TO SYSTEMATIC HELPING

While the Elizabethan Poor Law of 1601 set in motion principles that remain relevant, the roots of the social work profession are found in the extensive volunteer movement during the formative years of the United States. Social work owes its existence to volunteerism (Sherr, 2008). Volunteers have founded relief societies, children's homes, day care programs, recreation services, family and child welfare associations, mental health associations, and almost every other field of practice in the profession (Anderson & Ambrosino, 1992). As with the Poor Law, the journey from private volunteering to an established profession makes for inherent tensions and challenges that influence current and future practice.

To appreciate the inherent tensions and challenges, students need to understand how important volunteerism is to American society. Having the freedom to organize, associate, and serve people as volunteers is vital to a functioning democracy. As Ellis and Noyes (1990) point out, the more citizens involve themselves as volunteers in the community, the closer they come to making the ideals of democracy a reality. When Alex de Tocqueville visited the United States in the early 1830s, he concluded that the key to democracy was the freedom and disposition of Americans to come together as volunteers for the common good. He observed that Americans of all ages, all different socioeconomic backgrounds, from all regions of the country, are always gathering together as volunteers for all sorts of reasons (Tocqueville, 1835/1966, p. 485). For instance, in the seventeenth century, volunteers worked together to assist in building construction, collective cattle herding, and labor sharing (Barck & Lefler, 1958; Earle, 1923). Volunteers also worked together to erect churches that functioned as meeting places for all types of community purposes as well as places of worship (Rines, 1936). Even government took the form of volunteers coming together for town meetings where people selected unpaid volunteer officials to serve as clerks of the market, town criers, and surveyors for highways.

Gathering together in volunteer societies was also the initial way of caring for the poor beyond the church and the family. Throughout the eighteenth and nineteenth centuries, volunteer societies were responsible for advocating for children's rights, women's rights, rights of African Americans, fair labor practices, better medical practices, and the humane treatment of the mentally ill (Carter, 1926; Cubberly, 1944; Dunlop, 1965; Laidler, 1968). Even the social reform advances of the Progressive Era depended on volunteer societies (Hofstadter, 1963). Volunteer societies, for example, lobbied for government to take more responsibility for social welfare; communities to temper the zealousness for economic prosperity with the protection of human rights; and efforts to care and provide social services for the poor and disenfranchised to become more systematic.

The COS movement and the Settlement House movement represented volunteer efforts that applied systematic methods to serve the poor. The two volunteer movements also emerged to become significant precursors to the social work profession. The COS consisted of volunteers who assisted families in meeting their physical, economic, emotional, and spiritual needs. In 1877, the Reverend S. Humphrey Gurteen established the first COS in Buffalo, New York, to provide an alternative method to indiscriminate giving for helping the poor (Pumphrey & Pumphrey, 1961). The COS used volunteer cooperation to make services systematic and efficient. Volunteer leaders serving on executive councils usually led COS organizations.

The councils trained direct service volunteers, commonly referred to as "family visitors," to screen applicants, conduct family histories, and manage cases to make informed choices about the best way to provide support for different families (Putnam, 1887). Most social workers consider the COS movement as the forebearer of microlevel practice or direct practice with individuals and families. Many social workers also consider Mary Richmond, one of the leaders of the COS movement, as one of the matriarchs of social work because she identified and documented a theory of practice in her books *Friendly Visiting Among the Poor* (1899) and *Social Diagnosis* (1917).

The Settlement House movement also emerged as a systematic effort of volunteers. Perhaps more than any other person, Jane Addams was the matriarch of the Settlement House movement and is considered to be another matriarch of the social work profession. As a volunteer member of the Woman's City Club of Chicago, Addams turned an old and battered building into the Hull House. The Hull House brought together residents of the house with volunteers to advocate for better health care, sanitation, working conditions, and housing conditions. The Settlement House movement is considered by most social workers as the precursor to macrolevel practice, which is commonly referred to as practice with communities and organizations.

FROM SYSTEMATIC HELPING TO SOCIAL WORK AS A PROFESSION

Beyond representing the potential of volunteers working together in cooperation, the COS movement and Settlement House movement marked the shift toward professional helping. The two movements occurred during industrialization. With industrialization came growing numbers of people in need of services living away from their extended families, their churches, or any other means of informal support. Cadres of professionally trained volunteers to coordinate services, conduct comprehensive assessments, and keep clear records became necessary to serve the poor and needy (Morales, Sheafor, & Scott, 2012). These professionally trained volunteers eventually became known as social workers.

As social work emerged as an established occupation, attention turned to its development as a legitimate profession. In addition to the volunteer movements, a few schools began offering formal training (e.g., New York School of Philanthropy, Philadelphia Training School for Social Work, Boston School of Social Work, and Atlanta School of Social Work) and social work expanded into other practice areas such as medical social work, mental health, prisons, employment, and schools (Barker, 1999). Also, NCCC formed as the first professional organization to allow social workers to discuss social problems and study the characteristics of effective practice. NCCC was a precursor to NASW. It was also the organization that provided social work with one of our most influential events, Abraham Flexner's address at the 1915 NCCC convention.

At the 1915 NCCC convention, Dr. Flexner, an accepted authority on the study of professions, was invited to present his analysis of whether social work was a profession. Apparently, the organizers of the convention assumed Flexner would offer them assurance that social work was, or was about to become, a full-fledged profession similar to medicine, law, and engineering. They were not prepared for the possibility that he would draw the opposite conclusion.

At the beginning of the presentation, Flexner (1915) distinguished between the relative use of the term "professional" and the absolute use of the term "profession." To Flexner, the term "professional" loosely describes someone who devotes his or her time to a specific activity, be it baseball, basketball, dancing, acting, bartending, or truck driving. In contrast, he considered the term "profession" to describe a limited group of activities that meet a certain predetermined set of objective criteria. He spelled out six criteria that separate a profession from all other occupations. He then used the criteria to assess whether social work was a profession.

1. Professions involve activities that are essentially intellectual—the thinking process is the main instrument applied to address problems. Individuals who freely use their intelligence as part of a profession are often held accountable for the outcomes. To Flexner the activities of a social worker were definitely intellectual. He stated, "The worker must possess fine powers of analysis and discrimination, breadth and flexibility of sympathy, sound judgment, skill in utilizing whatever resources are available, facility in devising new combinations. These operations are assuredly of intellectual quality" (Flexner, 1915, p. 17).

2. Professions derive their own raw material from science and learning—the thinking process uses information specifically learned for the given field instead of drawing on knowledge and experience that is easily accessible from general sources of information. Flexner indicated that social workers perform a mediating function with material developed by other fields instead of using raw material that they developed. He questioned whether the social worker was a professional or the person that brings professional activity into action. He stated, "The very variety of the situations [a social worker] encounters compels him [or her] to be not a professional agent so much as the mediator invoking this or that professional agency" (Flexner, 1915, p. 17).

3. Professions apply learning in a way that is practical—the thinking process and the development of raw knowledge have a clear-cut end that is recognized and sanctioned by society. To Flexner, social work did not have definitive ends that distinguished it from other professions. Instead, he viewed social work as being in touch with many professions rather than as a profession in and of itself. "It appears not so much a definite field as an aspect of work in many fields" (Flexner, 1915, p. 18).

4. Professions use a transmittable technique that requires education—there are specific objects a practitioner must master before gaining entry into the profession. In addition, there is an

agreed-on standard as to the admission requirements and the content and length of education. Flexner viewed the fields of social work as too numerous and diverse to organize a single educational discipline. Although he determined schools of social work to be important, he posited that the content was not technically professional. Instead, he characterized the education of social workers as supplemental and "broadly cultural in a variety of realms of civic and social interest" (Flexner, 1915, p. 18).

5. Professions are self-organized—the activities of a profession are so definitive, so absorbing in interest, so richly engaging in duties and responsibilities that individuals and their families tend to organize around a strong nucleus. As Flexner pointed out in his presentation, the annual conventions testified to the development of professional self-identity that leads to self-organization.

6. Professions become increasingly altruistic in motivation—as time goes on, devotion to the common well-being of society will become more and more an accepted mark of the professional activities. Eventually the interests of individual practitioners of a given profession will gradually yield before the increasing realization of responsibility to the larger social environment. To Flexner, this is the one criterion where social work exceeds most other occupations. Although he would not officially call social work a profession, he did acknowledge that social work's professional spirit, in many ways, is what mattered most. He stated, "The unselfish devotion of those who have chosen to give themselves to making the world a fitter place to live in can fill social work with the professional spirit and thus to some extent lift it above all the distinctions which I have been at pains to make" (Flexner, 1915, p. 19).

In summary, Flexner described social workers as intelligent, kindhearted, and resourceful people who perform an important mediating function. In his opinion, however, social work was not a profession. What happened thereafter, and still continues to occur, was an all-out attempt by social workers to demonstrate to colleagues from other disciplines, to clients, to society, and most important to ourselves that social work was and is a profession.

This attempt to prove ourselves created another unique tension and challenge relevant for current and future social workers. On the one hand, efforts to solidify the place of the profession resulted in substantial gains and progress for social workers. On the other hand, as some have warned (Brueggemann, 2002; McKnight, 1995; Specht & Courtney, 1994), the quest (and perhaps obsession) for achieving and maintaining professional status may have come at the cost of abandoning our roots as the profession that existed first and foremost to care and advocate for the poor, indigent, and disenfranchised. We believe that this tension is ever present, is something that every social worker should wrestle with, and is a tension that students need to recognize and embrace as part of becoming competent practitioners. Let's briefly assess the two most significant developments coming after Flexner's address that can be viewed as both advances and challenges to social workers.

Self-Organization

Responding to the notion that self-organization is an attribute of a profession, a great amount of effort was and still is devoted to social work professional organizations. The tension and challenge for social work is deciding which organizations and how many organizations should represent the profession. For instance, social workers established NASW in 1955 by consolidating seven different organizations (NASW, 2012a): the American Association of Social Workers, the American Association of Psychiatric Social Workers, the American Association of Group Workers, the Association for the Study of Community Organization, the American Association of Medical Social Workers, the National Association of School Social Workers, and the Social Work Research Group. The formation of

NASW has served many social workers well as far as enhancing professional status, establishing a unified code of ethics, and establishing and maintaining standards of practice. The question that remains relevant is, however, Is it better for the profession to have social workers unified and represented by one organization or to have social workers belonging to different organizations?

Social workers and social work educators have differences of opinion about the benefits and challenges of a unified social work organization. Some in social work want to see one organization to enhance our position among other helping professions and to be more effective in advocating for just social policies. In fact, in 2007 leaders of many of the major social work organizations met and developed the *Wingspread Resolution on Social Work Unification* in which they pledged to form one professional social work organization by 2012 (NASW, 2007). Other social workers believe that professional organizations emphasizing specialized purposes and specialized fields of practice may serve and represent the interests of social workers in those fields better than one organization.

This debate has its historical roots in the Flexner address and will continue to be an issue for social work in the foreseeable future. Although the resolution has yet to become a reality, there is definitely overlap and partnership among organizations, especially among social work education organizations. At the same time, there are more than forty social work organizations (NASW, 2012b), suggesting that many social workers see a place for different organizations serving and representing the profession. What is important for students to remember is that this tension is part of social work. Recognize it. Embrace it. And, in time, develop your own informed position about this tension.

Raw Knowledge Base and a Practical and Clear-Cut End

The search for a distinctive knowledge base and practice methods preoccupied social work in the decades following Flexner, and continues to garner attention. Shortly after the 1915 convention, social work became infatuated with psychiatry and Freudian psychology, which conveniently offered two advantages in terms of achieving professional status. First, adopting psychiatry and Freudian psychology allowed social work to claim adherence to a specific knowledge base that would satisfy the gap pointed out by Flexner. In the decades following his presentation, several leading social workers promoted their new knowledge base. Eventually, psychiatric social work became a distinct field of practice, and Freudian psychology (and the theories derived from Freudian psychology) became a primary theoretical lens in most other areas of social work practice.

Second, psychiatry and Freudian psychology offered social work the opportunity to associate its practice methods with the medical model of practice. Aligning with the medical model created a distinction between social workers and ordinary concerned volunteers, to that of trained experts that provided treatment. Instead of emphasizing the larger environmental causes of poverty and other community problems, under the medical model social workers study the problems of their clients (individuals, groups, or communities), diagnose the problems (or strengths), prescribe action steps, and evaluate the outcomes.

Many social workers and social work educators disagree on the appropriateness and effectiveness of the medical model of practice. Regardless, the influence of this approach permeates the profession. Whether working in child and family services, foster care, mental health, substance abuse, gerontology, or with communities and organizations, most social workers commonly conceptualize practice in ways influenced by the medical model. Indeed, the four-step generalist practice method of engagement, assessment, intervention, and evaluation, described above as part of competent social work practice, is rooted in the medical model.

While the field's adoption of psychiatry and Freudian psychology helped legitimize social work as a profession, it created at least two inherent tensions and challenges that remain pertinent. Although social work claimed adherence to a specific knowledge base, the reality is that the profession still does not have its own specialized body of knowledge. Social work also wrestles with the relationship between direct and indirect practice.

Social work does not have its own specialized knowledge base. In this regard, Flexner is correct. The variety of circumstances faced in social work practice requires knowledge from multiple fields used in a distinctive way infused by the values and priorities of the profession. For example, systems theory emerged from the field of biology; the ecological perspective is derived from anthropology, sociology, and psychology; life course theory is rooted in psychology and sociology; and social exchange theory evolved from psychology, anthropology, and economics (Robbins, Chatterjee, & Canda, 1998).

The lack of knowledge that is unique to social work is not the result of a lack of effort. After the convention, the profession became preoccupied with the task of developing discipline-specific knowledge. In fact, some in social work remain preoccupied. In some cases, social workers attempted to claim different theories as discovered and applied primarily in social work practice. For example, Robinson (1931) advocated for the psychoanalytic contributions made through social work practice, Hollis (1970) for the psychosocial approach, Smalley (1970) for the functional approach, Thomas (1973) for behavioral modification, and Saleeby (2002) for the strengths perspective. Nevertheless, each theoretical framework mentioned is ultimately rooted in knowledge developed by another field. Other social workers attempted to develop social work knowledge through scientific research. Perhaps the best example is Thyer (2002) who, just over a decade ago, candidly admitted to spending his entire career searching for a knowledge base that social work could claim as its own. After twenty-five years of work, he reluctantly concluded that it is impossible to identify unique social work contributions to knowledge in any given area of practice research.

The preoccupation with identifying a unique knowledge base is a tension and challenge in that it detracts from our purpose. On every other account, the profession of social work is undeniably secure. We have a unified code of ethics, established licensure and credentials, and agreed-on curriculums for social work education. Also, the job outlook for trained social workers is more optimistic than that of all other human service professions. Social workers are the main providers of social welfare and mental health services in the United States and are growing in numbers in other fields, such as substance abuse, aging, school, health care, and employment assistance (U.S. Department of Labor, 2012). The reality, however, is that the lack of a social work knowledge base remains an issue for enough social workers that the tension and challenge remains. It is important for students to recognize and embrace this tension and, in time, develop an informed position.

The other tension created from adopting psychiatry and Freudian psychology is the relationship between direct (micro) and indirect (macro) practice. Viewed from a broad perspective, social work's unique contribution as a profession to society is our attention to individuals *and* the environment. Students learn early on that in the context of social work the term "clients" connotes a broad concept that, given the specific circumstances, encompasses individuals, families, small groups, organizations, and even entire communities. Nevertheless, as students interact with different faculty members, take different courses, and begin networking with other social workers, they will also experience the relationship between direct and indirect practice from an insider's perspective.

Viewed from the inside, students will likely observe that social work educators and practitioners tend to emphasize one area of practice over the other. In fact, in most MSW programs the curriculum requires students to choose a concentration or specialization in their second year of the program. As part of that choice, students often have to decide whether to focus more on direct or on indirect practice, while also learning that they *are supposed to* appreciate both as equally relevant to competent social work practice.

A decade after Flexner's presentation, Jane Addams' comments capture the essence of this tension. While acknowledging the benefits to the profession, she questioned social work's fascination with psychiatry, psychotherapy, and the medical-model approach to practice. Speaking at a social work meeting, she made the following request (Addams, 1926): "I should like now to ask a favor of the psychiatric social workers. They are the newest and most popular among us. They are taking great care of the individual who is brought to them, whether he comes as a free nursery child, or whether he comes from the courts. Perhaps we can ask them that they go outside this individual analysis and give us a little social psychiatric work" (p. 7). She then reminded her colleagues that social work practice must always involve partnering with other people in the community who are closest to the poor to help create environmental conditions that allow people to enhance their own well-being.

After years of experience, both authors—one who tends to emphasize direct practice and the other who emphasizes indirect practice—admit that Addams' words remain relevant. We appreciate and respect each other. We are broadly aware that competent social work practice involves direct and indirect practice. Still, when discussing a specific client circumstance or a specific social problem, we experience the tension and challenge of approaching a particular situation with a macro *and* a micro perspective. It is important for students to recognize and embrace this tension as unique to social work.

CURRENT TRENDS FOR THE SOCIAL WORK PROFESSION

As the next generation of social workers, students should enter the field knowing that, although there have been tensions and challenges, social work is indeed a profession. Assessed by almost any measure (e.g., job outlook, state appropriations, and state licensure), social work has achieved sanction as the profession that helps people enhance their well-being through improving interactions with their social environment. Students should be aware of current trends that will likely create opportunities and challenges for social work in the future. We briefly review some of the current trends below and eagerly look forward to students contributing to the direction of our profession in the years ahead.

Globalization

Our world is becoming increasingly interconnected. With greater access to the Internet, for example, people experiencing events locally can share with people from around the world within minutes. When we consider the well-being of individuals and their communities, the needs and concerns go far beyond the confines of a single geographic area. We really do live in a global community where decisions of one community about the environment, the economy, and the culture affect those in every other community (Midgley, 1997). In the same way, as people in different regions become interdependent, they share a growing responsibility to resolve or reduce social problems and provide services to people needing assistance.

As the profession dedicated to serving individuals and improving social conditions, social work has become global. The evolving efforts to address international social issues, the diverse approaches to providing social welfare, and the expanding countries in need of professionally trained social workers have created new ways for the profession to fulfill its mission. The ability to exchange information with social workers from different countries also makes it possible to learn from each other and to improve practice outcomes. The globalization of social work, however, also brings about challenges. For instance, it can be overwhelming to consider the knowledge, values, and skills needed for social work practice in just one country or region. Given the need for a global perspective, how can social workers learn all they need to know for competent practice? Moreover, people from different countries have diverse views and approaches to understanding and addressing social issues. They may also have different conceptions of the role of social workers. How can social work be broad enough to embrace diverse views about different social issues, while also maintaining our purpose of enhancing the well-being of individuals and communities?

Morales and colleagues (2012) ask the next generation of social workers to "evolve a concept of social work that will bridge the differing philosophies of society's role in meeting human needs and yet maintain [social work's] unique mission" (p. 227). We humbly suggest such a concept does not exist. Instead, we encourage the next generation of social workers to allocate all of their time and energy to addressing real social problems, while recognizing the challenges of globalization as similar to some of the other inherent tensions and challenges that make the social work profession unique.

Evidence-Based Practice

Social workers have always been, and always will be, concerned with providing effective services. Still, in an era of increasing accountability, the need to demonstrate service effectiveness in our profession is greater than at any other time. The public, as it should, expects the expenditure of financial resources to produce tangible benefits. Regardless of whether programs receive direct out-of-pocket payments from clients or indirect funds from tax dollars, social workers have to *prove* that the funds will result in measured outcomes, using data gathered from empirical research.

Social workers are concerned with providing the best possible service, but the profession has also maintained an uneasy relationship between empirical research and social work practice. The beginning of almost any social work research book describes a strained and tenuous connection (e.g., Rubin & Babbie, 2010; Yegidis, Weinbach, &

Myers, 2011). Researchers claim practitioners shun empirical studies, instead relying on humanitarian impulses, authoritative guidance from consultants and supervisors, and anecdotal practices to make decisions. Practitioners assert that researchers conduct studies that are too obscure, present findings that are difficult to understand, and do not directly influence their work. In perhaps the most scathing assessment of the tenuous relationship, Gambrill (2001), a social work researcher and scholar, suggested that social work practitioners bamboozle the public by relying on authority, tradition, and good intentions rather than on empirical research.

EBP represents a potential step forward in bridging the chasm that exists between social work researchers and practitioners. If taught and implemented consistently, we believe the EBP model has the potential to mend the connection between researchers and practitioners by merging their roles. EBP is a twofold process in which social workers combine practice expertise and unique circumstances with the best scientific evidence available on which to base their practice decisions. EBP also applies to examining outcomes of interventions and determining how to assess the findings when contemplating future practice decisions (Rubin, 2008). Barker (2003) defines EBP in social work as a "type of intervention in which the professional social worker uses research as a practice and problem-solving tool; collects data systematically to monitor the intervention; specifies problems, techniques, and outcomes in measurable terms; and systematically evaluates the effectiveness of the intervention used" (p. 141).

The adoption and implementation of EBP in social work also gives rise to inherent tensions and challenges unique to the profession. EBP originates in the field of medicine (Sackett, Richardson, Rosenberg, & Haynes, 2000). Physicians use the steps in the EBP process in making treatment planning decisions with patients. In social work, EBP aligns more closely with situations where social workers assess the needs of individual clients, develop predetermined measurable outcomes, and use interventions supported by empirical research. Social work practice, however, is much broader than the situations in which EBP is a good fit. The process of working with larger groups, organizations, and communities does not always follow such a succinct and linear pathway. The goals and objectives will not be as clear and as measurable from the outset. They can even evolve in the midst of practice. So, as the EBP model brings the promise of merging empirical research and practice, the historical challenge of defining and emphasizing social work practice as involving direct and indirect practice remains.

EBP in social work also rekindles the tension and challenge of defining a discipline-specific knowledge base in social work. In medicine, where EBP fits well, when physicians search for the best available evidence, they normally draw from a vast collection of rigorous medical research. Medical research often involves studies with a higher degree of internal and external validity, which means physicians can be fairly sure that the findings are useful and relevant for their patients. If a certain prescription drug, for instance, was found to be effective for a particular ailment, they can conclude that their patients suffering from similar ailments might benefit from the same prescription. In contrast, when social workers seek the best available evidence, they will often find it very difficult to ascertain the findings of rigorous research studies that fit their practice needs. Rubin (2008) is correct when he suggests that the degree to which an intervention in social work is considered evidence based depends on the quality and number of empirical studies demonstrating its effects. The challenge for social work is that situations and issues confronting individuals, groups, families, and communities are so diverse that it is nearly impossible for social work research to develop rigorous studies with enough internal and external validity to guide all the necessary practice decisions. In this regard, Flexner is correct—

social work is too diverse and too broad to have its own discipline-specific knowledge base gained through scientific inquiry. We believe students need to understand and wrestle with this tension.

The Role of Licensure

The public regulation of social work through licensure is another trend that benefits and challenges the profession. When states began licensing social workers in the late 1960s and early 1970s, it represented an important milestone because it implied public and legal recognition of social workers as professionals (Hardcastle, 1977). State licensure creates title protection for social workers as a distinctive helping profession with the authority and autonomy to define different levels of practice. Licensure also protects the public by holding social workers accountable in the delivery of services based on established and agreed-on standards. If clients believe they have been subject to malpractice or unethical conduct, state licensure boards give them a legitimate forum to seek remuneration and protection. Consequently, if boards determine social workers were practicing unethically, they have the power to suspend or revoke licensure.

The proliferation of licensure is also a source of inherent tension and challenge for the profession. One question the profession struggles with, for example, is, Does licensure adequately capture all the roles of social workers? Remember, social work's purpose and approach to practice is unique in that (1) our primary concern is for providing services to the most vulnerable and oppressed; and (2) we attend to advocating for community conditions that allow people to enhance their own well-being, inasmuch as we provide direct practice to individuals. Stated differently, initiating a social movement advocating for fair wages, writing a white paper to influence policy on sexual orientation, or lobbying local, state, or federal officials to support a bill that provides resources for victims of human trafficking are just as much part of social work practice as is working with someone struggling with a mental illness or disability.

As with the challenge of EBP, licensure seems more congruent with social work narrowly defined as direct (or even clinical) practice. Again, our dual purpose, our unifying mandate to advocate for human rights and justice, and our broad approach to practice, all create an inherent tension students need to recognize and embrace as part of becoming professional social workers.

The Influence of Private Nonprofit and Faith-Based Organizations in Social Work

The American social welfare system has shifted drastically over the past three decades. Before 1980, social services were traditionally provided by public agencies. The past thirty years, however, have seen the gradual emergence of private nonprofit, private for-profit, and volunteer organizations. Along with this shift, there has been a concerted effort to strengthen the private nonprofit sector, while encouraging more volunteerism and greater involvement of faith-based services (Gronbjerg & Never, 2002). Beginning with the Reagan administration, religious organizations and other private volunteer groups have been encouraged to accept greater responsibility for the needy (Denton, 1982). Although belonging to different political parties, President Bill Clinton, President George H. Bush, and First Lady Nancy Reagan worked together throughout the 1990s to encourage more volunteerism (G. H. W. Bush, 1991; Hayslett, 1997). Likewise, Democrat and Republican leaders officially welcomed faith-based organizations into the circle of service providers by including Charitable Choice in section § 104 of the Personal Responsibility and Work Opportunity Reconciliation Act of 1996 (P.L. 104-193). Continuing to support more volunteerism and faith-based services, President George W. Bush established the White House Office of Faith-Based and Community Initiatives to work closely with corresponding units in the departments of Labor, Health and Human Services, Housing and Urban Development, Justice, and Education (Cnaan & Boddie, 2002). More recently, President Barack Obama created the Office of Faith-based and Neighborhood Partnerships (2012) that exists to (1) strengthen the role of community organizations in the economic recovery; (2) reduce unintended pregnancies, support maternal and child health, and reduce the need for abortion; (3) promote responsible fatherhood and strong communities; and (4) promote interfaith dialogue and cooperation (Office of Faith-based and Neighborhood Partnerships, 2012, para. 1).

The emergence of private nonprofit and faith-based organizations brings about opportunities, tensions, and challenges for social work. As the primary profession in the development, provision, and evaluation of social services (CSWE, 2008), social work must decide how to fulfill its purpose and function, given the economic realities and changing landscape of social welfare delivery. Some in social work refer to the current shift in social welfare policy as devolution—a term used to elicit caution and to suggest the current shift represents a step backward to a time when there were no federal social welfare programs and no social services delivered by professionally trained social workers (Wineburg, 2001). O'Neill (2002), for example, reports the profession is turning to volunteers to fill many traditional social work jobs in answer to the shortage of resources. Others in social work, however, see the current era from a historical perspective that started with volunteers being primarily responsible for social welfare, to volunteers advocating for government participation, to government and professional social workers becoming responsible to, finally, the current era where society recognizes the need for an optimal balance of shared responsibility among public, private, professional, volunteer, secular, and sectarian social welfare services (Sherr & Straughan, 2005).

Although written more than a decade ago, we believe White's (1997) description of the current era of social work remains relevant for students entering the field today. Assessing the current landscape of social welfare, she stated, "A golden opportunity may be presenting itself to influence public opinion, and hence public policy, on such issues as welfare reform and crime through the involvement of more citizens who will see and begin to understand what we encounter in our daily work and through our research" (p. 317).

SUMMARY

This chapter examined the emergence of social work as a profession. Recognizing, embracing, and wrestling with the tensions and challenges that are unique to our profession is part of developing the professional identity of social worker. We are hopeful that students will seize the opportunity White (1997) describes as they enter the profession. To do so, students need to engage in ethical social work practice with individuals, families, groups, and communities.

DISCUSSION QUESTIONS

In this chapter's discussion questions, we continue the theme of asking you to engage in self-reflection. We ask that you consider each question, keeping in mind your career goals, on historical and current issues and tensions within the social work profession.

Self-reflection questions regarding historical and current context:

1. Throughout recorded history, there is evidence of varying views about poor and disenfranchised individuals. What is your personal view regarding the notion of worthy versus unworthy poor? Has your view changed over time? Who are the people that helped shape your view? What are the circumstances that helped shape your view? What institutions have helped shape your view? And, perhaps most important, how do you think your view will help or hinder your work with vulnerable populations with which social workers interact?

2. What is your view on the roles of the public, private, and volunteer sectors in the provision of social services? Has your view

changed over time? Who helped shape your view? What circumstances helped shape your view? What institutions helped shape
your view? Again, and perhaps most important, how do you think
your view will help or hinder your work with vulnerable populations with which social workers interact?

3. What does and/or does not appeal to you as you consider various roles of social work practice concerning both direct and indirect practice?

4. Even now, as you are being introduced to the field of social work
and deciding if it is the right career for you, you should begin
thinking about what it means to be a good social work practitioner. Is it important for social workers to be able to demonstrate effective practice? Why or why not?

5. Revisiting your answers to the discussion questions regarding
professional licensure, credentialing, and organizational membership from chapter 6, and keeping in mind the tension mentioned
in this chapter regarding various areas of practice, how do you
feel about these tensions? What do you need to consider as you
explore licensure, credentialing, and membership in professional
organizations?

6. As mentioned in this chapter, one strength of social work is that
it is a broad profession that will offer a wide variety of career
choices; however, this same strength may be considered by some
to be a weakness in that it is too broad to be considered a profession on par with other professions. What are your views on
the tension between the mission of social work and the need for
professional legitimacy?

7. Discuss any concerns you have about social work as your chosen
profession with your instructor and your classmates. Our hope is
that your development of self-reflection processes and habits
now will greatly enhance your professional development as social
work practitioners in the future.

REFERENCES

Addams, J. (1926). How much social work can a community afford? From the ethical point of view. In *Jane Addams papers* (Series 3, pp. 1–10). Swarthmore, PA: Swarthmore College Peace Collection.

Anderson, S. C., & Ambrosino, R. N. (1992). Should volunteers be used as direct service givers? In E. Gambrill & R. Pruger (Eds.), *Controversial issues in social work* (pp. 174–175). Boston: Allyn & Bacon.

Axinn, J., & Levin, H. (1982). *Social welfare: A history of the American response to need* (2nd ed.). New York: Harper and Row.

Barck, O. T., & Lefler, H. T. (1958). *Colonial America.* New York: Macmillan.

Barker, R. L. (1999). *Milestones in the development of social work and social welfare.* Washington, DC: NASW Press.

Barker, R. L. (2003). *The social work dictionary.* Washington, DC: National Association of Social Workers (NASW).

Brueggemann, W. G. (2002). *The practice of macro social work.* Belmont, CA: Brooks/Cole.

Bush, G. H. W. (1991, January 29). *State of the union address: Envisioning one thousand points of light.* Retrieved from http://www.infoplease.com/ipa/A0900156.html

Carter, C. F. (1926). *When railroads were new.* New York: Simmons-Boardman.

Chambers, C. A. (1967). *Seedtime of reform: American social services and social action, 1918–1933.* Ann Arbor: University of Michigan Press.

Cnaan, R. A. (1999). Our hidden safety net. *Brookings Review, 12*(2), 50–53.

Cnaan, R. A. (2002). *The invisible caring hand: American congregations and the provision of welfare.* New York: New York University Press.

Cnaan, R. A., & Boddie, S. C. (2002). Charitable choice and faith-based welfare: A call for social work. *Social Work, 47*(3), 224–236.

Colby, I., & Dziegielewski, S. (2010). *Introduction to social work:The people's profession* (2nd ed.). Chicago: Lyceum.

Cole, B. (1973). *Perspectives in public welfare:A history* (3rd printing).Washington, DC: Government Printing Office.

Council on Social Work Education (CSWE). (2008). *Educational policy and accreditation standards.* Alexandria,VA: Author. Retrieved from http://www.cswe.org/File.aspx?id=13780

Cubberly, E. P. (1944). *Public school administration.* New York: Houghton Mifflin.

Denton, H. H. (1982, April 14). Reagan urges more church aid for need. *Washington Post,* p. A3.

Dunlop, R. (1965). *Doctors of the American frontier.* New York: Doubleday.

Earle, A. M. (1923). *Home life in colonial days.* New York: Macmillan.

Ellis, S. J., & Noyes, K. H. (1990). *By the people:A history of Americans as volunteers.* San Francisco: Jossey-Bass.

Faherty,V. E. (2006). Social welfare before the Elizabethan Poor Laws:The early Christian tradition,AD 33 to 313. *Journal of Sociology and Social Welfare, 33*(2), 107–122.

Flexner,A. (1915). Is social work a profession? In National Conference of Charities and Corrections, *Proceedings of the National Conference of Charities and Corrections at the forty-second annual session held in Baltimore, Maryland, May 12–19, 1915.* Chicago: Hildmann.

Gambrill, E. (2001). Social work:An authority-based profession. *Research on Social Work Practice, 11,* 166–175.

Gronbjerg, K. A., & Never, B. (2002). *Performing different types of volunteer work:The role of religious and other networks.* Paper presented at the annual meeting of the Society for the Scientific Study of Religion, Salt Lake City, UT.

Hardcastle, D. A. (1977). Public regulation of social work. *Social Work, 22*(1), 14–19.

Hayslett, C. M. (1997, April). Volunteering positively impacts nation's future. *Daily Beacon.* Retrieved from http://utdaily beacon.com/opinion/columns/untitled-column-by-chandra-hayslett/1997/apr/29/volunteering-positively-impacts-nations-future/

Hofstadter, R. (Ed.). (1963). *The progressive movement, 1900–1915.* Englewood Cliffs, NJ: Prentice-Hall.

Hollis, F. (1970). The psychosocial approach to the practice of casework. In R. W. Roberts & R. H. Nee (Eds.), *Theories of social casework.* Chicago: University of Chicago Press.

Jansson, B. (1988). *The reluctant welfare state: A history of American social welfare policies.* Belmont, CA: Wadsworth.

Katz, M. B. (1996). *In the shadow of the poorhouse: A social history of welfare in America.* New York: Basic Books.

Kurzman, P. A. (1970). Poor relief in medieval England: The forgotten chapter in the history of social welfare. *Child Welfare, 49*(9), 495–499.

Laidler, H. W. (1968). *Boycotts and the labor struggle.* New York: Russell & Russell.

McKnight, J. (1995). *The careless society: Community and its counterfeits.* New York: Basic Books.

Midgley, J. (1997). Social work in international contexts: Challenges and opportunities for 21st century. In M. Reisch & E. Gambrill (Eds.), *Social Work in the 21st century* (pp. 59–67). Thousand Oaks, CA: Pine Forge Press.

Morales, A. T., Sheafor, B. W., & Scott, M. E. (2012). *Social work: A profession of many faces* (12th ed.). Upper Saddle River, NJ: Allyn & Bacon.

National Association of Social Workers (NASW). (2007). Re-engineering our structure for the future. *NASW News, 52*(8). Retrieved from http://www.naswdc.org/pubs/news/2007/09/deSilva.asp

National Association of Social Workers (NASW). (2012a). *NASW.* Retrieved from http://www.naswdc.org/pressroom/features/general/nasw.asp

National Association of Social Workers (NASW). (2012b). *Social work organizations.* Retrieved from http://www.naswdc.org/swportal/swo1/

Office of Faith-based and Neighborhood Partnerships. (2012). *Policy goals.* Retrieved from http://www.whitehouse.gov/administration/eop/ofbnp/policy

O'Neill, J. V. (2002). Paraprofessionals: Answer to shortage? *NASW News, 47*(6), 3.

Personal Responsibility and Work Opportunity Reconciliation Act of 1996, P.L. 104–193, 110 stat. 2105.

Pumphrey, R. E., & Pumphrey, M. W. (Eds.). (1961). *The heritage of American social work.* New York: Columbia University Press.

Putnam, M. C. (1887). Friendly visiting. *Proceedings of the 14th annual conference of charities and corrections* (pp. 255–260). Boston: A. Williams.

Richmond, M. E. (1899). *Friendly visiting among the poor.* New York: MacMillan.

Richmond, M. E. (1917). *Social diagnosis.* Philadelphia: Russell Sage.

Rines, E. F. (1936). *Old historic churches of America.* New York: Macmillan.

Robbins, S. P., Chatterjee, P., & Canda, E. R. (1998). *Contemporary human behavior theory: A critical perspective for social work.* Needham Heights, MA: Allyn & Bacon.

Robinson, V. (1931). Psychoanalytic contributions to social case work treatment. In *Proceedings of the National Conference of Social Work.* Chicago: University of Chicago Press.

Rubin, A. (2008). *Practitioner's guide for using research in evidence-based practice.* Hoboken, NJ: Wiley & Sons.

Rubin, A., & Babbie, E. R. (2010). *Research methods for social work* (7th ed.). Belmont, CA: Brooks/Cole.

Sackett, D. L., Richardson, W. S., Rosenberg, W., & Haynes, R. B. (2000). *Evidence-based medicine: How to practice and teach EBM* (2nd ed.). New York: Churchill Livingstone.

Saleeby, D. (2002). *The strengths perspective in social work.* Boston: Allyn & Bacon.

Sherr, M. E. (2008). *Social work with volunteers.* Chicago: Lyceum.

Sherr, M. E., & Straughan, H. H. (2005). Volunteerism, social work, and the church: A historic overview and look into the future. *Social work and Christianity, 32*(2), 97–115.

Smalley, R. (1970). The functional approach to casework practice. In R. W. Roberts & R. H. Nee (Eds.), *Theories of social casework.* Chicago: University of Chicago Press.

Specht, H., & Courtney, M. E. (1994). *Unfaithful angels: How social work has abandoned its mission.* New York: Free Press.

Thomas, E. (1973). Behavioral modification and casework. In R. W. Roberts & R. H. Nee (Eds.), *Theories of social casework.* Chicago: University of Chicago Press.

Thyer, B. A. (2002). Developing discipline-specific knowledge for social work: Is it possible? *Journal of Social Work Education, 38*(1), 101–113.

Tocqueville, A. de. (1966). *Democracy in America* (J. P. Mayer & M. Lerner Eds.). New York: Harper and Row. (Original work published 1835).

Trattner, W. I. (1999). *From poor law to welfare state: A history of social welfare in America.* New York: Free Press.

U.S. Department of Labor (2012). *Occupational outlook handbook.* Retrieved from http://www.bls.gov/ooh/Community-and-Social-Service/Social-workers.htm

White, B. (1997). The summit place for America's future: A place for social work? *Social Work, 42*(4), 317–318.

Wineburg, R. J. (2001). *A limited partnership: The politics of religion, welfare, and social service.* New York: Columbia University Press.

Yegidis, B. L., Weinbach, R. W., & Myers, L. L. (2011). *Research methods for social workers* (7th ed.). Upper Saddle River, NJ: Allyn & Bacon.

CHAPTER EIGHT

Ethical Social Work Practice

Along with the historical tensions and challenges unique to our profession, a set of values has emerged unifying all of social work practice. These shared values are one of the reasons social work is such a dynamic international profession. Social work values are rooted in the profession's purpose. Recall from chapter 2 that the purpose of social work is to enhance the well-being of individuals, groups, and communities, and to create societal conditions that help individuals, groups, and communities to enhance their own well-being. Social workers speak different languages, practice in different countries, and work in agencies that consist of a variety of clients. Social workers will invariably continue to disagree about the primacy and effectiveness of direct and indirect practice. Amidst the areas of diversity and reasons for disagreement, the purpose and emerging values of social work unify the profession.

Ethical social work practice is also synonymous with competence-based social work. The point of students understanding the purpose of the profession, engaging in continuing self-reflection, and emphasizing professional identity is to prepare them to synthesize *why they do* with *what they do*. Stated differently, when students graduate with a degree in social work from a program accredited by CSWE, they have demonstrated the ability to incorporate the purpose and values of social work into their professional interactions with clients (individuals, groups, organizations, and communities), resulting in both ethical and competence-based practice.

We begin chapter 8 by introducing students to the values, ethical principles, and subsequent standards that guide social work practice. We then briefly examine the need to tolerate complexity and ambiguity in applying the NASW Code of Ethics when dealing with ethical dilemmas. We conclude this chapter by reviewing one model that students can use to help make practice decisions when faced with ethical dilemmas. Four new case vignettes (two in the chapter and two as part of the discussion questions) give students the opportunity to address ethical dilemmas common to social workers.

THE VALUES AND ETHICAL PRINCIPLES OF SOCIAL WORK

At the heart of social work are its values. Values are preferences or assumptions about what is worthwhile or important. Values affect how social workers practice with individuals, groups, and communities. Values also influence the broader goals of the profession. Rooted in the profession's purpose, social work values are the source of ethical principles. Ethical principles guide what people in communities have agreed is good and bad (Kirst-Ashman, 2009).

The NASW Code of Ethics represents a concrete expression of social work values, ethical principles, and standards. This code establishes guidelines for practice, helps social workers address ethical dilemmas, and provides accountability to the public by providing criteria used to assess the conduct of social workers. We strongly encourage students to become familiar with the code from the start of their careers and learn how to adhere to it in practice. Students can access and review the code online at http://www.naswdc.org/

pubs/code/code.asp. We next discuss the preamble of the NASW Code of Ethics, and then briefly review the six core values and ethical principles outlined in this document.

Preamble

The preamble of the NASW Code of Ethics provides a succinct description of the purpose of social work. The values, ethical principles, and standards are derived from the preamble. We encourage students to review the preamble often as they progress through their coursework and enter the profession. Even as experienced social workers and social work educators, we often review the preamble ourselves as a source of motivation and a reminder of *why we do, what we do.* As stated in the code,

> The primary mission of the social work profession is to enhance human wellbeing and help meet the basic human needs of all people, with particular attention to the needs and empowerment of people who are vulnerable, oppressed, and living in poverty. A historic and defining feature of social work is the profession's focus on individual wellbeing in a social context and the wellbeing of society. Fundamental to social work is attention to the environmental forces that create, contribute to, and address problems in living.
>
> Social workers promote social justice and social change with and on behalf of clients. "Clients" is used inclusively to refer to individuals, families, groups, organizations, and communities. Social workers are sensitive to cultural and ethnic diversity and strive to end discrimination, oppression, poverty, and other forms of social injustice. These activities may be in the form of direct practice, community organizing, supervision, consultation administration, advocacy, social and political action, policy development and implementation, education, and research and evaluation. Social workers seek to enhance the capacity of people to address their own needs. Social workers also seek to promote the responsiveness of organizations, communities, and other social institutions to individuals' needs and social problems.

Value One: Service

Consistent with the purpose of enhancing well-being, social workers enter into helping relationships to serve. When social workers interact with individuals, groups, or communities, they place the needs of others before their own. Although social workers are professionals that earn incomes, the importance of serving others often leads them to engage in practice as volunteers.

"Ethical Principle: Social workers' primary goal is to help people in need and to address social problems."

The value of service is more than an elusive ideal. Social workers direct their knowledge, values, and skills toward serving people in need and addressing social problems. This emphasis on serving people in need and addressing social problems is distinct to the social work profession. We encourage students to contemplate what this ethical principle means as they consider careers in social work. Although some social workers go into private practice as clinicians serving individuals in need who can afford treatment, most social workers serve clients who are vulnerable and experiencing the effects of oppression, and who are living in poverty.

Value Two: Social Justice

Promoting social justice is an ever-present primary purpose of all social work practice. Social workers recognize that environmental forces often create and contribute to problems that prevent individuals and communities from thriving. They use direct and indirect practice methods to help people cope with difficult circumstances, while supporting efforts that make it possible for every person to have the opportunity to flourish.

"Ethical Principle: Social workers challenge social injustice."

Ethical practice for every social worker involves seeking to confront injustices that prevent or challenge the well-being of others. Social workers take up efforts to address and alleviate social problems such as hunger, lack of education, discrimination, inaccessible health care, inadequate housing, unfair wages, and poverty. Moreover, social workers seek to partner with and empower people who are vulnerable and oppressed to challenge social and economic injustices on their own. Students need to think carefully about these ethical principles as they consider careers in social work. Becoming a social worker means more than serving people as clients to help meet their needs: it also means making a commitment to addressing or alleviating the reasons clients need to see a social worker in the first place. In a very real sense, ethical and competent social work practice involves always trying to work ourselves out of a job.

Value Three: Dignity and Worth of the Person

Social workers recognize that all people are autonomous and worthy individuals. Social workers also recognize that people are diverse yet share some characteristics. Valuing the dignity and worth of people means that social workers appreciate, and even celebrate, characteristics that make each person and group unique. It also means that social workers know that all people have goals, aspirations, wants, and needs that influence their well-being.

"Ethical Principle: Social workers respect the inherent dignity and worth of the person."

Social workers view people as always being capable of growing and adapting. They believe people all have strengths that can be mobilized to address personal problems and that can be used together with others to address social problems. Social workers also believe that people have the ability and capacity to make their own decisions. Social workers do not enter into professional helping relationships as "experts" and do not view the clients as "patients." Instead, the professional relationship is reciprocal, with social workers promoting self-determination and clients taking responsibility for their own actions and decisions.

Value Four: Importance of Human Relationships

If all of social work values represent the heart of the profession, human relationships represent the vehicle by which the heart carries out its purpose; in other words, human relationships represent the means by which the values carry out their purpose. Social workers appreciate human relationships in general as a key part of wellbeing and as a key mechanism for change in the community. Social workers are also acutely aware of the importance of human relationships in practice with clients (individuals, groups, organizations, and communities).

"Ethical Principle: Social workers recognize the central importance of human relationships."

Building trusting professional relationships is perhaps the most important component of social work. In fact, the role of human relationships is so important that nearly everything students learn prepares them to deliberately incorporate their knowledge, values, and skills into reciprocal professional relationships with clients. As we often advise students who are considering social work as a career, just as pursuing a degree in fine art or music requires intense study of the knowledge and skills needed to create art or perform music, social work requires intense study of knowledge and skills for the conscious use of human relationships needed for competent practice.

Value Five: Integrity

Integrity is the value that ties ethical practice and competence-based practice together as essentially overlapping concepts. When social workers engage in practice, they seek to keep the highest ethical standards. Part of developing the personal identity needed for practice is learning the history, mission, and ethical principles of social work while remaining aware of all that it means to be a social worker when engaging in practice with clients. Practicing with integrity involves social workers recognizing that in everything they do they represent the interests of clients, organizations, other helping professions, the social work profession, and society.

"Ethical Principle: Social workers behave in a trustworthy manner."

Social workers enter into trusting, helping relationships as authentic and sincere professionals. They commit themselves to being honest and genuine with clients as they incorporate their knowledge, values, and skills to provide assistance. Behaving in a trustworthy manner also involves maintaining awareness of one's own personal feelings and keeping them in check when engaging in professional relationships. Clients must always be the focus of practice. Remember, social workers value self-determination, except in a few extreme circumstances (e.g., if there is the potential for clients to harm themselves or others), and acknowledge that clients have a right to make their own decisions and take their own actions. Within the reciprocal trusting professional relationship, social workers interact as objective helpers. As objective helpers, they avoid steering clients to decisions or actions the social workers themselves might choose or think is best. Instead, social workers guide clients in assessing their choices and considering the potential consequences of their choices.

Value Six: Competence

The final value described in the NASW Code of Ethics is competence. Competence as a value means that social workers stay aware of their knowledge and skills as professional helpers. They remain careful to only practice within their areas of proficiency, while also remaining committed to expanding their knowledge and skills.

"Ethical Principle: Social workers practice within their areas of competence and develop and enhance their professional expertise."

Social workers know that they are not experts in every field of practice or proficient using every method and skill available to help clients. Social work education at the BSW and the first year of the MSW provides an introduction to generalist practice. The second or advanced year of the MSW provides additional training in one or, at most, two areas of specialization in practice. Students cannot possibly graduate knowing everything they will ever need to know throughout their careers. Instead, social work education gives students a foundation of knowledge, values, and skills that make it possible for them to become competent practitioners and for them to incorporate new areas of knowledge and skills to enhance their professional expertise. Graduating as competent social workers, therefore, means social workers with a new MSW degree or social workers with a new BSW degree are ready to monitor their practice to make sure they work only within their areas of proficiency while remaining committed to developing as a professional through lifelong learning.

ETHICAL STANDARDS

Ethical standards are derived from ethical principles. They are enforceable guidelines of conduct approved and self-regulated by a specific profession (Kirst-Ashman, 2009). The professional conduct of social workers in the United States is guided by standards listed in the NASW Code of Ethics. The standards are listed according to six areas of ethical responsibility for all social workers. These standards concern (1) social workers' ethical responsibilities to clients, (2) to colleagues, (3) in practice settings, (4) as professionals, (5) to the social work profession, and (6) to the broader society.

Students need to now go to the NASW Web site and review all of the standards listed in the six areas of ethical responsibility. They will find the NASW Code of Ethics at http://www.naswdc.org/pubs/code/code.asp. We recommend that students keep the Web site open and available as they read the rest of this chapter. Students may need to review certain standards as we focus on ethical dilemmas.

ETHICAL DILEMMAS

The unique mission of social work offers incredible flexibility and opportunity for students to contribute to society as professional helpers. Along with flexibility and opportunity, students must learn to make decisions while tolerating the complexity and even the ambiguity that comes from being a social worker. The dual emphasis on the well-being of individuals and of communities means that social workers are often in situations where they must make difficult choices between two or more alternative actions. These situations are called ethical dilemmas.

Ethical dilemmas are very common in social work. Ethical dilemmas occur when social workers must choose between two or more relevant, but contradictory, standards, and/or when every alternative available to social workers results in an undesirable outcome for one or more persons (Loewenberg, Dolgoff, & Harrington, 2000). Students will find that very little in social work practice is black or white (i.e., inherently right or wrong). Instead, social work practice is mostly gray: professionals enter into helping relationships with diverse people (whether working with them as individuals, in groups, or as representatives of communities and organizations) and use a myriad of knowledge, values, and skills to offer assistance to them in a multitude of circumstances, influenced by unique contexts.

Consider the case vignettes so far in the book. The preceding case vignettes describe situations where the social workers must choose how to proceed next. In almost every situation, the decision involves an ethical dilemma. For example, Ian Hawthorne (case vignette 2.1) must decide what to do when he learns that Logan was absent for two days even though he was not sick and did not have any other reason to miss school. Doris Lieberman (case vignette 3.3) has to decide what to do about the 355 guests paying $360 each to attend a fundraising banquet where they expect to hear from one of the Milwaukee Brewers as the guest speaker. Kristen

Lancaster (case vignette 5.2) has to decide how to respond to her supervisor's concern for confidentiality and dual relationships in Kristen's proposal to allow her to provide the parenting classes in McCall, Idaho. In all three examples, the social workers have to make decisions where there are two or more relevant, but contradictory, standards to consider. Moreover, all the available decisions will likely result in undesirable outcomes for at least one person. Now let's consider the ethical dilemmas described in the following two case vignettes.

CASE VIGNETTE 8.1. CAMESHA TALBERT

Background

Camesha Talbert pursued social work as a career after six years of working as a recreation coordinator at a community senior center. She enjoyed working with older people but believed earning her social work degree would give her more options. Camesha looked for social work programs that would allow her to keep her current employment. As a single mom with three children, she could not afford to go back to school without working. She applied and was accepted into an MSW program that offered a hybrid curriculum. (A hybrid curriculum uses a combination of in-class and online instruction to deliver the courses.) For two years, Camesha traveled to campus once a month to attend three-hour intensive seminars. She also engaged in online instruction from 7:00 to 10:00 p.m. every Tuesday and Thursday evenings. A few months after finishing her MSW, Camesha left the senior center to become a social worker for a home care and hospice agency.

The Context

The home care and hospice agency is an interdisciplinary health agency. Nurses, health aides, social workers, occupational and physical therapists, speech therapists, nutritionists, and chaplains work in teams to care for people in their own homes. The home-care program provides health-care services to people who wish to stay at home while recovering from an injury or illness, or while recuperating from a recent hospital stay. The hospice program offers palliative care for people suffering from a terminal illness. Instead of focusing on the active recovery from illness, palliative care emphasizes comforting people by addressing physical or emotional issues that are causing them pain. Hospice care is often different from home health care in that the services seek to address the needs of the family as well as the patients.

Camesha is a social worker for one of the interdisciplinary hospice teams. As the social worker on the team, she is responsible for building relationships with the hospice patients, the families, and all the other potential members of support systems assisting with care. Her primary tasks involve completing an initial social history, assisting patients and their families in making health-care decisions based on their own self-determination, ensuring end-of-life wishes are documented and known by assisting with advance directives and do not resuscitate (DNR) orders, coordinating services of other local agencies providing assistance, assisting with all the paperwork, assisting with funeral planning, and identifying emotional and spiritual needs of patients and their loved ones. Camesha also helps families after death occurs. She helps with paperwork, assesses and makes referrals for grief counseling, and provides follow-up care to determine if loved ones have any needs as they cope with their loss.

Camesha spends most of her time in the agency car and at the homes of clients. She sees four to five clients a day from Monday to Thursday. After each visit, she sits in her car and uses her cell phone to complete her social histories and progress reports by calling into the automated dictation services. Every Friday she goes into the office for the weekly team meeting. She also reviews and signs all of the social histories and progress reports she dictated during the week.

The Situation

The administrative leadership of the agency consists of an executive director, a director of development, a medical director, and a director of social work. The last Friday of each month, all the social workers meet for group supervision facilitated by Miss Bryant, the director of social work. The director of social work also goes with social workers on a home visit each year and writes a review of their work for their personnel files. It was Camesha's turn for a review. This was Camesha's first home visit with the director.

The morning of her review, the director asked Camesha to meet for lunch to go over Mr. Hartwell's case file. Camesha does not normally review cases in public. Since the director of social work asked her, however, she agreed. The plan was for Camesha to stop by Miss Bryant's office before noon so she could ride with her to the restaurant. At 11:45, Camesha packed her belongings and proceeded to pick up the director. As she approached her office, she noticed Miss Bryant drinking from a silver flask. When Miss Bryant looked up and saw Camesha coming, she quickly covered the flask and scrambled to put it in the bottom drawer of her desk. Although she knew what she had seen, Camesha acted as if she had not seen the director drinking.

At the restaurant, Miss Bryant ordered a glass of wine before lunch and three more glasses during the meal. As Miss Bryant began discussing Mr. Hartwell's case, Camesha was uncomfortable because her colleague was speaking in a very loud voice. As Miss Bryant asked her a question or made a comment, Camesha tried to respond as quietly and discreetly as possible. She was concerned for Mr. Hartwell's right to confidentiality. Toward the end of the meal, Miss Bryant started rambling on and on about her recent divorce. As Camesha looked across the table, she saw a hurt, emotionally raw, and intoxicated woman who also happened to be her director. Things only got worse at Mr. Hartwell's residence. Instead of observing Camesha at the home visit, Miss Bryant became an embarrassing distraction.

Mr. Hartwell was suffering from the end stages of chronic obstructive pulmonary disease (known as COPD). After his last exam, the doctor determined his condition was terminal and made the referral for hospice care. As Camesha sat down in his living room to talk with Mr. Hartwell, she saw Miss Bryant from the corner of her eye looking at and opening up the drawers and cabinets of the hutch in the dining room. Miss Bryant then made her way to a bookshelf filled with photo albums and started paging through the pictures. As she walked over to sit down on the couch across from Camesha, she tripped on the cat, fell onto the coffee table, and knocked everything to the floor. Camesha spent the rest of the home visit with Mr. Hartwell cleaning up the mess and rescheduling another visit for later in the week.

As Camesha and Miss Bryant headed back to the office, Camesha could not believe what had just happened. The next day, the director handed Camesha her report and walked away without saying anything. Miss Bryant had given Camesha a glowing review. Feeling shocked and confused, Camesha sat down to dictate her progress note from her visit with Mr. Hartwell and wondered what she should do.

CASE VIGNETTE 8.2. JENNIFER IBARRA

Background

Growing up in Asherton, Texas, Jennifer had helped her mother run a day care out of their home. Her father was the pastor of one of the largest churches in the area. Given their occupations and a population of fewer than two thousand, the Ibarra family knew almost everyone in the city. When it came time for Jennifer to go to college, she knew she wanted to do something where she could serve and help people. In her sophomore year, she completed all of her pre-cognates and the introduction to social work course. Then she applied and was admitted to the BSW program. She did so well in school that she earned a full scholarship to another university to earn her MSW degree. Because she had graduated with her BSW, she qualified for advanced standing and was able to finish her MSW in twelve additional months. She now practices social work as a primary clinician at a family counseling center supported by all of the churches in the community.

The Context

The family counseling center is a private nonprofit agency located in Dimmit County, Texas. Dimmit County has a population of approximately 10,000. The center is located in Carrizo Springs, the county seat, nine miles from Asherton. The center provides mental health and family counseling, case management, and medication management services for children and families. The center generates revenues from three sources—fees collected for services, monthly contributions from almost every church in the county, and funds from a contract with the DHW. As the only provider for counseling in the county, the DHW contracts with the center to provide counseling services for foster parents. Jennifer's position with the center is funded by the contract. She spends most of her time providing time-limited supportive counseling to foster parents. She also facilitates a support group for new foster parents every Thursday evening.

The Situation

After writing a progress note and returning the case file from a previous client to the file room, Jennifer walked to the reception area to meet with Mrs. Reyes and Jarod. Mrs. Reyes has been a foster parent for the past six years. Jarod is her fourth foster child. He is twelve years old and has been living with Mrs. Reyes for almost a year. The DHW removed Jarod from his home because he was being abused repeatedly by his stepfather. Jarod's mother is allowed to have supervised visits with Jarod every other month, but Jarod cannot return home to his mother as long as she continues living with the stepfather. Mrs. Reyes and Jarod were referred to the family counseling center by a school social worker after he had a fight with someone at school. Jarod had never been in a fight at school before.

When the school social worker discovered that Jarod had recently been put in foster care, she thought that he and Mrs. Reyes could benefit from talking to someone at the center.

Jennifer had met with Mrs. Reyes and Jarod for one hour a week for the past six weeks. She focused most of their sessions on helping Jarod cope effectively with his mixed emotions. On the one hand, Jarod knew his mother loved him. On the other hand, he could not understand why she stayed with his stepfather. During the sessions, it also seemed as if Jarod liked Mrs. Reyes. He told Jennifer how much he enjoyed her. She also observed how warm and supportive they seemed to be in their interactions. Together, Mrs. Reyes and Jarod developed and implemented an intervention strategy to cope with his emotions. For the past six weeks, Jarod had kept a picture diary where he drew pictures that described his emotions; if he wanted to, he could share the pictures with Mrs. Reyes. The intervention strategy appeared to be effective, as he has not had any other altercations. Mrs. Reyes also shared that his teachers reported he seemed more engaged with his peers in class and during recess. This was their last session with Jennifer.

Jennifer used the last session to review the progress Mrs. Reyes and Jarod made during their time together. She praised Jarod for embracing the picture diary and for his willingness to share it with Mrs. Reyes. When she asked Jarod if he planned to continue with the diary, he shared that he loved to draw and was considering entering some of his drawings in a contest at school. Toward the end of the session, Mrs. Reyes thanked Jennifer. She then reached into her purse and pulled out what seemed to be a thank-you card. Mrs. Reyes told Jennifer that she wanted to get her something to express her appreciation for helping them. When she opened the card, Jennifer found two tickets to a San Antonio Spurs basketball game. Before Jennifer could say anything, Mrs. Reyes said that she noticed the Spurs coffee mug on her desk and thought she would surprise her with tickets. After Jennifer opened the card, Jarod moved toward her and gave her a hug. Jennifer smiled briefly at Mrs. Reyes and Jarod, then looked down for a moment to pause and gather her thoughts. The tickets were worth $100 or more. She loved the Spurs and appreciated the gesture, but she was not comfortable accepting the gift. She also did not want to offend Mrs. Reyes and Jarod. He had been doing so well and she did not want to say or do anything as they terminated to stifle his progress. She looked up and wondered what to do.

Camesha Talbert and Jennifer Ibarra find themselves faced with ethical dilemmas from circumstances that are fairly common in social work. Camesha is in an awkward situation with Miss Bryant, who is her supervisor and also the director. Camesha seems to be fairly new at the home health and hospice agency. This is the first time Miss Bryant has gone with her to observe her work. In their time together, Camesha observed Miss Bryant drinking at lunch and at work, talking loudly in a public place about a client without regard for his right to privacy and confidentiality, and acting inappropriately during the home visit. In fact, Miss Bryant's behavior was so distracting that Camesha had to work with Mr. Hartwell to clean up the mess Miss Bryant had caused and to schedule another appointment. The next day, Camesha received a positive review from the director, but Camesha knew that Miss Bryant had not really observed her work. Does she simply accept the positive review, forget what happened, and go on with her work at the agency? What if Miss Bryant were to act like this on all of the visits? How may her behavior interfere with other clients? Maybe the director needs help. Does Camesha say something to someone? If so, what does she say, and to whom does she say it? If she says something, will it put her job in jeopardy? How will it influence her relationship with Miss Bryant and her other colleagues?

Jennifer Ibarra is also in a difficult situation. When social workers enter into professional relationships, clients may feel a sense of gratitude. Mrs. Reyes is grateful for how well Jarod is doing and wanted to do something to express her appreciation for the assistance she received. Jennifer recognized the gesture from Mrs. Reyes as an expression of thankfulness. She has likely received thank-you cards from other clients in the past. However, this time the card included a gift that Jennifer knew was quite expensive. Should she accept the tickets? Is it appropriate or inappropriate for her to accept the tickets? If the latter, why would it be inappropriate? Should she give them back? If she does, what should she say to Mrs. Reyes and Jarod?

Making ethical decisions in social work is an important practice behavior that requires knowledge, values, skills, and experience. As competent social workers, Camesha, Jennifer, and the social workers from the other cases have the ability to apply the code of ethics with strategies of ethical reasoning to respond to their ethical dilemmas. Students will need to learn to make ethical decisions as they progress toward earning their social work degrees. We use the rest of this chapter to present a general ethical decision-making model students can use to practice addressing ethical dilemmas. We conclude by providing students two additional cases to practice using the model.

A MODEL FOR MAKING ETHICAL DECISIONS

Response to ethical dilemmas in social work practice is seldom a simple act. The complexities of entering into professional helping relationships make it almost impossible to point to a single discrete decision as the right response. Rather, ethical decision making is usually influenced by many factors, including the context, the people involved, the values in conflict, and the previous decisions. Making ethical decisions, therefore, comes with the following caveat: ethical decision making is far too complex for a simple one-size-fits-all model. Students should consider any model, including the one we present, as merely a guide to help them evaluate all that is involved before making a decision. Students or social workers can use the same model to assess the same situation and still choose different, though equally viable, responses.

Figure 8.1 lists the steps of one general decision-making model used for addressing ethical dilemmas in social work practice (Loewenberg et al., 2000, p. 63). Let us briefly use the steps to consider the situation facing Jennifer Ibarra.

Figure 8.1. A General Ethical Decision-Making Model

Step

1 Identify the problem.

2 Identify all the persons and institutions involved.

3 Determine who should be involved in the decision making.

4 Identify the values relevant to the problem.

5 Identify the goals and objectives.

6 Identify alternative intervention strategies and targets.

7 Assess the effectiveness and efficiency of each alternative.

8 Select the most appropriate strategy.

9 Implement the selected strategy.

10 Monitor the implementation.

11 Evaluate the results and identify additional problems.

Step 1. Identify the Problem.

During her last session of working with Mrs. Reyes and Jarod, Jennifer receives a thank-you card containing two tickets valued at more than $100 to attend a San Antonio Spurs basketball game. Mrs. Reyes intended the gift as a thoughtful gesture to express her appreciation for her work with Jarod.

The factors contributing to the problem seem to center on the type of relationships that exists among Jennifer, Mrs. Reyes, and Jarod. If Jennifer and Mrs. Reyes were in a personal relationship as friends, the gift may be completely appropriate and she could accept it without hesitation. Deciding what to do and how to respond within the context of a professional helping relationship is not as simple. Mrs. Reyes and Jarod worked with Jennifer for six weeks because she is a trained professional working for an agency contracted by the DHW to provide supportive counseling to foster parents. Jennifer also entered into the helping relationship as a representative of the social work profession. She, therefore, must apply the standards of the NASW Code of Ethics to guide her professional decisions and actions.

Step 2. Identify All the Persons and Institutions Involved.

At first glance, it may seem as if the situation involves only Jennifer, Mrs. Reyes, and Jarod. The reality is that multiple people and institutions are involved. Social workers, even private practitioners, *never* practice in a vacuum or in isolation. When social workers practice, they at all times have ethical responsibilities to clients, to colleagues, in practice settings, as professionals, to the social work profession, and to the broader society. Jennifer entered into a professional helping relationship with Mrs. Reyes and Jarod knowing she has ethical responsibilities to them, to her colleagues at the family counseling center, indirectly to her colleagues at DHW, to herself as a professional, to the social work profession, and to society.

In deciding how to respond to the gift, she needs to consider what is best for the clients. In this case, what decision is of most benefit to Mrs. Reyes and Jarod? How could her decision influence their interactions with other people at the counseling center? Jennifer also needs to be aware of agency policy guiding her interactions, the stipulations set forth in the contract with the DHW, and the standards of the NASW Code of Ethics. Finally, she needs to consider the potential effects of her decision for other social workers. How does her decision contribute to or hinder the profession in fulfilling our sanctioned purpose to society?

Step 3. Determine Who Should Be Involved in the Decision Making.

It seems the case calls for Jennifer to respond immediately to Mrs. Reyes and Jarod. She is the only one directly involved in decision making. However, other people in the agency may also be involved, though indirectly. For example, Jennifer probably has a direct supervisor that meets with her periodically. She and the supervisor may have talked about agency policy and procedures for handling gifts from clients. Jennifer may also participate in clinical staff meetings where a group of interdisciplinary professionals gather to review cases. The group may have discussed cases from other clients where other staff members responded to similar situations. Again, social workers *never* practice in a vacuum or in isolation.

Step 4. Identify the Values Relevant to the Problem.

As with any ethical dilemma, there were personal and professional values relevant to the problem. Mrs. Reyes appreciated the service she received from Jennifer and wanted to express her gratitude. She probably believes that it is important to be generous and to be thankful when people provide assistance.

Jennifer is a social worker. As a competent practitioner, she has the interpersonal skills to develop rapport with clients. Her ability to develop rapport makes it possible for her to provide effective services. She probably values working with different people in professional helping relationships. It is also natural for her to appreciate when clients thank her for their work together. As a social worker, however, professional values must guide her practice. Though all of the professional values are in some way applicable, the values of service and integrity seem most pertinent in this situation. Given the importance in social work to enter into relationships to serve others, Jennifer has to consider how her decision contributes to her helping Mrs. Reyes and Jarod. She also needs to consider how her decision contributes to her practicing with the highest of ethical standards. Remember that practicing with integrity means that in everything Jennifer does she is representing the interests of clients, her colleagues, herself as a professional, the social work profession, and the broader society. She must keep Mrs. Reyes and Jarod as the focus of practice. Practicing with integrity means she needs to place their needs before her own needs.

Step 5. Identify the Goals and Objectives.

Jennifer entered into a professional helping relationship to provide supportive counseling services to Mrs. Reyes and Jarod. It seems that the goals of their relationship were to help Jarod cope with the transition to foster care and to help Mrs. Reyes support Jarod in his transition. At the time of the incident, Mrs. Reyes' intentions were to express her appreciation and gratitude. Jennifer was focused on termination. She reviewed the progress they had made and sought to encourage Jarod to continue what had made him successful over the six weeks of their sessions. After receiving the thank-you card with the tickets, her objectives probably include how to respond appropriately to Mrs. Reyes' gesture while maintaining the trusting relationship that made it possible for their sessions to be so effective. Jennifer also needs to make sure her response fits within the policies and procedures of the agency as well as the standards of the NASW Code of Ethics.

Step 6. Identify Alternative Intervention Strategies and Targets.

It appears that Jennifer has a few alternatives. She could, in fact, accept the gift, thank Mrs. Reyes and Jarod, and wish them well while Jarod continues living with Mrs. Reyes in foster care. By accepting the gift, Jennifer validates Mrs. Reyes' desire to express her gratitude. Accepting the gift, however, seems to emphasize Jennifer as the target of this strategy. She benefits as much or more from the exchange than do Mrs. Reyes and Jarod. Remember, Jennifer earns her salary as a social worker with the family counseling center. The center probably received compensation either from revenue generated from the contract with the DHW and/or from fees-for-service collected from Mrs. Reyes. The tickets are essentially additional compensation for Jennifer.

The other alternatives involve returning the tickets. She could keep the card and return the tickets or return the card and the tickets. Jennifer can also decide what she can say so that she validates Mrs. Reyes' intentions while explaining that she cannot accept the tickets. Mrs. Reyes and Jarod seem to be the targets of any of the alternatives that involve returning the tickets. For instance, Jennifer could ask Jarod to step outside so she can speak with Mrs. Reyes alone for a minute. She could thank Mrs. Reyes for the gesture, empathize with her intentions, and explain why she cannot accept the tickets. Jennifer also could suggest to Mrs. Reyes that she keep the tickets and take Jarod to the game. She could tell her that taking him to the game could serve as a positive reinforcement for how well he has been doing lately and to express her care for him as her foster child.

Step 7. Assess the Effectiveness and Efficiency of Each Alternative.

The alternatives need to be assessed in terms of the goals for the clients, the agency, the profession, and for Jennifer. Accepting the gift may seem efficient and even effective for Jennifer and the clients. The last session would end rather smoothly and Mrs. Reyes and Jarod would leave with the emotional satisfaction that comes with such an expression of generosity. The benefits would be short term, though, because accepting the tickets could cause more problems after the initial emotions dissipate. After the clients leave, Jennifer will have to write her progress note. Does she write about the thank-you card and gift in the note? Does she tell her colleagues and/or her supervisor about the tickets? If she feels uncomfortable doing so, it may indicate that she should not accept the gift. Accepting the gift may also encourage Mrs. Reyes to offer gifts to other helping professionals. Jennifer needs to consider that Mrs. Reyes may now believe that every time she receives support for one of her foster children she will need to purchase an elaborate gift. It is also likely that accepting the tickets would not be congruent with the goals of the agency or the values of the social work profession.

The way Jennifer returns the tickets will probably determine how effective and efficient her future interactions are with Mrs. Reyes and Jarod. Although she cannot control how Mrs. Reyes and Jarod will respond, she has to try to balance the need to communicate appreciation with explaining why she cannot accept the tickets. Jennifer also needs to make sure that her response is congruent with agency policy and the code of ethics. She will want to terminate her work with Mrs. Reyes and Jarod in a way that reinforces their trust in her and the agency, that allows her to follow up, and that makes it easier for other helping professionals to work with them in the future.

Step 8. Select the Most Appropriate Strategy.

When social workers address ethical dilemmas, the most appropriate strategy is usually not that obvious. In fact, different social workers can apply the steps of the decision-making model and still choose different strategies. The combination of developing the knowledge, values, and skills necessary for competent practice, and the practice wisdom that develops after years of experience with adequate supervision can help social workers select appropriate strategies.

As we have suggested thus far, the ethical dilemma facing Jennifer seems to require two levels of decision making. She has to decide whether to accept the tickets, and she has to decide how to respond to Mrs. Reyes and Jarod. Given the circumstances, we believe Jennifer should consider thanking Mrs. Reyes for her gesture, which would normalize her feelings of appreciation and gratitude and reinforce the progress Jarod has made. In addition, we believe she should keep the card, but explain that as a professional social worker and employee of the family counseling center she cannot accept the tickets.

Step 9. Implement the Selected Strategy.

Depending on the specifics of an ethical dilemma, social workers may have an opportunity to work through the decision-making steps slowly and seek guidance from colleagues and/or a supervisor before responding. Jennifer is confronted with an ethical dilemma where she has to decide and implement her strategy almost immediately. She has to rely on her training and experience to choose and implement an appropriate strategy before Mrs. Reyes and Jarod leave her office. Implementing the strategy described in step 8 seems to be a reasonable response.

Step 10. Monitor the Implementation.

When Jennifer responds to Mrs. Reyes and Jarod, she needs to monitor their verbal and nonverbal communication. After six weeks of sessions, it appears Jarod has made considerable progress developing healthy ways to cope with his emotions. As Jennifer thanks them and explains why she cannot accept the tickets, she must attend to what they say that may indicate a setback. In the same way, she must attend to their facial expressions and other gestures. Although she cannot completely control their reaction, by paying close attention she can adapt and alter her words, her tone, or her body language to reinforce their progress and express her appreciation for their gratitude.

Step 11. Evaluate the Results and Identify Additional Problems.

Jennifer can evaluate the short-term and long-term outcomes of her responses. After Mrs. Reyes and Jarod leave, she will have the opportunity to sit down, reflect on the session, and write a progress note. She also can evaluate the outcome when she talks to them at follow-up.

There seem to be at least a few additional issues that Jennifer can identify and perhaps address. As Mrs. Reyes continues as a foster parent, she will probably have further interactions with social workers and other professional staff that provide supportive services. The way Jennifer responds to the ethical dilemma will likely influence how Mrs. Reyes interacts with other professional helpers. Will Mrs. Reyes continue providing gifts after working with someone? Will she leave feeling hurt? Will her experiences with Jennifer influence how willing she is to seek help in the future from another social worker? These are the type of problems Jennifer needs to be aware of as she evaluates her response.

SUMMARY

Responding effectively to ethical dilemmas is a significant part of practicing as competent social workers. The dynamic focus on the well-being of individuals, families, groups, and communities often puts social workers in positions where they must make decisions that involve competing interests. Competent social workers draw from their knowledge, values, skills, and experience to assess competing interests and make sound ethical decisions. We encourage students to use the general ethical decision model as they practice incorporating what they learn to address ethical dilemmas. Just remember that the model is only a guide. Students must still be able to tolerate the complexity and ambiguity often characteristic of social work practice.

DISCUSSION QUESTIONS

In this chapter's discussion questions, we provide two additional case vignettes so that you can practice addressing ethical dilemmas. We also continue the theme of asking you to engage in self-reflection. We ask that you consider each question, keeping in mind your career goals, the historical and current issues, and the tensions within the social work profession.

CASE VIGNETTE 8.3. CATHY JENNINGS

Background

After her youngest daughter finished college, Cathy Jennings decided to return to school. When she met with an admissions counselor in the admissions office, she shared her interest in working with children and families needing support. The counselor recommended that she look into social work. The following day, Cathy met with the social work department head, who described all of the ways she could work with children and families in social work. Because she already had a bachelor's degree, Cathy applied and was admitted to the MSW program. A few years later, she graduated, earned her license, and accepted a position working as a clinician in a psychiatric unit at the local community hospital.

The Context

The psychiatric unit consisted of three programs. There was a twenty-seven-bed short-term inpatient facility where clients could be admitted for up to thirty days, a partial hospital program where clients stayed at the hospital from 8:00 a.m. to 2:00 p.m. for up to fourteen days, and an outpatient office where the hospital provided mental health and substance abuse counseling services. A multidisciplinary staff of psychiatrists, nurses, licensed clinical social workers, and certified substance abuse counselors worked in the unit.

Cathy worked primarily with clients admitted to the inpatient facility. She was responsible for completing social histories of every client within twenty-four hours of being admitted. She also cofacilitated a therapy group, a psycho-education group, and a medication management group each day. Her other responsibilities included discharge planning and being on call once a month to provide psychiatric evaluations in the emergency room.

The Situation

It was Cathy's weekend to be on call. Just as she was finishing her dinner at home, she received a text message letting her know that one of the physicians requested a psychiatric evaluation. She quickly ran upstairs to put on her shoes and then headed to the hospital. When she arrived, one of the nurses met her in the lobby and walked her back to meet the client. As they walked, the nurse described Ms. Flores as a twenty-six-year-old female brought to the emergency room after her sister found her lying unconscious on the floor of the living room. She was unconscious after swallowing a whole bottle of acetaminophen. She regained consciousness after the doctor had revived her and pumped her stomach. Once she was stable, the doctor ordered a psychiatric evaluation so she could determine appropriate follow-up care. The nurse informed Cathy that Ms. Flores did not have health insurance. She was waiting in room 7 with her sister.

Cathy walked in and introduced herself to Ms. Flores and her sister. She then got the empty chair from across the room, put it next to the bed and sat down, and asked Ms. Flores to describe what had happened. Ms. Flores shared that their mother had died last week. Her cousin had called her and her sister from El Salvador to give them the bad news. She told Cathy that since last week she had felt numb. She also shared that she could not remember taking the pills. All she remembered was falling asleep and then waking up in the hospital. Next, Cathy asked about her living situation. Specifically, she wanted to know if Ms. Flores lived with someone who could watch over her. She learned that Ms. Flores and her sister shared a two-bedroom apartment. The two of them, however, worked different shifts. Ms. Flores worked during the day as a housekeeper for a large hotel. Her sister worked as an assistant manager at a twenty-four-hour convenience store in the evenings. Cathy also learned that she and her sister had only been living in the United States for eleven months. Neither of them owned a car and they did not know the area very well.

After listening to Ms. Flores and her sister, Cathy told them that since Ms. Flores attempted to take her own life, she had to contact the attending psychiatrist, Dr. Tauger, to develop an appropriate plan. She left the room, walked down the hall to the nursing station, then sat down to call the psychiatrist. As Cathy was describing the situation over the phone, Dr. Tauger interrupted to ask if Ms. Flores had insurance. After learning that she did not have insurance, the psychiatrist gave Cathy two choices: commit Ms. Flores and transfer her to the state hospital for seventy-two hours of observation, or send her home with her sister.

Cathy knew that the state hospital was six hours away from them. Sending Ms. Flores that far away could be very traumatic. She would be transported by a police officer to the other side of the state and away from her sister, who was her only close friend or family member in the United States. Cathy was also concerned about sending her home with her sister. She knew that Ms. Flores would be alone in the evenings since her sister could not miss work. Cathy tried convincing Dr. Tauger to admit her to their psychiatric unit for observation, but she would not change her mind. She asked Cathy to call her back when she had decided. If Cathy decided to commit Ms. Flores, Dr. Tauger would come down to the hospital to sign the order. Cathy put down the phone, pulled out a commitment order and a release order, and then wondered what she should do.

CASE VIGNETTE 8.4. JORDAN ZILLNER

Background

Jordan always knew he would eventually do something in the helping professions. His mother was a school psychologist for a residential children's home. His father had a private practice as a licensed substance abuse counselor. After exploring his options, he decided to pursue a degree in social work. In his sophomore year, Jordan applied and was selected for the state stipend/certification program. Through the program, the state covered his tuition and provided a modest living stipend for the last two years of school in return for at least two years of work for the state DSS. Jordan completed his BSW and was hired as a social worker in the adult protective services unit in the same county where he had done his field internship.

The Context

Jordan has three responsibilities as a social worker in the adult protective services unit. First, he investigates cases of alleged abuse, neglect, or exploitation of adults. Second, he writes a report of his investigation and develops an initial service plan for the adult protective treatment team. Third, he rotates with other social workers in the unit to screen incoming calls from the people reporting potential abuses.

The Situation

After receiving a referral from the intake worker, Jordan went to visit with Ms. Strickland. Ms. Strickland was a seventy-two-year-old woman who lived with her son. The referral indicated that a few days before a neighbor had called adult protective services after Ms. Strickland showed up at her home asking for a ride to the grocery store. This was the first time she had ever asked for a ride to the store because her son usually takes her. The neighbor described her as having bruises on her wrists. When Jordan arrived at the home, Ms. Strickland invited him into the living room. Jordan explained that he was a social worker from adult protective services and that he was there to follow up on a referral. Ms. Strickland thanked Jordan for coming by but assured him that everything was fine. Looking down at her wrists, Jordan asked her if she could explain how she got the bruises. Ms. Strickland turned away, telling him again that everything was fine. She then looked back at Jordan and shared that her son had been angry with her the other day for losing his cell phone. She was cleaning the house and moved it to another room, then she could not remember where she had put it. She told Jordan that it really was not a big deal.

Ms. Strickland then asked Jordan to leave before her son returned home. She explained that her son was the only family she had left. She did not want Jordan to cause trouble. Jordan explained that he could help her. In a stern but shaken voice, Ms. Strickland told Jordan that she did not want his help, especially if his help meant that she was going to have to leave her home to go live in a nursing home. She then walked over, opened the front door, and pleaded with Jordan to leave. Jordan sighed, walked over to the doorway, turned to Ms. Strickland, and wondered what to do next.

For each of the preceding vignettes, use the NASW Code of Ethics and relevant literature (i.e., the EBP) to do the following:

Step 1. Identify the problem.

Step 2. Identify all the persons and institutions involved.

Step 3. Determine who should be involved in the decision making.

Step 4. Identify the values relevant to the problem.

Step 5. Identify the goals and objectives.

Step 6. Identify alternative intervention strategies and targets.

Step 7. Assess the effectiveness and efficiency of each alternative.

Step 8. Select the most appropriate strategy.

Step 9. Implement the selected strategy.

Step 10. Monitor the implementation.

Step 11. Evaluate the results and identify additional problems.

In addition to the steps in the ethical decision-making model above, please answer the following self-reflection questions regarding the preceding two case vignettes:

1. What personal values influenced your decision making in each of the preceding cases?

2. Did aspects of either case cause you particular discomfort? If so, discuss those aspects with your fellow students and/or instructor.

3. Did you have any conflicts between your personal values and the applicable ethical principles from the NASW Code of Ethics or social work literature related to either case? If so, how did you resolve those conflicts? Are you comfortable with how you resolved those conflicts? If not, consider discussing it further with your instructor.

REFERENCES

Kirst-Ashman, K. K. (2009). *Introduction to social work and social welfare: Critical thinking perspective* (3rd ed.). Belmont, CA: Brooks/Cole.

Loewenberg, F. M., Dolgoff, R., & Harrington, D. (2000). *Ethical decisions for social work practice* (6th ed.). Itasca, IL: Peacock.

CHAPTER NINE

Human Rights and Justice

CASE VIGNETTE 9.1. VIOLET SCOTT

Background

Violet Scott was the first person in her family to go to college. Her mom and dad did not finish high school, but they worked very hard to provide for Violet and her two younger sisters. Her dad worked as a plumber's assistant, while her mom worked as a custodian at an elementary school. Every day, Violet and her sisters would go to the Boys and Girls Club after-school program, where they worked on their homework and played with other children until one of their parents came to take them home. It was at the Boys and Girls Club where Violet met Katherine, who was the supervisor of the after-school program. She was also a social worker who happened to spend a lot of time talking with Violet through the years. After attending a career fair at her high school, Violet met with Katherine to talk about what she was going to do after she graduated. It was during that conversation that Violet realized that she wanted to go to college and become a social worker.

During the next few months, Katherine worked with the school guidance counselor to help Violet get into college. She helped her select a few colleges with social work programs, study for the entrance exams, complete the applications for admissions, and apply for financial aid. The following winter, Violet was accepted into three of the four schools she considered. She chose one school that provided a generous scholarship covering most of her tuition and offered her a work-study position. Five years later, she earned her BSW, completed an advanced-standing MSW program, and then went to work as a manager of a group home for at-risk youth. Because Violet had done her internship at the group home, when the former manager left for another position she recommended Violet as her replacement to the owner. The owner hired Violet two weeks after she graduated with her MSW.

The Context

The group home provided safe, long-term residence and support for twelve teenaged girls. Most of the girls were referred to the group home by the Department of Children and Family Services (DCFS) after repeated abuse by at least one of their parents. Two of the girls were so abusive to their younger siblings that their parents had had no choice but to work with DCFS to find them an alternative safe place to live outside their homes. Even though the younger siblings were not abused by their parents, DCFS was still responsible for making sure they were living in a safe environment. Eight of the girls were African American, and the other four were European American. The girls ranged in age from thirteen to seventeen.

As the group home manager, Violet supervised a staff of six people. She was responsible for making sure that at least two adults were at the home at all times. She also led the staff in developing the rules for the home and establishing protocols for responding to different types of emergency situations. Every other morning at 10:00, Violet facilitated a staff meeting. She used the staff meeting to organize transportation needs for the girls, plan activities for the weekends, and provide support for staff dealing with specific behavioral issues in the home. During the week, Violet spent most of her time interacting with the girls. She planned and facilitated a check-in group each afternoon where the girls had an opportunity to talk about their days. She also kept her schedule free from appointments between 5:00 to 8:00 in the evenings so she would be available to help the girls with their homework and talk with them individually. Violet ate dinner with the girls almost every evening. She thought eating dinner with them was important to develop and maintain their trust and to show the girls that she really cared. The only time she did not stay for dinner was when she took time off from work.

The Situation

In August, Violet attended a high school orientation with Erica, a fifteen-year-old African American girl who had been living in the home for the past fourteen months. Erica had moved into the group home after her mother received a seven-year prison sentence after being found guilty of assault and battery. Erica had no other family willing to let her live with them so the courts referred her to DCFS, who arranged for her to move to the group home. Erica thrived after moving into the home. Knowing she had a safe, structured, and peaceful place to live, she adapted quickly, and developed trusting relationships with the staff and the other girls. She was also a good student who was eager to begin high school.

Two weeks before high school orientation, Violet helped Erica fill out and turn in her class schedule for the fall semester. Erica had done so well in her last year of middle school that she qualified for the gifted and talented courses at the high school. She looked forward to attending the high school orientation so she could meet the teachers and the other students in the gifted and talented sections. She also wanted to see the classrooms. When the assistant principal handed Erica her official schedule, she and Violet noticed she had been placed in the regular classes. Before they could say anything, the assistant principal explained that although Erica technically qualified for the gifted and talented courses, she and the principal thought that, given her unique living situation, she might fit in better with students in the regular sections. Erica was deeply upset and disappointed. Violet was also upset. She was concerned that the school administrators had made a decision about Erica based on her race and her residence instead of on her academic record. She pulled the assistant principal aside, away from Erica, to share her concerns. When they were alone, she told the assistant principal that Erica would not accept the current schedule and that she wanted it adjusted to reflect the courses Erica requested and was qualified to take. The assistant principal shared that she could not make that change on her own but would schedule a meeting the next morning with the principal and Violet. The following morning, as Violet headed to the high school, she wondered what she should say and do next.

CASE VIGNETTE 9.2. DUSTIN SHELDON

Background

Dustin returned to school after twenty-three years as a pastor. In his application to graduate school, he shared that after years of preaching to his congregation, he wanted to spend the rest of his life serving and ministering alongside others, helping those in need. For the next two and a half years, he attended an evening and weekend MSW program that allowed him to work during the day. Within a month after graduation, a nonprofit housing coalition hired him as a case manager to work with families who were struggling to pay their bills.

The Context

Dustin worked with a caseload of thirty-one families. The families usually requested help from the coalition for three reasons.

Some families were renting either a house or an apartment and were struggling to pay their rent. Other families wanted help with purchasing their first home. Another group of families sought help from the coalition to prevent foreclosure. In addition to working with individual families, Dustin facilitated a budgeting support group for couples every Tuesday evening at a local church. The group was sponsored by the coalition, but the church provided the space for the sessions. The mayor, a member of the church where Dustin was the pastor, appointed him to serve on a local housing and planning commission for the city. Dustin thought serving on the commission as a social worker was important so he could be an advocate for the families that come to the coalition. He also thought it was important as a case manager to network with as many real estate agents and landlords as possible.

The Situation

Mr. and Mrs. Vargas came to the housing coalition after they had fallen two months behind on their rent. Mr. Vargas worked as a mechanic at a car dealership. Mrs. Vargas worked for a house-cleaning service. Their combined incomes put them in a difficult position: they make barely enough to cover their normal expenses, while they make too much to qualify for any assistance. They lived at the Westbrook Apartment Village, a spread-out complex with fifty-eight apartment units. In his initial meeting, Dustin reviewed their income, helped them develop a budget, and negotiated a payment plan between them and the landlord that would catch them up on the rent within six months.

During his monthly follow-up sessions with Mr. and Mrs. Vargas, Dustin noticed how high their utility bills were each month. They lived in a one-bedroom apartment, yet their electric and water bills were almost as high as his, and he lived in a large home. Troubled by their expenses, Dustin decided to search the expense records of a few other families that came to the coalition who also lived at the

Westbrook Apartment Village. In his search, he discovered that all of the families living in the apartment complex had unreasonably high utility bills. He thought that the unreasonably high utility bills might be a primary reason these families have had trouble meeting their expenses. He wondered what he could do to help them.

CASE VIGNETTE 9.3. TERESA BROWN

Background

Teresa started her social work program interested in working with older adults. She envisioned herself working either in a nursing home or a hospital setting as a medical social worker. The field instructor in her BSW program interviewed Teresa for her field placement and then sent her to interview with the social worker at an assisted living facility in the community. Her interview went well and the social worker invited her to do her field internship with them. The social worker also agreed to be her field instructor.

Teresa learned a great deal from completing her internship at the assisted living program. Through her field contract, she did a variety of activities that allowed her to demonstrate the knowledge, values, and skills of a generalist competent social worker. She also confirmed her desire to practice as a social worker with older adults, but in a way that was different from how she had first envisioned it. Throughout her coursework and internship experience, Teresa discovered that she was drawn toward organizational and community practice. Although she knew that practice with larger systems is the responsibility of every competent social worker, she decided she wanted to do something that focused more on macro practice and less on working directly with older adults as individual clients. She applied and was admitted for advanced standing in an MSW program where she specialized in community practice. After graduation, she was hired by the Area Agency on Aging in her local community.

The Context

The Area Agency on Aging provided programs, services, and information for older adults and their families. The purpose of everything the agency does was to help older adults remain in the community instead of moving to nursing facilities. The organization provided family caregiver support programs, information about short-term and long-term care options, and consumer education and protection. Teresa was a social worker in the consumer education and protection program. She developed, planned, and coordinated workshops that provide information so people can make informed choices as they get older. The topics for the workshops ranged from healthy eating and exercise to financial planning in retirement. Teresa also spent a significant portion of her time as a consumer advocate. Although she did not work in the ombudsman program, she often worked with social workers in the program when they discovered a pattern of complaints from multiple residents about the same agency or business, or about the same issue.

The Situation

As Teresa left the office at the end of the day, Valerie Williams, the director of the ombudsman program, walked with her to the parking lot. Valerie asked Teresa if she could join her staff in their weekly meeting in the morning. She did not have time to give her all the details, but told her they needed her help and input. Teresa looked down at her calendar on her cell phone, noticed that she was free in the morning, and told Valerie she would be there.

Teresa arrived at 8:00 the following morning. She went to her desk, checked her voicemail, and then headed to the other side of the building to attend the ombudsman meeting. At the meeting, Valerie and her staff shared their concerns about a recent increase in the number of calls from people reporting that they were not receiving the monthly checks from their reverse mortgages. Within the past two months, they had received more than two dozen calls from older adults or their families. Valerie told Teresa that her staff was looking into the individual cases and thought that Teresa should investigate what was going on from a broader perspective. The meeting concluded with everyone agreeing to meet the following week so Teresa could give them an update on what she learned and what she planned to do to begin addressing the issue. Teresa left the meeting, went back to her desk, pulled out a legal pad, and wondered where to begin.

The three case vignettes demonstrate, once again, the uniqueness of social work. Social work is a broad field that can involve working with many different population groups, in different settings, and at different levels of practice. In the midst of this diversity, social workers share particular knowledge, values, and skills that unify the profession. The importance of advancing human rights and social and economic justice is a key competence that unifies the profession.

Violet Scott, Dustin Sheldon, and Teresa Brown work in positions where they engage in different levels of practice. Violet works primarily with individual clients, Dustin with families or small groups, and Teresa with larger groups and organizations. However, the three of them share core professional values that undergird all they do. For example, they believe in the right to well-being as individuals, groups, and communities; the right to self-determination; and the inherent dignity and worth of all people. They were trained with the knowledge and skills to advance human rights, and social and economic justice. As social workers representing the profession, they share a responsibility to incorporate social justice practices wherever and with whomever they engage in practice. As you continue contemplating whether social work is the right field for you, consider social workers' professional commitment to advance human rights and social and economic justice.

HUMAN RIGHTS, JUSTICE, AND WELL-BEING

An important part of developing the professional identity needed for social work is grasping the interconnections between human rights, justice, and well-being. Recall that the primary purpose—*why* we *do*—of social work is to enhance or restore well-being for individuals, groups, and communities. As social workers engage in helping relationships for the purpose of enhancing well-being, the concept of human rights becomes important because it contributes to our understanding of what we mean by well-being. Social workers believe that all people have basic human rights, such as freedom, safety, privacy, an adequate standard of living, health care, and education. These human rights are essential for enhancing and restoring well-being. In fact, it is fair to state that social workers believe well-being is a basic human right, regardless of his or her position in society. We encourage students to learn more about human rights by reading through the Universal Declaration of Human Rights, adopted by the United Nations in 1948, found at http://www.un.org/en/documents/udhr/index.shtml.

The concept of justice becomes relevant as social workers seek to enhance or restore well-being. Just as all people have basic human rights, social workers recognize that forms and mechanisms of oppression and discrimination prevent some people from exercising those rights. As competent practitioners, therefore, social workers must be prepared to assess underlying practices of oppression and discrimination that can negatively influence well-being, and be prepared to do something about it in their work with individuals, groups, and communities.

DIFFICULT BUT IMPORTANT QUESTIONS

Up to this point in the book, we have avoided two difficult but essential questions. These two questions warrant consideration from anyone thinking of pursuing social work as a career. Furthermore, we believe that competent social workers should consider exploring these questions continuously as part of their commitment to lifelong learning as professional helpers. Read the following two questions and then pause to think about them for a few minutes.

1. What is well-being?
2. What is social justice?

If you gave the questions considerable attention, we imagine that you discovered that they are very difficult to answer. Some might find these two questions almost unanswerable. The questions are difficult because they require a search inward into the depths of our beliefs. Simple, coy, or rationalized intellectual responses cannot adequately address them.

The questions, moreover, have been and continue to be the focus of many great thinkers from different fields including philosophy, theology, religious studies, and the sciences. And yet, inasmuch as the social work profession exists to enhance well-being and emphasize human rights and social and economic justice, most social work educators and practitioners tend to overlook these central questions. Indeed, the questions invoke deeply personal responses that may differ from one social worker to the next. Questions that involve such personal responses are difficult to address in a course or a textbook.

It is our contention that how students attempt to answer these two questions will directly influence and inform their practice. We further believe that exploring these questions represents the point at which their personal identity and their professional identity as social workers intersect. It is one thing to define social work and present the purpose of the profession as we did in chapter 2, list the six core values of social work as we did in chapter 8, and then let students know how important human rights and justice are to the profession. It is quite another thing to ask students to commit to a blind adherence to a life of enhancing well-being, advancing human rights, and advocating for social justice when they have had very little opportunity or encouragement to explore what exactly they are working toward and why they should care in the first place.

Consider again the three social workers in the case vignettes. Why should Violet care enough to advocate for Erica? Why should Dustin care enough to look into the utility bills for Mr. and Mrs. Vargas? Why should Teresa care enough to investigate and protect older persons in her community from potentially unscrupulous businesses? Their conscious views and beliefs in regards to answering the two questions, combined with their professional identity and training as social workers, is what makes them competent professionals with the knowledge, skills, and determination to be effective change agents in these situations.

We use the rest of the chapter to present a brief overview of how a few prominent scholars have attempted to address these two questions. A few words of caution are warranted, however, before we continue. The overview will not provide students with any concrete answers. Instead, the overview is intended as a starting point for students to continue exploring their own answers to the questions. It is also important to remember that the authors' views presented came about after years of rigorous and meticulous work from people, who in some instances dedicated their entire careers to focusing on these questions. The few paragraphs used here to summarize the premises of a few prominent scholars will inevitably be an oversimplification of their work. At the end of the section, we provide a list of additional resources and encourage students to read them as they continue exploring these questions as they engage in lifelong learning.

WHAT IS WELL-BEING?

There are essentially three broad perspectives on well-being—the hedonist perspective, the desires perspective, and the objective list perspective. The three views overlap in that they view the concept of well-being as describing what is fundamentally good for a person. All three perspectives are far from being the so-called right answer. Each has serious challenges that are too expansive and elaborate to describe below. For the purpose of providing a starting point, however, the brief paragraphs that follow are sufficient. We encourage students to remain critical and analytical as they work toward developing their own descriptions of well-being.

The Hedonist Perspective

The hedonist perspective describes well-being as consisting of the greatest balance of pleasure over pain. This view was first expressed by Socrates in the Platonic dialogue, *Protagoras* (Plato c. 4 BCE/1976, pp. 351 b–c). There are currently two forms of hedonism used to describe well-being. The *simple hedonist view of well-being* is that the more pleasure people can pack into their lives, the better, while the more pain in their lives, the worse their lives will be. The only aspects of experience that matter from the simple hedonist view of well-being are duration and intensity of experiences (Bentham, 1789/1996). The alternative to simple hedonism is *evaluative hedonism*. In addition to duration and intensity of experience, evaluative hedonism considers the quality of experiences. In other words, this view of well-being distinguishes between higher and lower pleasures. The claim is that some pleasures, by their very nature, are more valuable than others. For example, the pleasures of reading a good book or volunteering time to help people in need are, by their very nature, more valuable than any amount of basic animal pleasures, such as eating, sleeping, drinking, or engaging in sex. The evaluative hedonist view of well-being, moreover, posits that people experiencing both types of pleasures are normally capable judges who will usually choose higher pleasures whenever they are accessible and possible (Mill, 1863/1998).

The Desires Perspective

The desires perspective of well-being differs from hedonism. Instead of seeking out pleasure, well-being is thought to occur as a consequence of experiencing satisfaction in obtaining or fulfilling one's desires. Historically, desire theories emerged from the field of economics. Economists realized that pleasure and pain are inside people's heads and are hard to measure—especially when we have to start weighing different people's experiences against one another. As an alternative, economists began to see people's well-being as consisting of the satisfaction of fulfilling their preferences or desires. This view made it possible to rank order preferences and develop methods for assessing the value of obtaining preference satisfaction (Heathwood, 2006, 2011).

As with the hedonistic perspective, there are two primary forms of desire theory used to describe well-being. *Present desire theory* assumes a short-term view of well-being, where people are better off when their current or immediate desires are fulfilled. *Informed comprehensive desire theory* assumes that well-being results from the level of desire-satisfaction experienced through an entire life span. More than just a summation of the number of desires fulfilled, this view considers people to be capable of prioritizing their desires and choosing options that will benefit their lives as a whole. Well-being, therefore, results when people experience desire-satisfaction from preferences they choose after being fully informed about all the facts available used to prioritize their desires (Griffin, 1986).

The Objective List Perspective

The objective list perspective goes beyond the desire-satisfaction view of well-being. This perspective assumes, as the name suggests, that people can agree on a list of items that, if experienced or achieved, constitute well-being. Of the three perspectives, the objective list perspective moves the concept of well-being away from experiencing pleasure and avoiding pain. Instead, here well-being is the result of figuring out and obtaining what is good for people. The shift in focus, of course, begs the question, "What should go on the list?" There are two primary approaches used to address what should be on the list. The simplest and most straightforward answer comes from Aristotle, who suggested that the list must include every possible good. In this view, people experience well-being when they experience or obtain every possible thing listed as a good (Aristotle, c. 4 BCE/2000). The other approach is known as perfectionism. In this view, the list should include items that contribute to perfecting human nature. Well-being is experienced, therefore, when people experience or obtain things listed that help them realize their true nature as human beings (Hurka, 1993).

WHAT IS SOCIAL JUSTICE?

Similar to the three perspectives of well-being, there are three central theories of social justice—utilitarianism, social justice as fairness, and libertarianism. The first two (utilitarianism and social justice as fairness) emphasize a societal or communal approach that brings about social justice for individuals. A libertarian approach emphasizes individual freedom of choice as the root of social justice for society.

Utilitarianism

According to utilitarianism, a just society exists to the extent that laws and institutions of society help to promote the greatest overall happiness of its members. After reading such a statement, we hope students ask themselves, "What is overall happiness and how do we determine the overall happiness of all the members of a society?" These questions are the primary focus of the most influential utilitarian scholars. For example, John Stuart Mill (1863/1998), perhaps the most influential utilitarian of the nineteenth century, considered freedom to be a basic human need, necessary for overall happiness. According to Mill, political and economic liberties were crucial for happiness. More specifically, he posited that the political liberties of democracy—such as freedom of speech, freedom of the press, freedom of assembly, and freedom of worship—were essential to the happiness of every person. Without such political liberties, he argued, people would be prevented from effectively pursuing their own conception of a good and satisfying life.

More recently, James P. Sterba (1995) suggested there are, at minimum, certain basic needs that must be satisfied in order for overall happiness to even be possible. According to him, every person has a need for food, shelter, medical care, protection, companionship, and self-development. Such needs are considered by Sterba to be universal. People are alike in having such needs regardless of how diverse they are in regard to the other needs, desires, or ends. Furthermore, the physical and mental well-being of people in a community can be seriously endangered if these basic needs are not satisfied.

Taken together, from a utilitarian perspective social justice exists when the institutions of society (i.e., its government, its laws, and its economy) create an environment where as many people as possible have the means and opportunities to achieve their chosen conception of a desirable life. Advocating for social justice, therefore, in the utilitarian view, involves efforts to reform the institutions of society toward this goal.

Social Justice as Fairness

The notion of social justice as fairness is a reformulation of utilitarianism that comes from John Rawls (1971). Rawls considered the utilitarian perspective of social justice flawed because such a view put individuals at an undesirable and unfair risk of being sacrificed for the overall happiness of society. In contrast, he suggested that elements of social justice should be determined from a hypothetical situation he called the original position (OP).

In the OP, people are stipulated to be in a rather peculiar state that could never be realized in actuality. They are imagined to have simpler motivation than people in fact have and to be ignorant of certain facts about themselves that no rational person in fact could be ignorant of; they are imagined to be simply self-interested in motivation and to have no knowledge of their own particular interests. They are assumed to know that they have to choose the fundamental principles of organization for the basic institutions of their society; given the risks posed by the choice, they are assumed to have adopted a cautious rule for choosing among the alternative principles put up for consideration. Rawls calls this rule the Maximum Rule of Choice. According to this rule, people would choose the alternative whose worst possible outcome would be no worse than the worst possible outcome of any other alternative.

As Rawls argued, people in the OP are behind a veil of ignorance where none of them knows any of his or her abilities, desires, or interests. The only way, therefore, that people can look out for themselves is to look out for everyone. In other words, people can only look out for themselves by choosing principles that do not favor any type of person over any other; there is no type of person that one might not turn out to be, and so it is only in this way that one can guarantee that one will not be disadvantaged by the principles chosen. Moreover, from the OP, all forms of oppression and discrimination cannot logically exist. Instead, fairness alone would be the only trait guiding decisions about social justice.

As a result, according to Rawls, if people were given the opportunity to start from the OP and choose the fundamental principles by which the basic institutions in society would be organized and evaluated, they would choose two principles of social justice—the equal liberties principle and the difference principle. The *equal liberties principle* is that each person is to have the maximum civil liberties compatible with the same liberty for all. The *difference principle* is that inequalities are permissible only when they can be expected to work to the advantage of everyone, especially to the advantage of the most vulnerable. Also, the positions, offices, and roles to which the inequalities attach must be open to all under conditions of fair equality of opportunity.

To summarize the *justice as fairness perspective*, social justice exists when the institutions of society (i.e., its government, its laws, and its economy) ensure that people have the maximum civil liberties compatible with the same liberty for all. And, when in an effort to maximize civil liberties differences become necessary, the differences work to the advantage of everyone, especially the most vulnerable. Advocating for social justice, therefore, in the justice as fairness view, involves efforts to reform the institutions of society toward functioning in such a way as to emphasize these two principles.

Libertarianism

As the name suggests, libertarianism emphasizes individual liberty as the central and exclusive concern of social justice. A just society, according to the libertarian, must grant and protect the liberty or freedom of each individual to pursue his or her desired ends (Hospers, 2007). In the libertarian view, social justice is possible only if individuals have the freedom to choose their own ends and freedom to pursue them without interference from others. This may seem to imply that the libertarian holds that everyone should be able to do whatever he or she wants, but really the libertarian holds no such view. The libertarian view is that each person should have the same freedom to pursue his or her chosen ends, that each is obligated to refrain from interfering with others in their freedom to pursue their ends, and that the function of the state is solely to protect the freedom of individuals to pursue their chosen ends. The libertarian, therefore, conceives of everyone as having certain rights, which protect his or her liberty to pursue a desirable kind of life.

The libertarian view of rights is similar to Rawls' view (1971), in which he stressed the maximum of civil liberties. The two views differ, however, in the relative importance attributed to property rights. Whereas Rawls restricts the principles of social justice to civil liberties, libertarians emphasize property rights as essential to the individual freedom of choice and action. Property rights, according to libertarians, include more than owning land or real estate. They include anything that people can call their own property such as their cars, their jewelry, their books, and even their ideas. Moreover, libertarians are specific in how people are to acquire their property. People cannot just take things from others; rather, people have the unrestricted right to acquire possessions, and to acquire those possessions noncoercively with money or services bartered voluntarily. As Hospers (2007) posits, for people to be truly free, they should have the right to acquire ownership, they should have the right to own the means of production, and they should have the full rights of bequeathal—the right to pass on or hand down their possessions.

For libertarians, social justice exists when the institutions of society (i.e., its government, its laws, and its economy) remain as unregulated as possible. People must have the right to individual property rights, the right to free association, and the right to trade with one another without coercion or fraud. The welfare system; social security; Medicare and Medicaid; anti-trust laws; and laws against racial, religious, and gender discrimination in hiring and promotion are one and all unacceptable to libertarians. Each involves an unjust interference with individual liberty as the libertarian understands individual liberty. People should be free to dispose of their property as they see fit and to associate with whomever they choose. Advocating for social justice, therefore, in the libertarian view, involves efforts to deregulate the institutions of society to minimize the amount of intrusion into the lives of individuals.

Box 9.1 provides students with a beginning list of resources on well-being and social justice. We encourage students intending to pursue careers in social work to continue exploring what well-being and social justice mean to them as they engage in lifelong learning.

Box 9.1. Beginning List of Readings on Well-Being and Social Justice

Aristotle. *The Complete Works of Aristotle*. Edited by J. Barnes. Princeton, NJ: Princeton University Press, 1984.

Aristotle. *Nicomachean Ethics*. Edited by R. Crisp. Cambridge, England: Cambridge University Press, 2000.

J. Bentham. *An Introduction to the Principles of Morals and Legislation*. Edited by J. Burns and A. Hart. Oxford, England: Clarendon Press, 1996 (original work published 1789).

R. Crisp. *Reasons and the Good*. Oxford, England: Clarendon Press, 2006.

F. Feldman. *Pleasure and the Good Life*. Oxford, England: Clarendon Press, 2004.

J. Griffin. *Well-being*. Oxford, England: Clarendon Press, 1986.

D. Haybron. *The Pursuit of Unhappiness*. Oxford, England: Clarendon Press, 2008.

D. Hospers. *Libertarianism: A Political Philosophy for Tomorrow*. Lincoln, NE: Authors Choice Press, 2007.

T. Hurka. *Perfectionism*. Oxford, England: Clarendon Press, 1993.

R. Kraut. *What Is Good and Why*. Cambridge, MA: Harvard University Press, 2007.

R. Layard. *Happiness: Lessons from a New Science*. London: Penguin, 2005.

J. S. Mill. *Utilitarianism*. Edited by R. Crisp. Oxford: Oxford University Press, 1998 (original work published 1863).

G. E. Moore. *Principia Ethica*. Cambridge, England: Cambridge University Press, 1903.

R. Nozick. *Anarchy, State, and Utopia*. Oxford, England: Basil Blackwell, 1974.

M. Nussbaum and A. Sen, editors. *The Quality of Life*. Oxford, England: Clarendon Press, 1993.

D. Parfit. *Reasons and Persons*. Oxford, England: Clarendon Press, 1984.

Plato. *Protagoras*. Edited and translated by C. C. W. Taylor. Oxford, England: Clarendon Press, 1976.

J. Rawls. *A Theory of Justice*. Cambridge, MA: Harvard University Press, 1971.

J. Raz. *The Morality of Freedom*. Oxford, England: Clarendon Press, 1986.

J. Raz. "The Role of Well-being." *Philosophical Perspectives, 18*, 269–294.

M. J. Sandel. *Justice: What's the Right Thing to Do?* New York: Farrar, Straus, and Giroux, 2010.

T. Scanlon. *What Do We Owe to Each Other?* Cambridge, MA: Belknap Press, 1998.

J. P. Sterba. *Contemporary Social and Political Philosophy*. Belmont, CA: Wadsworth Publishing, 1995.

W. Sumner. *Welfare, Happiness, and Ethics*. Oxford, England: Clarendon Press, 1996.

V. Tiberius. *The Reflective Life*. New York: Oxford University Press, 2008.

N. White. *A Brief History of Happiness*. Malden, MA: Blackwell, 2006.

SUMMARY

Advancing human rights and social and economic justice is central to competent social work practice. With our thirty years of collective experience, it is clear to us that the professional mandate to incorporate social justice practices is what distinguishes social work from other helping professions.

You need to take your professional commitment to human rights and justice seriously as you contemplate becoming a social worker. As part of developing the professional identity needed for competent social work, we encourage you to examine what well-being and social justice mean, in theoretical and practical terms, as part of your commitment to lifelong learning. Keep in mind that what is important is developing self-awareness of how you tend to describe well-being and social justice and how your description influences your practice. It is important to respect how other people may describe the same concepts. Culture, nationality, gender, race, sexual orientation, religious beliefs, family background, and individual life trajectory may shape how people think about human rights, well-being, and justice. As competent social workers, we must appreciate the diversity that shapes human experience. Diversity in practice is the focus of the next chapter.

DISCUSSION QUESTIONS

For each of the three vignettes presented in this chapter, use the NASW Code of Ethics and relevant literature (e.g., the EBP) to

Step 1. Identify the problem.

Step 2. Identify all the persons and institutions involved.

Step 3. Determine who should be involved in the decision making.

Step 4. Identify the values relevant to the problem.

Step 5. Identify the goals and objectives.

Step 6. Identify alternative intervention strategies and targets.

Step 7. Assess the effectiveness and efficiency of each alternative.

Step 8. Select the most appropriate strategy.

Step 9. Implement the selected strategy.

Step 10. Monitor the implementation.

Step 11. Evaluate the results and identify additional problems.

In addition to the steps in the ethical decision-making model above, please answer the following self-reflection questions regarding well-being and social justice:

1. What are your personal preferences at this stage of your personal journey regarding the meaning of well-being? Which perspective or combination of perspectives most clearly mirrors your personal perspective? What conclusions can you draw about how your personal perspective aligns with the social work values and principles?

2. How would you define social justice in your own words? How well does your perspective of the meaning of social justice align with the ideas presented in this chapter? How well do they align with social work values and ethics?

3. Did you have any conflicts between your personal values and perspectives and the ethical principles espoused in the NASW Code of Ethics? If so, how will you reconcile those conflicts?

REFERENCES

Aristotle (2000). In R. Crisp (Ed.), *Nicomachean ethics.* Cambridge: Cambridge University Press (Original work published c. 4 BCE).

Bentham, J. (1996). In J. Burns & A. Hart (Eds.), *An introduction to the principles of morals and legislation.* Oxford: Clarendon Press (Original work published 1789).

Griffin, J. (1986). *Well-being.* Oxford: Clarendon Press.

Heathwood, C. (2006). Desire-satisfactionism and hedonism. *Philosophical Studies, 128,* 539–563.

Heathwood, C. (2011). Desire-based theories of reasons, pleasure, and welfare. *Oxford Studies in Metaethics, 6,* 79–106.

Hospers, D. (2007). *Libertarianism: A political philosophy for tomorrow.* Lincoln, NE: Authors Choice Press.

Hurka, T. (1993). *Perfectionism.* Oxford: Clarendon Press.

Mill, J. S. (1998). In R. Crisp (Ed.), *Utilitarianism.* Oxford: Oxford University Press. (Original work published 1863).

Plato (1976). In C.C. W. Taylor (Ed. and Trans.), *Protagoras.* Oxford: Clarendon Press (Original work published c. 4 BCE).

Rawls, J. (1971). *A theory of justice.* Cambridge, MA: Harvard University Press.

Sterba, J. P. (1995). *Contemporary social and political philosophy.* Belmont, CA: Wadsworth.

CHAPTER TEN

Diversity in Practice

Almost everything we learn and do in social work is interconnected. Our purpose, our history, our mission, and our knowledge, values, and skills overlap and intersect in such a way that when competent social workers engage in practice, things fit seamlessly for the benefit of the people and communities we serve. From the outside looking in, the observable practices of social workers might seem simple. For example when Violet Scott, the social worker from case vignette 9.1, fills out Erica's paperwork, accompanies her to school, and decides to talk with the assistant principal, her actions themselves seem quite clear and straightforward. From the outside looking in, it may seem as if anyone could have executed those tasks with or without specific training as a social worker. The reality, of course, is that Violet is a trained competent professional. She brings to her interactions with Erica, or with any other client (individual, group, organization, or community), the knowledge of an array of human behavior theories and practice methods, the values, the history, and the professional identity of a social worker, and the awareness and commitment to human rights and social and economic justice. In other words, the observable actions in her work with Erica are the result of deliberate engagement and assessment of the situation, informed by her knowledge, values, and skills acquired in her training and experience as a social worker.

In the same way, the foundations of social work are interconnected. By now students should understand that everything we cover in this book is part of the fundamental basis for social work practice. Stated differently, the material provides the root from which students can develop the personal self-awareness and professional identity needed to incorporate the material from other social work courses to become competent social workers. Diversity in practice, therefore, is more than an arbitrary characteristic. It is of primary importance to anything and everything we do as social workers.

Let's briefly review the key points made thus far, with the purpose of making it clear that diversity in practice logically fits as part of the core of social work.

The foundational key points about social work covered so far include the following:

- Social work is a complex and dynamic profession.
- The purpose of social work is to enhance or restore well-being.
- Social work practice involves working with individuals, families, groups, and communities.
- Social work is more than a scientific field of study. Social workers actually *care*.
- Social work is rooted in the core values of service, social justice, dignity and worth of the person, importance of human relationships, integrity, and competence.
- Social workers incorporate a broad knowledge base, and professional values and skills, with a high degree of personal self-awareness, to develop the professional identity needed for competent practice.

• The broad scope and focus of competent practice has brought, and will continue to bring, inherent tensions for the profession.

• Social workers believe that all people have basic human rights, such as self-determination, freedom, safety, privacy, an adequate standard of living, health care, and education.

The foundational key points addressed in this chapter are the following:

• As part of valuing self-determination, freedom, and the other basic human rights of *all* people, social workers appreciate and celebrate *all* the dimensions of diversity.

• Social workers recognize that difference and diversity can bring about opportunities for oppression, marginalization, and alienation, as well as for privilege and power. Social workers, therefore, make a commitment to advocate for social and economic justice in everything they do in practice.

Chapter 11 introduces students to various dimensions of diversity. The focus here in chapter 10 is to help students understand *why* diversity is so important to social work. We believe that understanding *why* diversity is so important is critical for establishing the foundation for competent practice. Students who decide to continue progressing toward achieving their BSW or MSW degree need to incorporate the appreciation and celebration of diversity into the core of their professional identity as social workers. We want to make sure students understand how important diversity is to competent practice as they decide if social work is the right field for them.

A LOGICAL AND CENTRAL VALUE OF SOCIAL WORK

Stated simply, perhaps more than in any other profession social workers appreciate and celebrate diversity in practice. The emphasis on diversity and difference is linked to two overlapping factors.

First, social workers emphasize the primary importance of individuals as the key to enhancing and restoring well-being. Second, social workers value the delicate balance of similarity and uniqueness of individuals and groups as a foundation to community well-being.

The individual is the center of practice in social work. Social workers view all people as having inherent worth as human beings. We may not agree with or approve of what some people do with their lives, but we consider everyone as a valued member of society. The primary importance of individuals is emphasized in the NASW (2006) Code of Ethics. Recall from chapter 8 that the code addresses six ethical standards: responsibilities (1) to clients, (2) to colleagues, (3) in practice settings, (4) as professionals, (5) to the social work profession, and (6) in the broader society.

The code addresses the responsibilities to clients first because of the commitment to the centrality of individuals in social work. Standard 1.01, the very first statement in the code, addresses commitment to clients: "Social workers' primary responsibility is to promote the wellbeing of clients" (p. 7). Standard 1.02 addresses self-determination: "Social workers respect and promote the right to self-determination and assist clients in their efforts to identify and clarify their goals" (p. 7). Both standards are consistent with diversity in practice.

Social workers recognize that in some ways people are alike and in other ways each person is unique. On the one hand, individuals and groups share common needs and wants such as health care, education, adequate housing, freedom, and safety. On the other hand, people have life experiences and capacities that make them unique. Social workers value and respect the differences in life experiences, talents, and desires that make people unique. In fact, social workers usually tailor helping strategies to a person's or group's uniqueness. Moreover, social workers believe that the overall quality of life for a community is enriched by understanding and celebrating differences. Instead of working to help people assimilate to their social environment, social workers advocate for a pluralistic society that accommodates a range of cultural beliefs, behaviors, languages, and customs.

DIVERSITY AND WELL-BEING

Advocating for a pluralistic society connects the value of diversity with the purpose of practice—enhancing or restoring well-being. Social workers avoid taking on the role of an expert who knows what is best for individuals, families, groups, or communities. Instead, social workers enter into reciprocal helping relationships where we work with clients to enhance *their* well-being, as *they* understand well-being, and practice to create communities that allow people to enhance their own well-being as *communities* understand well-being. When social workers engage in reciprocal relationships, we enter as lifelong learners committed to learning, working with, and appreciating all the varieties of humanism. We bring a broad range of knowledge, values, and skills that, when incorporated with our commitment to diversity, make us competent practitioners.

The people and institutions we engage with in practice do not always share the central importance of diversity. Differences can be celebrated, but they also can bring about opportunities for oppression. Perhaps more so than other helping professionals, social workers often find ourselves challenging the status quo as to how humans relate to one another. Often our practice involves encouraging individuals, groups, and communities to allow and embrace differences so that as many people as possible can enhance or restore their own well-being.

PRIVILEGE, OPPRESSION, AND EMPOWERMENT

The rest of chapter 10 examines the concepts of diversity in practice, especially with regard to privilege, oppression, and empowerment. Chapter 11 explores the dimensions of diversity. We encourage students to pay specific attention to their understanding of diversity in their personal reflections, and to take seriously the contemplation questions at the ends of both chapters: we developed those questions to help students explore their own thoughts and feelings as they relate to differences.

Privilege

Differences can lead to arbitrary classifications used to explain privilege and oppression. Individuals who belong to dominant groups are those within a society who by birth or by attainment are seen as normal and/or who have the ability to influence the definition of normal. Those with dominant group memberships gain cultural power based merely on their cultural identity (Hays, Dean, & Chang, 2007).

Belonging to a dominant group makes it more likely that individuals will experience privilege. Privilege is defined as the benefits, advantages, and immunities from prejudice and discrimination afforded to certain individuals within a society. Privilege contains five core components: (1) it is a special advantage, (2) it is granted because of dominant group membership or as a birthright, (3) it is related to a preferred status, (4) it benefits the recipient and excludes others, and (5) it may or may not be outside the privileged person's awareness (Black & Stone, 2005). In other words, the benefits of privilege are assigned to members of dominant groups whether they want them or not. Merely by being a member of a group that is considered privileged, an individual inherits the rights and benefits of that group.

Oppression

Oppression is the use of power to disenfranchise or marginalize particular individuals or groups. When differences exist between groups of people, members of one group (usually the dominant group) can use those differences as reasons for prejudice and discrimination. It can become difficult or even impossible for groups of people that are different from the dominant group to access resources or opportunity, or to have the freedom to define and pursue joy and happiness. As Schiele (1996) describes, oppression is the "systematic and deliberate strategy to suppress the power and potentiality of people by legitimizing and institutionalizing person-delimiting values such as materialism, fragmentation, individualism, and inordinate competition" (p. 288). Stated differently, if members of the dominant group intentionally or unintentionally view individuals from certain groups as being different based on the parameters the dominant group uses to describe what is normal, it becomes easier for members of the dominant group to dehumanize members of those other groups. All of a sudden, it becomes possible to apply a set of expectations for human rights and well-being that is different for some people than it is for others.

Oppression is experienced unevenly by different groups of people. Individuals belonging to groups within a society are, to a greater or lesser degree depending on how similar they are to individuals in the dominant group, expected to abide by the norms of the dominant group. In the same way, individuals belonging to groups outside the dominant group may suffer different levels of oppression. Young (1990) suggests there are five primary levels of oppression that can be used to examine the degree of vulnerability a group may experience. She calls the levels "the five faces of oppression." We believe her model is useful for students to know as they develop the professional identity needed for competent social work.

The Five Faces of Oppression

The five faces or levels of oppression are on a continuum of vulnerability. Rather than one universal description, known formerly as the "equality-of-oppressions" paradigm (Graham & Schiele, 2010), Young (1990) describes oppression as involving five increasingly problematic criteria. The criteria are exploitation, marginalization, powerlessness, cultural imperialism, and violence.

Exploitation occurs when differences in group characteristics are used by members of the dominant group to define the rules of work. When one group can define the rules of work, it makes it easier for that group to gain access to the cumulative wealth in society. People in other groups then are in a place of greater risk of not being compensated fairly for the value of their work. Over time, systemic and structural exploitation occurs in such a way that the differences in standard of living, the preferential access to positions of leadership, and the power where decisions about work and the levels of remuneration are made can seem normal or even natural. As Young (1990) states, exploitation is "a steady process of the transfer of results of labor of one social group to benefit another" (p. 49).

With the ability to define the rules of work, the dominant group also defines who is eligible or of use in the labor market. *Marginalization* occurs when the dominant group decides that "the system of labor cannot or will not use" certain people (Young, 1990, p. 53). Referred to by Young as "marginals," these people lack the skills needed to find and maintain gainful employment and, therefore, become thought of as economically dependent and irrelevant. The most obvious examples of people who are considered marginals are persons who, due to illness, stigmatization, and disabilities, cannot secure or are blocked from obtaining essential skills needed to leverage the labor market for well-compensated meaningful work.

Powerlessness is the third face of oppression. Although anyone who lacks control over the rules of work can experience exploitation or even be deemed as marginal and irrelevant, Young (1990) uses the term "powerlessness" to describe the extra burdens endured by people who are not professionals. Professionals are privileged in ways that nonprofessionals are not. Professionals generally exercise more power in the workplace, can work with considerably more autonomy, can make more money, and can elicit more societal respect because of their higher education level and the higher value placed on their work. Nonprofessionals (those with little or no advanced training) have very few of these privileges. Relative to professionals, people in nonprofessional occupations are often powerless in the workplace and become victims of the rules and decisions rendered by professionals.

While it is certainly possible for individuals from diverse groups to become professionals regardless of their unique characteristics, it can be very difficult. Conversely, individuals who belong to dominant groups tend to have greater access to the resources needed to reach professional status in the workplace. Although hard work and intelligence undoubtedly contribute to people from dominant groups gaining their place in the workforce, from a macro perspective having greater access to a good education and opportunities for employment makes it much more possible for members of the dominant group to achieve professional status.

As two White American males, the authors are well aware of how belonging to dominant groups made the pathway easier to earn advanced doctoral degrees and become social work educators. We also know that students come to social work from many different backgrounds. Over the years, we have found that, for the most part, members of the social work profession truly appreciate all of the dimensions of diversity in practice. What is important is that as students enter the profession, regardless of their background they must realize they are making a lifelong commitment to being aware of the roles of privilege and oppression. They must also realize they are making a lifelong commitment to diversity and advocating for social and economic justice so that differences are celebrated, rather than being used to arbitrarily justify advantages in the workplace.

Exploitation, marginalization, and powerlessness as forms of oppression are all concerned with differences used to justify the social divisions of labor. The last two forms of oppression deal more with the control a group has over determining the cultural history, meanings, and values of a society and influencing which meanings and values will be excluded.

Young (1990) describes *cultural imperialism*, the fourth face of oppression, as "the universalization of a dominant group's experience and culture, and its establishment as the norm" (p. 59). The measure of a group's cultural oppression is determined by the extent to which the cultural values and interpretations of a group are deemed marginal and/or nonexistent by the dominant group. Conversely, when the cultural values and interpretations of an oppressed group are similar to the dominant group, the oppressed group is not as likely to experience stigmatization.

The fifth and last face of oppression is *violence*. The primary meaning of violence for Young (1990) is physical abuse and victimization. Groups who are targets of various hate crimes and who live in constant fear of being physically attacked are included in this form of oppression. Violence, the most severe form of oppression according to Young, however, also includes groups who are disproportionately targets of lesser forms of aggression, such as harassment, intimidation, and ridicule.

Empowerment

The concept of empowerment is important to social work. The emphasis on empowerment in practice is another example of how almost everything we learn and do in social work is interconnected. Recall that we ended chapter 9 by suggesting that advancing human rights and social and economic justice is central to competent practice. Empowerment provides the theoretical foundation and the methods used to advance human rights and to advocate for social and economic justice.

Social workers view empowerment as both a theoretical model and as an approach or method to practice. Empowerment theories reflect a wide range of ideas and themes drawn from the fields of sociology, economics, political theory, liberation theology, feminist theory, as well as the social work tradition (Freeman, 1990; Freire, 1970, 1973; Simon, 1994; Solomon, 1976). Empowerment as an approach refers to the process by which individuals and groups gain power, access to resources, and control over their own lives (Gutierrez & Ortega, 1991; Lee, 1994).

For social work, empowerment applies to direct (micro) practice with individuals and indirect (macro) practice with communities (Solomon, 1976). When viewed as an intervention for individuals, empowerment involves working with clients to enhance their feelings of increased power and capacity to influence forces that affect their lives (Pinderhughes, 1983). In direct practice, the emphasis is on helping clients improve their own situations one issue at a time in their immediate social environment. When viewed as a model or strategy for practice with communities, empowerment involves advocating for changes in society leading to removal of structural barriers that prevent all groups of people from accessing the resources necessary for health and well-being (Langan, 1998; Townsend, 1998). A primary component of empowerment in social work is helping clients develop critical consciousness or critical awareness of how political structures affect individual and group experience and contribute to personal or group powerlessness. In fact, Lee (1994) and Gutierrez (1990), two leading scholars on empowerment, suggest that empowerment must involve developing critical consciousness at every level of social work practice—individual, interpersonal among groups, institutional, and political.

TWO CASES THROUGH THE LENSES OF PRIVILEGE, OPPRESSION, AND EMPOWERMENT

Let's take another look at Violet Scott's work (case vignette 9.1) with Erica. Recall that Erica is a fifteen-year-old African American girl who had been living in a group home for the past fourteen months. Erica was a good student who did so well in her last year of middle school that she qualified for gifted and talented courses at the high school. At orientation, Violet and Erica discovered that the high school principal and assistant principal had decided that Erica would fit better with students in the regular sections of classes. Analyzing

the case through the lenses of privilege, oppression, and empowerment, what was is it about the principal and assistant principal that
allowed them to make the decision? What was it about Erica that
influenced the decision to change her schedule? What will Violet
Scott have to do to address the situation?

It seems that the principal and assistant principal had a precon-
ceived expectation of the type of students that fit in the gifted and
talented section. Given their positions in the school, they were
using their professional status to define and reinforce their understanding of the norms for the school. From their perspective, Erica
did not fit within their parameters of someone that belonged in
advanced classes. For some reason, instead of using her grades as
the objective measure established by the school system to assess
academic placement, it seems they decided that in Erica's case
something else was more important. In other words, they were
using their role as school officials and professionals to reset the
rules of the school. It appears that Erica was the victim of several
layers of oppression including marginalization, powerlessness, and
cultural imperialism.

There were several characteristics that made Erica unique.
Although Violet as a competent social worker appreciated and celebrated the qualities that made Erica unique, the principal and assistant principal may have used those attributes to misjudge her. The
case does not provide specific details about what guided the decision of the two school officials. Something about Erica, nevertheless,
triggered their decision. Examining the situation through the lens of
oppression, it is quite possible that her age, her gender, her race, and
her living situation added up to make her different from the kinds of
students the school officials were used to seeing enter the gifted and
talented classes. That is, it seems that something about her being an
adolescent Black female living in a group home led the school officials to look past her academic record when making their decision.
Remember, if members of the dominant group, in this case the
school officials as professionals, intentionally or unintentionally view

individuals from certain groups as being different based on the parameters the dominant group uses to describe what is so-called normal, it becomes easier for the school officials to dehumanize those individuals. Conversely, to better grasp the concept of privilege, we think it is important for students to wrestle with two additional but related questions.

1. Would the school officials have made the same decision if the student was a White male living in a two-parent heterosexual household?
2. What would the school officials do if the parents of a White male student from a privileged background insisted that the school allow their child to register for gifted and talented classes even if the student had barely missed the academic qualifications?

Violet Scott needs to consider empowerment strategies at the individual and group levels to address the situation. Recall that at the end of the case Violet was heading to the high school the next morning to meet with the school principal and was wondering what she should say and do next. At the individual or micro level, her immediate objective likely involves persuading the principal to allow Erica to register for the gifted and talented classes. When talking with the principal, Violet will probably need to make the principal consciously aware that Erica qualifies for the courses as stated by the school guidelines and that she is indeed a very good student that fits with the other gifted students. Stated differently, she needs to help the principal see that Erica's age, gender, skin color, and living situation have nothing to do with her academic ability and fit with other advanced students.

Beyond advocating for Erica, Violet needs to use this opportunity to talk with the principal to raise his or her awareness about making arbitrary decisions about students based on anything other than academic achievement. Violet also should have the skills to examine the trends for placing students in classes within the school district, determine if Erica's experience is isolated or part of a pattern of injustice, and, if necessary, have the knowledge and skills to organize a group of concerned parents, professionals, and perhaps former students to take the issue before the school board. As a competent social worker, it is part of her professional responsibility to make sure that all students, regardless of their characteristics and background, have equal opportunities to excel at this school.

Now consider the case vignette of Teresa Rogers (case vignette 4.1). Recall that Teresa was leading a planning committee to develop Project Hope, a long-term residential facility that would give four single mothers and their children an opportunity to live in a safe environment while they found employment and saved enough money to rent or purchase their own homes. During one of the planning meetings, the committee was about to approve the proposed mission statement that read, "The Project Hope apartments exist to provide a supportive environment for residents to develop their independence." When Teresa asked if the group needed additional time to discuss approving the statement, a few members expressed concern that the mission statement may inadvertently encourage residents to choose not to remarry and to remain single. Analyzing the case through the lenses of privilege, oppression, and empowerment, why were some members of the committee concerned about encouraging independence? What was it about the potential residents that influenced their concern? What will Teresa Rogers need to do to address the situation?

Members of the Project Hope planning committee probably volunteered their time and energy because they genuinely supported the idea of the church providing this facility. Along with their support and enthusiasm, however, the members probably brought expectations and beliefs that informed their views about families. Specifically, members of the committee may hold the notion that a so-called normal family consists of two parents, one male and one female, and their children. Teresa, as a competent social worker, likely values the diversity of different families and the self-determination of potential residents to define family for themselves, but is leading a group of volunteers connected to her church that seem to believe they know what is best for the potential residents. The planning members were in a position of privilege where they assumed that their definition of family was indeed the universal definition of family. Stated differently, they were in a position to define the rules for what constituted a family for the potential residents. In addition to the support and services provided to them through Project Hope, the women entering the facility would also become subjected to cultural imperialism because the concepts of well-being and family had already been defined for them.

The Project Hope residential facility was being developed for single mothers. A church planning to offer a residential program to help single mothers is probably needed in the community. Social workers and other human service professionals will likely appreciate having the facility available as a potential resource. As a field intern, leading a planning committee to develop the program is good experience for Teresa Rogers. She is learning and applying valuable knowledge and skills for indirect practice. In addition to knowledge and skills, competent social work also involves learning and applying professional values in practice. Teresa has to realize that the program intends to serve single mothers with limited financial resources and options who seek help from Project Hope. As such, they are susceptible to being the victims of exploitation, marginalization, powerlessness, cultural imperialism, and even violence. While respecting and appreciating the values and concerns of the planning committee members, as a social worker Teresa needs to help the committee empathize and become critically aware of the potential residents' vulnerability. She may also want to consider encouraging the planning committee to include a few potential residents. By serving on the committee, the women can help other members become more attuned and more aware of the residents' needs.

SUMMARY

Diversity in practice is a core professional value of social work. It is linked to the primary importance of individual and community well-being. Unfortunately, the people and institutions we engage with in practice do not always embrace diversity. The same differences celebrated by social workers can also bring about opportunities for oppression. Social workers, therefore, must be aware of the roles of privilege, oppression, and empowerment in their practice. They also need to be aware of the various dimensions of diversity experienced in practice—the focus of the next chapter.

DISCUSSION QUESTIONS

Review the case vignettes of Jeremy Williams (case vignette 5.1) and Kristen Lancaster (case vignette 5.2) and address the following items for each case:

1. What role does privilege play in either case?
2. Which faces of oppression seem to be present in both cases?
3. What empowerment approaches can Jeremy and Kristen use to address their situations at the individual and group levels of intervention?

In addition to the questions about privilege, oppression, and empowerment, please answer the following self-reflection questions:

4. Can you self-identify as a member of a dominant group in your community? What are your feelings and thoughts about being a member of either a dominant group or an often-marginalized group in your community or in your society?
5. Do you have personal issues that may be in conflict with valuing diversity and social justice as presented in this chapter or in the NASW Code of Ethics? If so, what are they? We suggest that you discuss these with your class instructor or your academic advisor.

6. In what ways might a social worker's membership in either a privileged group or an oppressed group affect social work practice with a member of a different group? Discuss this with other members of your class and your instructor.

REFERENCES

Black, L. L., & Stone, D. (2005). Expanding the definition of privilege: The concept of social privilege. *Journal of Multicultural Counseling and Development, 33,* 243–255.

Freeman, M. (1990). Beyond women's issues: Feminism and social work. *Affilia, 5,* 72–89.

Freire, P. (1970). *Pedagogy of the oppressed.* New York: Seabury Press.

Freire, P. (1973). *Education for critical consciousness.* New York: Continuum.

Graham, M., & Schiele, J. H. (2010). Equality-of-oppressions and anti-discriminatory models in social work: Reflections from the USA and UK. *European Journal of Social Work, 13*(2), 231–244.

Gutierrez, L. M. (1990). Working with women of color: An empowerment perspective. *Social Work, 35*(2), 149–153.

Gutierrez, L. M., & Ortega, R. (1991). Developing methods to empower Latinos: The importance of group. *Social Work with Groups, 14*(2), 23–43.

Hays, D. G., Dean, J. K., & Chang, C. Y. (2007). Addressing privilege and oppression in counselor training and practice. A qualitative analysis. *Journal of Counseling and Development, 85,* 317–324.

Langan, M. (1998). Radical social work. In R. Adams, L. Dominelli, & M. Payne (Eds.), *Social work: Themes, issues, and critical debates* (pp. 253–272). London: Macmillan.

Lee, J. (1994). *The empowerment approach to social work practice.* New York: Columbia University Press.

National Association of Social Workers (NASW). (2006). Code of ethics. Washington, DC: Author.

Pinderhughes, E. B. (1983). Empowerment for our clients and for ourselves. *Social Casework, 64*(6), 331–338.

Schiele, J. H. (1996). Afrocentricity: An emerging paradigm in social work practice. *Social Work, 41*(3), 284–294.

Simon, B. (1994). *The empowerment tradition in American social work: A history.* New York: Columbia University Press.

Solomon, B. (1976). *Black empowerment: Social work in oppressed communities.* New York: Columbia University Press.

Townsend, E. (1998). *Good intentions overruled.* Toronto: University of Toronto Press.

Young, I. M. (1990). *Justice and the politics of difference.* Princeton, NJ: Princeton University Press.

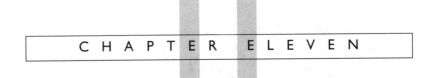

The Dimensions of Diversity

CASE VIGNETTE 11.1. NELSON HUFF

Background

Nelson returned to school after losing his job. He had worked for a company in Charlotte, North Carolina, that manufactured front doors for homes. Once new housing construction skidded to a halt at the start of the recession, his company laid off eight hundred employees. His position as the third shift supervisor was consolidated into the responsibilities of one supervisor for the entire company. After a few weeks of unsuccessfully looking for work, he decided to return to school. Between his financial aid and student loans, his wife's salary as a third-grade teacher, and help from his parents, he was able to enroll as a full-time student. He took classes for nine consecutive semesters, including summers, and was able to graduate with his BSW in three years. During his senior year he completed his field internship requirement with Mecklenburg County Adult Social Work Services (MCASWS). Two weeks after graduation he was hired to work in the centralized intake unit (CIU).

The Context

MCASWS provides comprehensive services to adults through-out the county. When adults need help, they contact the CIU. The CIU is staffed with twelve social workers. The social workers complete the initial assessments, make referrals for additional services, and then follow up to make sure clients arrive at their first appointments. CIU social workers will often make home visits to complete initial interviews when prospective clients are unable to travel to the office.

The CIU social workers usually refer clients to programs provided by ASWS. In addition to the CIU, ASWS offers caregiver support, kinship care support, and a guardianship program. The caregiver support program provides assistance to persons over sixty who are providing care for a family member or other loved one at home. The kinship program provides services for grandparents raising children. The guardianship program provides services to individuals who have been declared mentally incompetent and who have no one else to assume responsibility for their financial affairs. There is also an adult protective services unit that investigates alleged abuse, neglect, or exploitation of persons over the age of eighteen, and a program designed to assist older and disabled adults to maintain their independence. As part of the CIU, Nelson receives more than 150 phone calls, completes between seventy and eighty-five assessments, and makes between forty to sixty referrals for additional services each month.

The Situation

Shortly after returning from lunch, Nelson received a phone call from a nurse at an emergency room at one of the hospitals. The nurse shared that the hospital had recently treated Seo-yun Kim, a seventy-two-year-old Korean woman, for second-degree burns to her hands after she slipped while cooking. The nurse explained that the woman lives with her son and daughter-in-law. They both work outside the home, leaving Seo-yun alone to care for herself during the day. The nurse requested that MCASWS send someone to interview Seo-yun and her family. Nelson filled out the initial screening form, checked with his supervisor, signed out one of the agency vehicles, and then headed to the hospital.

When Nelson arrived at the hospital, he checked in at the front desk and was escorted by the nurse to meet with Seo-yun in one of the triage rooms. In the room, Seo-yun was sitting on the edge of the exam table. Ji-hun, her son, was sitting in a chair next to her. Nelson pulled the remaining empty chair to the other side of the exam table, sat down, and introduced himself. He explained that he worked for Mecklenburg County ASWS and that he had received a call from the nurse to come down to the hospital. He shared that he was there to learn more about what happened, how things were going at home, and to determine if ASWS could help them.

Ji-hun and Seo-yun both spoke English. Ji-hun began by explaining that his mother came to live with him after his father died last year. Although Ji-hun had lived in the United States since finishing college about thirty-five years ago, he explained that until last year his mother had never left Daegu, a large city in South Korea. He had brought his mother to the United States because she had no other place to live. Seo-yun added that living with her son has been very difficult. She explained that in Korea she had friends, could go out to the local markets, or walk to the park for morning exercise. In Charlotte, she felt trapped inside the house all day. She also felt guilty having to rely so much on Ji-hun and his wife. She told Nelson that her hands will heal. The burn was just an accident. What felt worse, she said, was being a burden to her family, having nothing to do, and no place to go on her own. As Nelson listened to Seo-yun speak, he began thinking about her background, how different it must be for her to live in Charlotte, and about the kinds of services potentially available through MCASWS. He also wondered what he should say and do next to help Seo-yun and her family.

CASE VIGNETTE 11.2. JULIE SHELTON

Background

Julie started out as an education major. She knew she wanted to work with children and thought she would become a teacher. After taking a few curriculum and instruction courses, however, she realized that she preferred working with kids one on one and in small groups. She also knew that she still wanted to work with kids in school. The spring semester of her sophomore year, she changed her major to social work. Two years later, she graduated with her BSW. The following month, she started her advanced-standing MSW program with a concentration in child and family practice. She also completed the two additional courses and required field placement in a school setting needed to earn her school social work certification. Shortly after graduating with her MSW, she started her position as a school social worker at the middle school of her local school district.

The Context

The school is one of two middle schools in the district. There are eight hundred students, fifty teachers, two guidance counselors, and two school social workers in her school. The school is located in an upper-middle-class rural suburb twenty-five miles from the nearest city. Regardless of the setting, the school draws from a diverse population because the district zoning cuts across several different communities. Although a significant percentage of students come from affluent homes, more than a third qualify for free or reduced breakfast and lunch.

As a school social worker, Julie provides individual prevention and intervention services to students and their families. For instance, she supports children and families when students are absent for extended periods of time, usually more than two days. She also serves as a liaison to help teachers and parents improve communication and increase parental involvement. When needed,

Julie provides brief counseling services, at least long enough to make an assessment so she can make appropriate referrals. On occasion, she serves as an advocate for students and families to the district.

The Situation

On just the fourth day of the school year, Julie received a referral from Mr. Sorenson, a sixth-grade home room teacher. Apparently, one of his students, Amelia Rostom, had missed her third day of school. Julie completed an absent request form, got Amelia's contact information from the front office, and called her home. When no one answered, she left a message on the answering machine. She then sent Amelia's mother an email. A few hours later, she received an emailed response from Amelia's mother indicating that she and her husband had concerns about Amelia at school and that they were looking into other options, including home schooling. Julie replied by email thanking the mom for responding and asking her if she could come to their home to talk about their concerns. The mom accepted Julie's offer and invited her to visit the next morning.

The following morning, Julie went to meet with Amelia and her mother. Their home was in one of the newer subdivisions built close to the middle school. When she arrived at their home, she walked up to the front of the house and rang the doorbell. A few minutes later, Amelia and her mother opened the door. They were both wearing *hijabs* (a headscarf worn by Muslim women). Her mother escorted her to the living room where she had coffee, tea, and pastries prepared. She invited Julie to sit down, and offered her a cup of tea and a pastry. Amelia and her mother sat down on the couch across from Julie.

Julie began by telling them how nice it was to meet them. She also said that she really appreciated their hospitality. She then shared with them that she had decided to come to their home because she was troubled knowing that in just the first week of school things were not going well for them. Amelia's mother responded by telling

Julie that she and her husband had been looking forward to their daughter going to school. It was one of the reasons they purchased their home in the neighborhood. At the end of the first day of school, however, Amelia came home crying. Julie turned toward Amelia to ask her what happened. Amelia explained that several teachers called her up to their desks at the end of their periods to let her know that she should really not be wearing her scarf at school. Then, after the last period, as she was getting her books out of her locker, a couple of students walked by making fun of her and saying mean things. The assistant principal talked to Amelia as she was leaving the building to let her know that it was against the school district dress code policy for students to wear hats in class. She asked her to come to school the next day without wearing her scarf.

Julie let out a sigh of disbelief. She then shared that she understands now why they had concerns. Julie also acknowledged the school did have a policy about students wearing hats in class. She explained that the school district implemented the policy a few years ago because some of the students were wearing hats that were inappropriate and offensive. She also added that school officials thought at the time that the policy would reinforce respect and order in the classroom. Amelia's mother answered that she understands why the school has that policy, but explained that a *hijab* is not a hat. She explained to Julie that Muslim women wear *hijabs* to be respectful and modest. She continued by letting Julie know that she and Amelia wear *hijabs* whenever they go out in public. She stated simply and respectfully that she and her husband could not allow Amelia to return to school without wearing a *hijab*.

Julie said she understood. She wanted Amelia to feel that her teachers and school officials respected her religious and cultural beliefs. She also wanted to advocate on their behalf so she could return to school. Julie recognized, however, that the district had a policy about wearing hats in class. She also knew that if Amelia missed too many days of school, she would be held back a year. She wondered what to do and say next.

CASE VIGNETTE 11.3. COOPER FLETCHER

Background

Cooper came from a wealthy family, and his parents sent him off to college in Vermont to study prelaw, accounting, business administration, or another field that would prepare him to earn a good living. Living in a three-bedroom apartment on the upper west side of Manhattan near Central Park, his parents knew how expensive it was to live in New York City. They also knew how much Cooper enjoyed volunteering. Since he entered the ninth grade, Cooper went with his parents every other weekend to prepare and serve food at a local church for people who were homeless. When Cooper called from college to tell his parents that he had changed his major to social work, they were a bit concerned, but ultimately not surprised. As he explained to his parents, he felt most alive and engaged when he helped people. Social work, he told them, gives him the opportunity to make helping people the focus of his career. His parents eventually supported his decision and continued paying for him to finish school. A few years later, they were thrilled when he was accepted into the advanced-standing MSW program at Columbia University. Cooper moved back home to begin graduate school three weeks after earning his BSW. He completed the summer courses and then entered the advanced year of the program. The following May, he graduated with his MSW. After passing his state licensure exam, he was hired as a hospice social worker at Hospice of New York.

The Context

Hospice of New York is a comprehensive agency that provides palliative care throughout the five boroughs of the city. Palliative care is for people facing a life-limiting or terminal illness. Whereas the focus of acute care is on curing patients, palliative care focuses on providing care and comfort to people who cannot be cured. The agency provides a range of services from in-patient residential care, pain medication monitoring, home health monitoring, social services and counseling, and bereavement services to support the families and friends after the death of a loved one.

As a hospice social worker, Cooper is assigned to a multidisciplinary team. The team consists of several nurses, a physical and occupational therapist, a nutritionist, volunteers, and a chaplain. His role on the team is to accompany one of the nurses to conduct initial visits and assessments, develop a comprehensive social history and support plan, build rapport with family and friends by providing care, provide limited in-home counseling, and coordinate all of the services provided by the rest of the team.

The Situation

Cooper scheduled a home visit with Neil Hurwitz for the early afternoon. He completed two intake assessments in the morning, stopped for lunch, and then went to Neil's apartment. Neil lived on the upper east side, just two blocks from Temple Israel, the synagogue he had attended since moving to the city eighteen years before. Until four months ago, he had worked as an assistant corporate finance manager for a major fashion design studio. He was referred to Hospice of New York by his oncologist after three years of surgeries, radiation, and chemotherapy. The oncologist indicated in her referral that Neil had originally been diagnosed with colon cancer. At his last exam however, she determined that his cancer had metastasized to his gallbladder, stomach, and lungs. Neil was forty-seven years old and had less than six months to live.

Neil had a good support system to help care for him. His parents also lived in New York. His sister lived in Great Neck on Long Island. Stephen, his partner for the past twenty-five years, was Neil's primary caregiver. Stephen was an independent real estate investor so he had the flexibility in his schedule to work from home as much as needed to care for his partner. Cooper arranged for Neil to have a volunteer companion visit from hospice three times a week. When the volunteer was there, Stephen was able to take the opportunity to run errands and have a few hours alone for respite each week.

Recently, Neil's health deteriorated to the point where he was confined to his bed. Once Neil was confined to his bed, Cooper helped Stephen rearrange the living room so they could fit a hospital bed in the center of the room. Putting the hospital bed into the living room made it easier for Neil to interact with people coming to the apartment.

The apartment was crowded for his visit with Neil this week. When Stephen opened the door, Cooper saw Neil's parents, his sister, brother-in-law, and their three children all standing around Neil in the living room. Neil and his family members were laughing as they finished watching a funny movie together. Once the movie ended, they each took their turn giving Neil hugs, then headed to the doorway. As they were leaving, his father turned back and told him he would take care of everything.

Once the family left, Stephen invited Cooper to sit near Neil. Neil grabbed Stephen's hand, turned toward Cooper, and told him they needed his help. Neil explained that his dad had just showed him a picture of the family cemetery plots he had purchased for everyone in the family. He said, "The plots are located at Beth-El Cemetery, which means that my dad thinks I am going to have a traditional Jewish funeral. Stephen and I decided that we want to be buried together someday in the same cemetery. Stephen is not Jewish and cannot be buried at Beth-El. We found another place where our different religious backgrounds will not matter. I want you to help me tell my parents and make sure my wishes are respected after I am gone." Cooper listened to Neil's request and thought about what he should do and say next.

TWO MEANINGS OF DIMENSIONS OF DIVERSITY

Chapter 10 introduced students to the importance of diversity in practice. Social workers appreciate and celebrate differences as part of valuing self-determination, freedom, and basic human rights. Diversity is part of what makes people unique and shapes human experiences. Difference and diversity can also bring about opportunities for oppression, marginalization, privilege, and power. Students must understand that by entering the field of social work they are making a professional commitment to advocate for social and economic justice in everything they do in practice.

This chapter emphasizes dimensions of diversity. The phrase "dimensions of diversity" has two overlapping meanings in social work. On the one hand, the phrase is an overarching term used to group various descriptions of differences. On the other hand, the phrase describes the concept or notion that competent social workers recognize the intersection of many factors that make individuals, families, groups, and communities unique.

Consider the three cases. Nelson Huff, for example, is working with Seo-yun, her son, and her daughter-in-law. Seo-yun is seventy-two-years-old and is from a large metropolitan area in South Korea. She is widowed, and moved away from her home town for the first time to live in Charlotte, North Carolina. Gender, age, culture, ethnicity, immigration status, living situation, class, and even religion are all dimensions of diversity that may be relevant to the case. Moreover, as a competent social worker, Nelson needs to recognize and assess how the dimensions intersect to make Seo-yun unique. Her unique circumstances will likely influence the effectiveness of the plan he develops with her and her family to provide assistance.

Julie Shelton is working with Amelia Rostom, her mother, the middle school principal, the teachers, and even the district. She has to consider the dimensions of diversity at the micro, mezzo, and macro levels of practice. In working with Amelia and her mother, Julie needs to be aware of at least gender identity, age, religion, culture, and ethnicity. She also has to be aware of the culture and context of the middle school, and the gender, class, and religion of the principal and teachers. She even has to understand the political context of the school district and the surrounding community. Specifically, she needs to understand the values and circumstances that led the district to create the "no hat" policy. Beyond the individual dimensions of diversity, Julie needs to recognize and assess the intersection of all the factors. For instance, if she plans to advocate for Amelia so she can wear a *hijab* in school, she will need to consider the religious views and practices of Amelia and her family as well as the political views and religious tolerance of the principal, superintendent, and perhaps even the school board. She may also need to consider the views and opinions of students and parents.

Neil Hurwitz asked Cooper to help him share his wishes with his parents. He wants Cooper to make sure his family respects his wishes when Neil is gone. As he decides what to do and say next, Cooper needs to consider several dimensions of diversity including age, sexual orientation, religion, and even social class. He also needs to assess the influence of these factors from the perspective of Neil, Stephen, Neil's parents, and other extended family members. Once again, in addition to recognizing the various differences, Cooper must assess how all of the factors come together to make the situation unique. For example, burial plots and funerals can be very expensive, especially in New York City. The intersection of age, social class, financial resources, and religious preferences often affect the options people and families have when they die. For Cooper, knowing that Neil is an adult, that he and Stephen have the funds to pay for the funeral, and being knowledgeable and attentive to Jewish funeral rituals will likely influence conversations with his parents.

CULTURAL COMPETENCE AND DIVERSITY: ANOTHER EXAMPLE OF AN INHERENT TENSION

Before we move on to exploring some of the different expressions of diversity, students need to be aware of another inherent tension.

Developing cultural competence in practice is important in social work. In fact, in 2008 the NASW delegate assembly amended its Code of Ethics to include a specific ethical standard regarding the cultural competence of social workers. The standard describes the following (NASW, 2008, 1.05):

1.05 Cultural Competence and Social Diversity

(a) Social workers should understand culture and its function in human behavior and society, recognizing the strengths that exist in all cultures.

(b) Social workers should have a knowledge base of their clients' cultures and be able to demonstrate competence in the provision of services that are sensitive to clients' cultures and to differences among people and cultural groups.

(c) Social workers should obtain education about and seek to understand the nature of social diversity and oppression with respect to race, ethnicity, national origin, color, sex, sexual orientation, gender identity or expression, age, marital status, political belief, religion, immigration status, and mental or physical disability.

As students learn, and as articulated in the NASW Code of Ethics, in order to understand culture, to have knowledge of their clients' cultures, and to recognize the nature of social diversity and oppression, students need to appreciate grouped differences. In other words, developing cultural competence involves seeking knowledge about the beliefs, values, and behaviors of different groups of people. The purpose of this knowledge is to give social workers an idea of how cultural differences can influence the selection and outcome of services. Having knowledge of cultures is important; however, social workers must also remember to appreciate the inherent dignity and worth of each individual. So while competent social workers focus on understanding how belonging to diverse groups shapes experiences for clients, they have to remember and, even *value*, that clients are unique. Section 1.02 of the code describes social workers as having an ethical responsibility to clients' self-determination. The lesson for students is to understand the inherent tension in social work to attend to group culture and differences at the same time that they view clients as unique. We encourage students to think about this tension as we look at different dimensions of diversity.

DIFFERENT DIMENSIONS OF DIVERSITY

Social workers engage in practice with clients representing very diverse groups. The various factors used to describe clients make it difficult to capture everything in one chapter. Students must, therefore, continuously seek to expand their knowledge of diversity as an essential part of lifelong learning and their professional identity. Our intention here is to provide a brief overview of some of the dimensions of diversity that students will likely experience in practice. Figure 11.1 presents a visual depiction of areas of diversity social workers may encounter in clients. Let's take a look at the dimensions presented.

Clients

Clients represent the most important dimension of diversity. There is almost always variation in how clients express and experience differences within and between the dimensions of diversity. The starting premise for competent social work practice is that each client is distinctive. The ongoing commitment to lifelong learning about diversity in social work exists because the profession recognizes that each individual, family, and community is unique. Remember that promoting the well-being of clients is the primary responsibility of social workers (NASW, 2008). Appreciating and understanding the role of differences is, therefore, essential to the extent that it helps us engage, assess, intervene, and evaluate our efforts to enhance the well-being of clients and create conditions for clients to enhance their own well-being.

Figure 11.1. Dimensions of Diversity

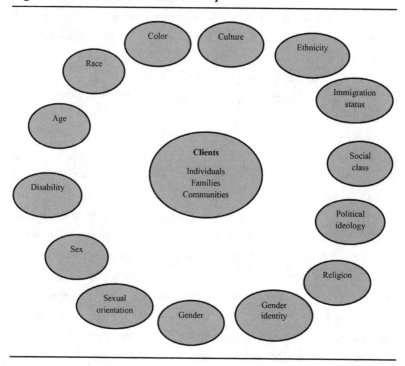

Sex, Gender, Gender Identity, and Sexual Orientation

At first glance, it may seem as if sex and gender are similar. In reality, social workers understand that they are separate dimensions of diversity. When used in the context of diversity, sex typically refers to the biological reproductive status of individuals (Craig, Harper, & Loat, 2004). In general, sex describes the biological difference between males and females and the body parts that determine whether someone is male or female. At a genetic level, however, the categories of male and female are insufficient labels to account for all of the variations that influence the sex of individuals. Genetic researchers and urologists know that people can be born with ambiguous genitalia, meaning that the chromosomes and biological parts do not fit the mutually exclusive categories normally used to define the sex of individuals. For instance, some people are born with ovaries as well as the external genitalia indicative of men, while others are born with the chromosomal karyotype indicative of men, without the male external genitalia (Bomalaski, 2005).

The dichotomous categories of male and female are even more problematic in gender and gender identity than when used to describe sex. Whereas biological factors inform the sex of individuals, a broad spectrum of biological factors, dispositional differences, and socially informed attitudes and behaviors influence gender. Stated simply, the associated differences in gender between men and women may result largely from the process of socialization (Butler, 1990; Eagly & Steffen, 1986; Jennings, 2006). Likewise, gender identity refers to the reflexive continuous process of people defining their position in the social world in reference to the social constructs of masculinity and femininity (Nakamura, 2008). Taken together with sex, students must realize that social workers engage in practice with clients who view themselves in different ways beyond the categories of male and female. The inherent complexities of the dimensions of sex and gender identity alone reinforce the notion that every client is unique.

The need to appreciate the uniqueness of clients is evidenced further by sexual orientation. As with gender identity, sexual orientation involves more than categorizing the attraction to people into dichotomous groups (Diamond & Butterworth, 2008). The patterns of attraction for people can be complex, making it very difficult to define sexual orientation with fixed categories (Nichols, 1988; Rust, 2002). In fact, research increasingly demonstrates that terms such as "gay," "lesbian," and "heterosexual," are problematic and inaccurate (Chivers, Rieger, Latty, & Bailey, 2005; Diamond, 2008; Rust, 2000). Instead, sexual orientation should be considered a fluid concept composed of the interactions of at least three factors—sexual identity, sexual behavior, and sexual attraction (Lindley, Walsemann, & Carter, 2012). As applied in practice, the specific desires for sexual intimacy, the range of actual behaviors, and the personal reflections on identity all contribute to the sexual orientation of clients.

Color and Race

Color and race are also important dimensions of diversity. These dimensions are complex; they overlap, again making every client unique. Color refers to the biological variations in phenotype that causes different shades of skin (Hall, 2003). Depending on the phenotype, people can have skin color ranging from very light to very dark.

Race is a social construct used to categorize and describe people with similar physiological traits such as hair texture, eyelid folds, facial features, and skin color (Hicks, 2004). Similar to the male and female labels used to describe sex and gender, the labels used to describe race are crude and inaccurate (D. Harris, 2002). The average genetic variations of individuals identified as being within the same race can be as great as any genetic variation between racial groups (Nash, 2011). In other words, it is possible, and even probable, for people identified racially as White to have features in common with people identified racially as Black, and vice versa.

As a social construct, there is also no universally accepted classification system of race. For instance, in a seminal study M. Harris (1970) discovered more than four hundred racial categories of people in Brazil. More recently, researchers in Puerto Rico described a continuum of at least twelve to nineteen racial categories (Duany, 2002). In the United States, the U.S. Census Bureau (2011) uses five categories of race: "White, Black or African American, American Indian or Alaska Native, Asian, and Native Hawaiian or Other Pacific Islander" (p. 2). Recognizing that some people may not identify with any of the five categories, the census bureau also includes the category "Some Other Race." Moreover, the bureau's definition of race summarizes the futility of trying to accurately sort people into groups based solely on this one dimension of diversity. It states, "The racial categories included in the census questionnaire generally reflect a social definition of race recognized in this country and not an attempt to define race biologically, anthropologically, or genetically. In addition, it is recognized that the categories of the race item include racial and national origin or sociocultural groups. People may choose to report more than one race to indicate their racial mixture, such as 'American Indian' and 'White.' People who identify their origin as Hispanic, Latino, or Spanish, may be of any race" (U.S. Census Bureau, 2012b, para. 2).

Ethnicity, Culture, and Immigration Status

The interaction of multiple factors of diversity is perhaps most apparent in attending to ethnicity, culture, and immigration status. And, although grouped separately to encourage students to think about every dimension, color and race are often considered interchangeable as well. Some social science researchers even question if race, ethnicity, and culture are distinct (Clark, Anderson, Clark, & Williams, 1999; LaVeist, 1996). Other researchers suggest that treating the concepts separately is important to emphasize that subgroups with unique cultures exist within groups of people labeled as having the same race and/or ethnicity (D. Harris, 1995; Phinney, 1996; Thompson, 1989). In recent social work literature, scholars seem divided in how they conceptualize and measure these dimensions (Barn, 2007; Hodge, Jackson, & Vaughn, 2010; Park, 2005; Yan, 2008).

Given our experience as social work practitioners, educators, and researchers, we contend that competent practice involves students appreciating each dimension separately *and* together. Consistent with other areas of the profession, this too is an inherent tension that exists for social work: our purpose is to enhance well-being of clients (individuals, families, groups, and communities) and not to figure out the conceptual and theoretical nuances of these terms. Practice with some clients may call for social workers to emphasize one dimension over others. In other instances, it may be more effective to consider them together. Here we describe ethnicity, culture, and immigration status using a helpful metaphor posited by Nagel (1994). As we describe the metaphor, we encourage students to wrestle with how they will make sense of these dimensions in their own practice with clients.

According to Nagel (1994), the image of a shopping cart is useful in understanding the three dimensions of diversity. *Ethnicity* determines the shape of the shopping cart. The size of the cart, the number of wheels, and the materials used to make the cart come together to create a shape that is observable to others. In the same way, ethnicity is observable. Ethnicity is primarily associated with the issue of boundaries. It is a social construction created and recreated as various groups of people intersect with one another. As a social construct, ethnicity consists of a combination of biological and environmental ascriptions. It is a fluidly evolving concept that always involves internal and external influences. Clients develop an ethnic identity based on a view of themselves and views held by others. Ethnic categories designate which people are members and which are not based on identification features that are noticeable at a particular time and place.

Culture determines what goes into the shopping cart. It is composed of factors such as art, music, dress, norms, beliefs, symbols, myths, and customs. Similar to ethnicity, culture is a social construct created and determined by individual and environmental influences. People pick and choose what goes into the shopping cart; these elements create their culture. Often what people put into their carts comes from a mixture of tradition, the past, the present, their families, and their own individual preferences. As with the contents inside any shopping cart, culture is constantly changing as people add new elements and discard others.

Immigration status can influence the shape and the contents of the shopping cart. On the one hand, national origin can coincide with ethnic identity as the physical appearance and environmental factors associated with different countries help shape the cart. On the other hand, immigration status can influence what goes into the cart as people blend elements from their home countries with living in a new location. The blending of elements is called acculturation.

People immigrating to a new country generally adopt one of four approaches to acculturation: assimilation, biculturalism, separation, or marginalization (Berry, 2006). *Assimilation* involves almost a complete merger with the new location. Although the shape of the cart looks different, the contents in the shopping cart look quite similar to contents of shopping carts of people from the new location. *Biculturalism* involves adopting some of the norms of the new host society, while maintaining cultural heritage and identity in the home. In this case, the contents of the cart look similar to carts of people from the new location, though at closer view, some of the core contents are from their nation of origin. *Separation* occurs when people seek to have nothing to do with their country of origin. In this case, individuals will do whatever they can to make sure their shopping carts look the same in shape and content with those in the new location. *Marginalization* describes people who try to avoid being identified with either their heritage or their host society. In other words, the shape and contents of their carts do not align with either location.

Religion, Political Ideology, and Social Class

A few additional factors can influence practice. Religion is a collection of belief systems, world views, and broad and diverse practices engaged in by individuals and the organizations (e.g., congregations, denominations, and religiously affiliated organizations) they form for these purposes (Bullis, 1996; Canda & Furman, 1999; Ellor, Netting, & Thibault, 1999). According to some estimates, there are roughly 4,200 religions in the world and more than four hundred past and present denominations in the United States (Association of Religion Data Archives, 2012). Political ideology refers to beliefs with respect to a set of interrelated social and economic issues such as abortion, same-sex marriage, job creation, taxation, import/export regulations, and the size and role of the military (Rosenwald, 2006; Verhulst, Eaves, & Hatemi, 2012). Social class refers to the increased chance that people with common experiences and economic conditions engage in similar thinking and actions (Dahrendorf, 1959). When social workers enter into helping relationships, it is important for them to recognize and appreciate that clients come from different backgrounds, hold different beliefs, and have their own views on a host of issues.

Age and Disability

Attending to the influence of age and disabilities is also essential in practice. Social workers need to think of age as a chronological and subjective dimension of diversity. Chronological age refers to the number of years people have been alive since their date of birth. Subjective age refers to the tendency of people to feel, think, and act younger or older than their chronological age (Mock & Eibach, 2011; Montepare, 2009). Discrepancies often exist between the two. Some clients feel, think, and act older than their age. Some clients feel, think, and act younger than their age (Galambos, Turner, & Tilton-Weaver, 2005; Rubin & Berntsen, 2006).

Age often defines the scope or area of practice. Some social workers work primarily with children and adolescents; others work with young or elderly adults. Regardless of the area of practice, social workers are likely to enter into helping relationships with clients of all different age groups. Nelson Huff, for example, is working with Seo-yun Kim, her son, and her daughter-in-law. Julie Shelton has to interact effectively with Amelia, her parents, teachers, the school principal, and the members of the school board. Cooper Fletcher has to navigate the relationships between Neil Hurwitz, Stephen, and his parents. In each of these cases, the chronological and subjective ages of the clients, the family members, and other relevant individuals may shape their experiences and expectations for dealing with their respective situations.

Disabilities can also shape client experiences. Disabilities are defined as impairments, activity limitations, or participation restrictions caused by an interaction between personal and environmental factors (World Health Organization [WHO], 2011a). They can occur because of physical, learning, and/or emotional conditions. Approximately 15 percent of the world's population lives with some form of a disability (WHO, 2011b). In the United States, nearly one in five people (over 56 million) has a disability (U.S. Census Bureau, 2012a). The prevalence of individuals with disabilities makes it essential for social workers to attend to this dimension of diversity.

SUMMARY

The core values of social work make it essential for students to incorporate diversity in practice into their professional identities. It is a part of practice that makes a commitment to lifelong learning so important. We imagine it may seem overwhelming for students to think about all the facets of diversity they need to attend to in practice. Just remember to balance the need for knowledge about different groups with the understanding that the intersection of the dimensions makes it imperative to approach clients as unique. Balancing both perspectives will come with experience and the ability for critical thinking—the focus of the next chapter.

DISCUSSION QUESTIONS

Review this chapter's case vignettes of Nelson Huff (case vignette 11.1), Julie Shelton (case vignette 11.2), and Cooper Fletcher (case vignette 11.3) and address the following items for each case:

Step 1. Identify the problem.

Step 2. Identify all the persons and institutions involved.

Step 3. Determine who should be involved in the decision making.

Step 4. Identify the values relevant to the problem.

Step 5. Identify the goals and objectives.

Step 6. Identify alternative intervention strategies and targets.

Step 7. Assess the effectiveness and efficiency of each alternative.

Step 8. Select the most appropriate strategy.

Step 9. Implement the selected strategy.

Step 10. Monitor the implementation.

Step 11. Evaluate the results and identify additional problems.

Please answer the following self-reflection questions regarding diversity:

1. With the assumption that each person is one-of-a-kind, what dimensions of diversity in this chapter help to shape your own uniqueness?

2. Are there dimensions of your own diversity that you believe may be devalued (or even elicit strong biases) by other people? If so, how does that make you feel?

3. Which of the dimensions of diversity mentioned in this chapter, if any, touch on or impinge on your own biases? In other words, can you identify any point along any of the dimensions where your own personal biases may lead to your not valuing that person's unique characteristic? What dimensions, if any, cause you internal discomfort?

4. Cultural competence is first and foremost about valuing diversity. If there are dimensions of diversity that cause you internal discomfort, what steps can you take to ensure you are conducting ethical social work practice with individuals who fall along extremes of those dimensions?

REFERENCES

Association of Religion Data Archives. (2012). Denominational profiles. Retrieved from http://www.thearda.com/Denoms/families/index.asp

Barn, R. (2007). "Race," ethnicity, and child welfare: A fine balancing act. *British Journal of Social Work, 37*(8), 1425–1434.

Berry, J. W. (2006). Stress perspectives on acculturation. In D. L. Sam & J. W. Berry (Eds.), *The Cambridge handbook of acculturation psychology* (pp. 43–57). Cambridge: University of Cambridge Press.

Bomalaski, D. M. (2005). A practical approach to intersex. *Urologic Nursing, 25*(1), 11–24.

Bullis, R. (1996). *Spirituality in social work practice*. Philadelphia: Taylor & Francis.

Butler, J. (1990). *Gender trouble: Feminism and the subversion of identity*. New York: Routledge.

Canda, E. R., & Furman, L. D. (1999). *Spiritual diversity in social work practice*. New York: Free Press.

Chivers, M. L., Rieger, G., Latty, E., & Bailey, J. M. (2005). A sex difference in the specificity of sexual arousal. *Psychological Science, 15*, 736–744.

Clark, R., Anderson, N. B., Clark, V. R., & Williams, D. R. (1999). Racism as a stressor for African Americans: A biopsychosocial model. *American Psychologist, 54*, 805–816.

Craig, I. W., Harper, E., & Loat, C. (2004). The genetic basis for sex differences in human behavior: Role of the sex chromosomes. *Annals of Human Genetics, 68*, 269–284.

Dahrendorf, R. (1959). *Class and class conflict in industrial societies.* Stanford, CA: Stanford University Press.

Diamond, L. M. (2008). *Sexual fluidity: Understanding women's love and desire.* Cambridge, MA: Harvard University Press.

Diamond, L. M., & Butterworth, M. (2008). Questioning gender and sexual identity: Dynamic links over time. *Sex Roles, 59,* 365–376.

Duany, J. (2002). *The Puerto Rican nation on the move: Identities on the island and in the United States.* Chapel Hill: University of North Carolina Press.

Eagly, A. H., & Steffen, V. J. (1986). Gender and aggressive behavior: A meta-analytic review of the social psychological literature. *Psychological Bulletin, 100,* 309–330.

Ellor, J. W., Netting, F. E., & Thibault, J. M. (1999). *Understanding religious and spiritual aspects of human service practice.* Columbia: University of South Carolina Press.

Galambos, N. L., Turner, P. K., & Tilton-Weaver, L. C. (2005). Chronological and subjective age in emerging adulthood: The crossover effect. *Journal of Adolescent Research, 20,* 538–556.

Hall, R. E. (2003). Skin color and post-colonial hierarchy: A global strategy for conflict resolution. *Journal of Psychology, 137*(1), 41–53.

Harris, D. R. (1995). Exploring the determinants of adult Black identity: Context and process. *Social Forces, 74,* 227–241.

Harris, D. R. (2002). Who is multiracial? Assessing the complexity of lived race. *American Sociological Review, 67*(4), 614–627.

Harris, M. (1970). Referential ambiguity in the calculus of Brazilian racial identity. *Southwestern Journal of Anthropology, 26*(1), 1–17.

Hicks, J. W. (2004). Ethnicity, race, and forensic psychiatry: Are we color-blind? *Journal of American Academy of Psychiatric Law, 32*(1), 21–33.

Hodge, D. R., Jackson, K. F., & Vaughn, M. G. (2010). Culturally sensitive interventions and health and behavioral health youth outcomes: A meta-analytic review. *Social Work in Health Care, 49*(5), 410–423.

Jennings, M. K. (2006). The gender gap in attitudes and beliefs about the place of women in American political life: A longitudinal, cross-generational analysis. *Politics & Gender, 2,* 193–219.

LaVeist, T. A. (1996). Why we should continue to study race . . . but do a better job: An essay on race, racism, and health. *Ethnicity and Disease, 6,* 21–23.

Lindley, L. L., Walsemann, K. M., & Carter, J. W. (2012). The association of sexual orientation measures with young adults' health-related outcomes. *American Journal of Public Health, 102*(6), 1177–1185.

Mock, S. E., & Eibach, R. P. (2011). Age prejudice moderates the effect of subjective age on psychological well-being: Evidence from a 10-year longitudinal study. *Psychology and Aging, 26,* 979–986.

Montepare, J. M. (2009). Subjective age: Toward a guiding lifespan framework. *International Journal of Behavioral Development, 33,* 42–46.

Nagel, J. (1994). Constructing ethnicity: Creating and recreating ethnic identity and culture. *Social Problems, 41*(1), 152–176.

Nakamura, M. (2008). Destabilizing gender identity. *Women's Studies Quarterly, 36*(3/4), 289–291.

Nash, C. (2011). Genetics, race, and relatedness: Human mobility and human diversity in the genographic project. *Annals of the Association of American Geographers, 102*(3), 667–684.

National Association of Social Workers (NASW). (2008). Code of ethics. Retrieved from http://www.naswdc.org/pubs/code/code.asp

Nichols, M. (1988). Bisexuality in women: Myths, realities, and implications for therapy. *Women and Therapy, 7,* 235–252.

Park, Y. (2005). Culture as deficit: A critical discourse analysis of the concept of culture in contemporary social work discourse. *Journal of Sociology and Social Welfare, 32*(3), 11–33.

Phinney, J. S. (1996). Understanding ethnic diversity. *American Behavioral Scientist, 40,* 143–153.

Rosenwald, M. (2006). Exploring the political ideologies of licensed social workers. *Social Work Research, 30,* 121–126.

Rubin, D. C., & Berntsen, D. (2006). People over forty feel 20% younger than their age: Subjective age across the life span. *Psychonomic Bulletin & Review, 13,* 776–780.

Rust, P. C. R. (2000). Alternatives to binary sexuality: Modeling bisexuality. In P. C. R. Rust (Ed.), *Bisexuality in the United States* (pp. 33–54). New York: Columbia University Press.

Rust, P. C. R. (2002). Bisexuality: The state of the union. *Annual Review of Sex Research, 13,* 180–240.

Thompson, R. H. (1989). *Theories of ethnicity: A critical appraisal.* New York. Greenwood Press.

U.S. Census Bureau (2011). *Overview of Race and Hispanic Origin: 2010.* Retrieved from http://www.census.gov/prod/cen2010/briefs/c2010br-02.pdf

U.S. Census Bureau. (2012a). *Nearly 1 in 5 people have a disability in the U.S., Census Bureau Reports.* Retrieved from http://www.census.gov/newsroom/releases/archives/miscellaneous/cb12-134.html

U.S. Census Bureau. (2012b). *What is race?* Retrieved from http://www.census.gov/population/race/

Verhulst, B., Eaves, L. J., & Hatemi, P. K. (2012). Correlation not causation: The relationship between personality traits and political ideologies. *American Journal of Political Science, 56*(1), 34–51.

World Health Organization (WHO). (2011a). *Disabilities.* Retrieved from http://www.who.int/topics/disabilities/en/

World Health Organization (WHO). (2011b). *Disability and health.* Retrieved from http://www.who.int/mediacentre/fact sheets/fs352/en/index.html

Yan, M. C. (2008). Exploring cultural tensions in cross-cultural social work practice. *Social Work, 53*(4), 317–328.

Critical Thinking

Throughout the previous chapters, we have incorporated a few primary themes that faculty will reinforce in other courses in the social work curriculum. By now, students should be able to describe social work as a broad, complex, and dynamic profession united in the purpose of enhancing the well-being of individuals, groups, and communities. Students should be able to understand and articulate some of the inherent tensions that come with being a social worker. Moreover, by now students should have a basic grasp of the notion that competent practice is much more than a technical method of helping people in need. Rather, it is the synthesis of persons with the professional identity of a social worker and the knowledge, values, and skills necessary to make sound judgments amidst the many unique and contextual situations they will encounter when working with clients. Critical thinking makes the synthesis of professional identity with knowledge, values, and skills possible. Stated differently, critical thinking is the link between *why we do* and *what we do* in social work.

DEFINING CRITICAL THINKING IN SOCIAL WORK

Critical thinking is at the heart of everything we do in social work. In fact, it is the link that makes competent practice possible. Students need critical thinking to engage with clients, to assess problems, and to develop and implement interventions at multiple levels of practice. Students will likely be working in settings where they collaborate with interdisciplinary professionals who bring different training and perspectives with them. They will need critical thinking to navigate their relationships with colleagues so they can contribute to providing effective services. Students must also learn to make nuanced judgments about complicated ethical dilemmas that have no clear or obvious solutions. They will need critical thinking to make decisions in unique client situations, often having to decide quickly, and in the context of at least some uncertainty. It is, therefore, important to examine the definition of critical thinking within the context of social work.

Definitions put forth by scholars tend to emphasize different aspects of critical thinking. Dobrzykowski (1994), for example, describes critical thinking as the ability to sift through multiple sources of information to derive plausible hypotheses. Gambrill (2005) emphasizes identifying and refuting fallacies in logic, considering contrary evidence, understanding statistical principles, and applying research findings to client problems as parts of critical thinking. Halpern (1997) stresses outcomes as most important. For Halpern, any thoughtful discernment directed toward increasing the probability of a desired outcome should be identified as critical thinking. Facione (1990) shares perhaps the most comprehensive definition, describing critical thinking as "purposeful, self-regulatory judgment which results in interpretation, analysis, evaluation and inference as well as the explanation of evidential, conceptual, methodological, criterion, or contextual considerations on which that judgment is based" (p. 3).

Critical thinking in social work involves facets of all these definitions. It also involves acknowledging the uniqueness of clients and situations. The ability to tolerate ambiguity, to draw on practice wisdom, and to incorporate innovation is essential to critical thinking in social work. The definition used in the EPAS captures the balance of systematic and contextual ways of making informed professional judgments. As described in the EPAS, critical thinking in social work involves (CSWE, 2008, para. 2.1.3)

• being knowledgeable about the principles of logic, scientific inquiry, and reasoned discernment;

• incorporating creativity and curiosity;

• distinguishing, appraising, and integrating research-based knowledge and practice wisdom;

• analyzing models of assessment, prevention, intervention, and evaluation; and

• demonstrating effective oral and written communication of professional judgments in working with individuals, families, groups, organizations, communities, and colleagues.

DEVELOPING THE ABILITY FOR SYSTEMATIC AND CONTEXTUAL KNOWING

Critical thinking in social work requires the ability to attend to systematic and contextual knowing. Competent social workers synthesize both ways of knowing so they are effective in practice. Recall, for example, the application of the two definitions used to understand dimensions of diversity. Social workers need knowledge of dimensions of diversity so they have insight into patterns that may influence work with clients from different groups. While recognizing potential patterns, social workers also attend to how dimensions of diversity contribute to making clients and their circumstances unique.

In the same way, ethical decision making in practice requires both ways of knowing. Recall that in chapter 8 we provided students with a general model for making ethical decisions (Loewenberg et al., 2000, p. 63). As we presented the model, we also provided the caveat that ethical decision making is far too complex for a one-size-fits-all model. Different social workers could use the same model (patterned way of knowing) to assess a situation and choose different, though equally viable, actions (influenced by contextual knowing).

The synthesis of patterned and contextual critical thinking makes it possible for social workers to arrive at different ethical decisions and actions. It also makes it possible for social workers to create new and innovative solutions to help clients and address social problems. Stated in simple terms, critical thinking in social work is the combination of thinking inside and outside the box when it comes to enhancing the well-being of clients. We use the rest of the chapter to provide students with two essential methods to develop both forms of critical thinking. We encourage students to contemplate the commitment needed for lifelong learning, which incorporates both methods into their professional identity.

The Five-Step Process of Evidence-Based Practice

EBP is a systematic approach to making sound judgments in practice. Recall from chapter 2, under the heading "A Definition of Social Work for the Future," that the definition of social work ends with the following statement, "Social workers select, use, and develop interventions based on the best available evidence." EBP is how social workers choose interventions based on the best available evidence. The purpose of EBP is to use critical thinking to make decisions in practice that lead to successful outcomes with clients. It involves social workers engaging in the following five steps (Rubin & Parrish, 2007, p. 407):

1. Formulating an answerable question regarding practice needs
2. Tracking down the best evidence available to answer that question

3. Critically appraising the scientific validity and usefulness of the evidence

4. Integrating the appraisal with one's clinical expertise and client values and circumstances and then applying it to practice decisions

5. Evaluating outcomes (with the use of single-case designs if feasible)

Let's briefly apply the five-step process to one of the case vignettes.

Review the case of Dustin Jordan (case vignette 2.3). Recall that Dustin is a social worker in the homeless program at the VA Medical Center in Oklahoma City. When he visits City Rescue Mission, the director introduces him to Terry Esherhut, a former technical sergeant in the Air Force who left the military to try to save his marriage. After moving in with his in-laws and being unable to find work, Terry started drinking, began using cocaine, and eventually separated from his wife and became homeless. After Dustin determined that Terry was eligible to receive services from the VA, he returned the next day to develop a plan.

Using the EBP process, Dustin must convert all of the information he has about Terry and his situation into answerable questions. Creating answerable questions in EBP involves constructing questions that can generate answers found in the research literature. Dustin needs to frame his questions to designate the client populations, the type of problems, interventions relevant to the problems, and measurable outcomes (Gibbs, 2003; Melnyk & Fineout-Overholt, 2002). For example, Dustin may consider the following answerable questions: What factors increase the probability of Terry, as an adult veteran, acquiring and maintaining permanent housing? If Terry receives drug and alcohol treatment, what is the probability of him remaining sober? If Terry receives vocational rehabilitation services, what is the probability of him finding and keeping a job that pays enough for him to secure permanent housing?

Dustin must now search for the best evidence with which to answer the questions. This step requires Dustin to have access to research literature and to have the critical thinking skills necessary to assess the relevance of potential studies. As a social work student, Dustin learned how to search electronic databases to find high-quality studies relevant to the circumstances involved in helping clients. After constructing answerable questions to help Terry, he could choose different combinations of specific terms used in the questions to identify and select studies to review. For example, Dustin could search for peer-reviewed sources that include a combination of key words and phrases such as veterans, treatment, alcohol, drugs, housing, and vocational rehabilitation. He then could select a reasonable number of credible studies to critically evaluate the evidence.

The third step of EBP involves Dustin critically evaluating the evidence for its validity and usefulness. As someone who graduated from a social work program accredited by CSWE, Dustin completed courses in statistics and social work research methods that prepared him to discern the credibility of research findings. He knows the elements involved in conducting methodologically rigorous research as well as the limitations of evidence discovered in studies using alternative approaches to collecting and analyzing data. When Dustin evaluates the evidence to help Terry Esherhut, for example, he knows he needs to determine the internal and external validity of each study. Internal validity in social work research refers to the certainty with which the outcome findings can be attributed to the examined intervention rather than other possible extraneous reasons. External validity refers to the degree to which the outcome findings may be replicated with different populations and in different contexts. As Dustin reviews evidence from studies to determine appropriate interventions for Terry, he needs to assess whether the research findings are indicative of the efficacy of the interventions or are the result of flaws in the research design. He also needs to assess the likelihood that the interventions he selects could result in similar outcomes for Terry. To do so, he will need to synthesize his practice wisdom with his ability to analyze the evidence from the research.

Step 4 of the EBP process involves integrating his knowledge of research with practice wisdom. Dustin knows that every client situation is unique. He knows he needs to consider his experience working with homeless veterans in Oklahoma City and the specific circumstances facing Terry to develop an effective plan. As Dustin evaluates the evidence, he needs to consider the resources offered in the community. For example, an effective program described in the literature is useful to Terry only if it is accessible in Oklahoma City. Dustin must also remember Terry is a unique individual. The combination of factors contributing to his situation and what will be helpful to him may be distinctive. For instance, Dustin may know of a religiously affiliated agency that provides a drug and alcohol treatment program. He may also know that the program has had good outcomes with adult veterans. If Terry is uncomfortable receiving treatment from a religiously affiliated agency, however, Dustin may need to refer him to a different agency.

Every practice situation provides an opportunity for social workers to improve services for clients. After implementing a plan based on the integration of practice wisdom with the best available evidence, Dustin completes the five-step EBP process by evaluating outcomes. By selecting interventions based on the best available evidence, Dustin increases the probability that Terry will benefit from his assistance. Using the EBP process, however, does not guarantee success. Invariably, programs with a higher probability of successful treatment do not work for everyone. Also, there is no guarantee that social workers and other human service professionals in a program in Oklahoma City will implement a program found to be effective with fidelity. In other words, staff at a local agency may use an empirically supported intervention but apply it inaccurately. Dustin must, therefore, monitor the efficacy of the intervention plan he develops with Terry.

Monitoring the efficacy of the intervention plan involves creating measurable goals with clients. Before initiating a plan, Dustin needs to establish expectations for success or improvement with Terry. A few possible expectations, for instance, could include the number of days of sobriety, the number of days in sustained employment, his ability to secure a stable living situation, and, subsequently, the number of days he lives at the same permanent residence. Dustin will then evaluate progress by periodically assessing the extent to which the intervention plan helps Terry meet his goals. He can then use that information to discern whether to continue the plan, adjust it, and, at some point, terminate his professional helping relationship with Terry. Moreover, Dustin can use the information from evaluating outcomes to inform his practice with other clients.

Remember that the term "clients" in social work refers to individuals, groups, families, organizations, and communities. Social workers can use the five-step EBP process in micro, mezzo, and macro practice with clients. Dustin could use the information from evaluating outcomes to improve his practice with other individuals, and he also could generate answerable questions to improve the services for veterans in his community. Suppose in his search for the best available evidence Dustin discovered a program for veterans that seemed to produce good outcomes, but that was not available in Oklahoma City. In addition to his immediate task of helping Terry, Dustin could construct answerable questions to intervene on behalf of all homeless veterans in the city. For instance, he could construct one of the following questions: What are the outcomes of the program identified in the research literature as compared with outcomes of programs currently provided in Oklahoma City? or Which implementation factors will increase the probability of bringing the new program to the community? Dustin could then follow the rest of the EBP process to determine if and how he should go about advocating to implement the new program in his community.

Self-Reflection

Contextual knowing is also part of critical thinking in social work. Social workers integrate what they know from logic, science, and research-based knowledge with practice wisdom. We believe that practice wisdom comes from the combination of experience with deliberate contemplation of everything learned. Deliberate contemplation is how social workers expand their ability for contextual knowing, which in turn contributes to their overall ability for critical thinking. Self-reflection is how social workers engage in deliberate contemplation. Self-reflection occurs when social workers enter into a continuous loop of learning and relearning informed by their experiences, their observations, their beliefs, and their exposure to new knowledge and new experiences that test what they already believe and know (Kolb, 1983; Zull, 2002). Students should envision a cyclical process that seems familiar—because it is the same contemplative cycle presented in chapter 5.

Giving students the opportunity to begin practicing self-reflection has been a primary theme of the book. Recall that in chapter 5 we provided a list of questions to help students begin exploring their own story, why they want to be social workers, and what they may want to do in the profession. We also provided questions in the discussion sections of each chapter designed to reinforce continuous self-reflection about the material.

Continuous self-reflection is essential for contextual knowing and is part of the commitment students make when they choose to become social workers. As students take other courses in social work, they will have assignments that provide additional opportunities for self-reflection. When students finally begin their field internships, faculty members will likely assign them weekly field logs that, again, provide opportunity for in-depth self-reflection. Making an informed decision about whether social work is a good fit as a career path is an important objective for an introductory course. We encourage students to think seriously about whether they are prepared to enter a field that involves so much introspection.

SUMMARY

We used the last eight chapters to accomplish a few goals. First, we sought to give students an in-depth look into one of the most rewarding, dynamic, and complex professions. Along the way, we described some of the inherent tensions that make social work unique. Next, we attempted to create an active, experiential learning experience. We wanted students to do more than simply read the chapters; rather, we encouraged them to begin the process of developing the professional identity needed for competent social work. As part of the process of developing professional identity, we provided opportunities for students to engage in continuous self-reflection. Our intentions were to share our enthusiasm and passion for the profession, while helping students make an informed decision about whether social work is the right career path for them. We welcome students who want to become social workers. We also hope that students going into a different field have benefitted from having such an in-depth introduction into the *why we do* of social work. We now transition to part III of the book, where we provide a brief overview of the helping process and describe some of the areas of social work practice.

DISCUSSION QUESTIONS

For practice, identify at least one of the vignettes provided in previous chapters that seems to fit your interests or represents an area that you would like to learn more about. It could even be a vignette that you had a difficult time addressing. Then, engage the vignette by practicing the five-step process for EBP by completing the following steps:

1. Formulate an answerable question regarding the practice needs identified in the vignette.

2. Track down the best evidence available to answer that question.

3. Critically appraise the scientific validity and usefulness of the evidence.

4. Integrate the appraisal with your clinical expertise and what you guess are the client's values and their circumstances and develop a brief plan for how you would implement a plan.

5. Discuss with your instructor how you might develop a plan for evaluating the effectiveness of your plan.

Self-reflection question:

To end this section of our book where we have discussed the *why we do* of social work, we ask that you very seriously consider the following question, remembering and perhaps reviewing what you have learned about our profession while considering your strengths, areas of needed improvement, and career goals. It is a simple question, but perhaps one of the most important questions you will ever answer:

Is social work the career for you?

REFERENCES

Council on Social Work Education (CSWE). (2008). *Educational policy and accreditation standards.* Retrieved from http://www .cswe.org/File.aspx?id=13780

Dobrzykowski, T. M. (1994). Teaching strategies to promote critical thinking skills in nursing staff. *Journal of Continuing Education in Nursing, 25*(6), 272–276.

Facione, P. A. (1990). *Critical thinking: A statement of expert consensus for purposes of educational assessment and instruction.* American Philosophical Association. ERIC Document Reproduction Service No. ED 315 423.

Gambrill, E. (2005). *Critical thinking in clinical practice: Improving the quality of judgments and decisions* (2nd ed.). Hoboken, NJ: Wiley & Sons.

Gibbs, L. E. (2003). *Evidence-based practice for the helping professions: A practical guide with integrated multimedia.* Pacific Grove, CA: Brooks/Cole.

Halpern, D. F. (1997). *Critical thinking across the curriculum.* Mahwah, NJ: Lawrence Erlbaum Associates.

Kolb, D. (1983). *Experiential learning: Experience as the source of learning and development.* New York: Prentice-Hall.

Loewenberg, F. M., Dolgoff, R., & Harrington, D. (2000). *Ethical decisions for social work practice* (6th ed.). Itasca, IL: Peacock.

Melnyk, B. M., & Fineout-Overholt, E. (2002). Key steps in implementing evidence-based practice: Asking compelling, searchable questions and searching for the best evidence. *Pediatric Nursing, 22,* 262–266.

Rubin, A., & Parrish, D. (2007). Challenges to the future of evidence-based practice in social work education. *Journal of Social Work Education, 43*(3), 405–428.

Zull, J. E. (2002). *The art of changing the brain: Enriching the practice of teaching by exploring the biology of learning.* Sterling, VA: Stylus.

PART III

Method of Practice and Where We Work

CHAPTER THIRTEEN

The Generalist
Method of Practice

Engage, Assess, Intervene, and Evaluate

Social workers share a unique professional identity, an identity characterized by a purpose that is noteworthy and values that are distinctive. The profession of social work exists to improve the lives of individuals and communities. The primary objective of social work practice is to enhance the well-being of people and create environmental conditions where everyone can thrive. Social workers emphasize the values of service, social justice, dignity and worth of the person, importance of human relationships, integrity, and competence. Competence-based social work occurs when social workers combine their professional identity (*why we do*) with the methods used (*what we do*) to help clients.

This chapter introduces students to the primary method in social work. The generalist method is the foundation of all social work practice. It consists of four steps—engagement, assessment, intervention, and evaluation. Social workers use this method to incorporate all other knowledge and skills—often tailoring the details of each step based on the context of the working environment and the specific clients. For instance, social service agencies serving children or the elderly may apply specific theories and treatment approaches for these age groups. As professionals working in those agencies, social workers incorporate the specific theories and approaches within the generalist method to serve their clients. In the same way, social workers advocating to develop a new program in a small rural town or a large metropolitan city may consider specific strategies needed in their given contexts, but they both are able to use the generalist method to implement their strategies. Let's use two new case vignettes to take a closer look at the four steps.

CASE VIGNETTE 13.1. INSOO PARK

Background

Insoo started in college as a nursing major. After completing her freshman year, she was not sure if she wanted to continue. She knew she wanted to do something to help people, but was not sure how. Her advisor in nursing recommended that she take introductory courses in early childhood development and social work. The advisor told her that registering for the two courses would expose her to other helping professions. If she still wanted to pursue her nursing degree, the courses would count as electives. Insoo listened to her advisor and took both intro classes during the fall of her sophomore year. The courses helped her realize she had no desire to work with small children and that she liked the holistic approach social workers use to help people. After the semester, she applied and was accepted into the social work major. Two and half years later, she graduated with her BSW. Six weeks after graduation, a home health-care agency hired her as a social work case manager.

The Context

Insoo works for Senior Home Care, a home health-care center that works to help older adults live as independently as possible, given their medical conditions. The agency provides a range of services including occupational and physical therapy, speech therapy, skilled nursing, and personal assistance such as help with bathing, dressing, eating, cooking, cleaning, grocery shopping, and transportation. As a social work case manager, Insoo makes initial visits with prospective clients within twenty-four hours after receiving a referral. She also completes comprehensive assessments, develops and implements intervention plans, and makes follow-up home visits. Insoo spends very little time in the office. In fact, she does most of her work in her car. She is either on the road traveling to see clients, in homes meeting with clients, on her cell phone arranging services, or in her car filling out paperwork. On Thursday afternoons, she meets with her supervisor and the other case managers for weekly group supervision to review their cases. Providing in-home case management also requires her to keep a flexible schedule. She rarely works a traditional eight-hour day.

The Situation

After finishing her weekly supervision, Insoo drove to the county hospital to meet with Mr. and Mrs. Carr. The hospital social worker had called Senior Home Care earlier in the day to make a referral for Mr. Carr: he was going to be discharged from the hospital the next day and needed home health-care assistance. Insoo scheduled the meeting for 5:30 in the evening because that was the earliest time Mrs. Carr could get to the hospital after work. When Insoo walked into his hospital room, Mr. and Mrs. Carr were finishing dinner. Mr. Carr was sitting up in bed, while his wife was sitting in a chair beside him. Insoo introduced herself as the social worker from Senior Home Care, and Mr. Carr invited her to sit in the empty chair against the window.

Insoo sat down, pulled out a folder with several forms, and then initiated the conversation. "I heard from the nurse that you will be discharged tomorrow. My role is to make sure you have the support you need to recover at home," she said. Mr. Carr shared that he was looking forward to leaving the hospital. He said the doctor told him the surgery to put in a pacemaker went as smoothly as could be expected. The doctor also had explained to Mr. Carr that he had to remain in bed for the first few days. Over the next several weeks, he also would need help with using the toilet, bathing, and other activities of daily living. The doctor had ordered Mr. Carr to avoid doing any manual labor or lifting more than five pounds. Finally, the doctor encouraged Mr. Carr to avoid getting upset.

Mrs. Carr, however, had some concerns. The nurse had showed her how to clean the area around the incision and change his bandages. Still, she was unsure of herself and anxious that she might do something to cause her husband harm. She also was concerned about taking care of her husband and working at the same time. It sounded to Mrs. Carr as if Mr. Carr would need someone at home during the day to take care of him. She explained that she worked full time and had already used up most of her sick leave. Mr. Carr retired two years ago. Even though he receives a pension, they still need her income to make ends meet. She shared that she could not afford to miss any more work. Insoo listened attentively to Mrs. Carr's concerns. She then wondered what she should say and do next.

CASE VIGNETTE 13.2. LAUREN AINSWORTH

Background

Lauren returned to college and earned her degree in social work after fourteen years of working as a sales rep for a large pharmaceutical company. By almost every measure, she was very successful. She consistently performed as one of the top sales persons, had received two promotions within the past twelve months, and made a very good living. Her success, however, also came with great sacrifice. Lauren traveled a lot for work. At first she enjoyed being on the go and being able to see so many places. After a few years of traveling hundreds of thousands of miles and spending more nights in hotels than in her home, she felt disconnected from friends and family. Just as important, she felt as if she wanted to work with children and families. When she had gone to college as an eighteen-year-old freshman, she had felt pressure from her parents to do something that would help her make a lot of money and be independent. Now that she had gained her independence, bought and completely paid for her own home, and saved enough money for retirement, she wanted to spend the rest of her life doing something she loved.

The Context

After graduation, Lauren accepted a job offer from Child Inclusion, an agency that provided services for children with behavioral, emotional, and learning disabilities. The agency offered intensive one-on-one counseling services and an after-school tutorial program. Child Inclusion received referrals for clients from schools, the DCFS, and from parents and other legal guardians. The state paid for most of the services, with families covering a small portion of the expenses. For three and a half years, Lauren worked as a behavioral counselor with a small caseload of clients. The executive director then made her the supervisor of the behavioral counseling program after her predecessor retired.

As supervisor, Lauren spent most of her time doing four things: (1) She coordinated the schedules of the thirty-six behavior counselors to make sure there was adequate coverage for all of the clients. (2) She provided monthly supervision and completed annual evaluations for every counselor. (3) She worked closely with the business manager to make sure the agency was submitting accurate billing for services. (4) Finally, every Tuesday at 10:00 a.m., she participated in the executive team meeting comprising herself, the supervisor of the after-school tutorial program, the executive director, the marketing/outreach coordinator, and the business manager.

The Situation

Toward the end of an executive team meeting, the executive director asked if there was anything else they needed to discuss before they adjourned. Lauren paused for a moment to see if her colleagues had anything to share. She then told the group that she had an issue to discuss. She began by explaining that creating consistent expectations and reinforcements for children at home and in school was important in order to provide successful one-on-one behavioral counseling. She then explained that at her last several supervision meetings, many of the counselors expressed heightened frustration. Their frustration centered around leaving their clients functioning relatively well on Friday afternoons, only to reengage with them on Monday mornings and realizing they were back to their destructive thinking and behavioral patterns. She shared that although she and her counselors knew how important it was to work closely with families, she wondered if the agency could do more to make sure parents and legal guardians knew they were supported and part of the treatment process.

When Lauren finished talking, the executive director asked the rest of the executive team if they had any thoughts or opinions before she responded. After a brief pause, the after-school supervisor added that she thought the agency could also do more to involve parents in helping clients with their homework. She continued, explaining that students come to them after school, work with the tutors, and then get picked up by their parents. There is minimal interaction between the tutors and the parents. The marketing/outreach coordinator confirmed that most of her interactions were with the school systems. Although parents complete the paperwork that allows the agency to work with their children, she rarely has direct communication with them.

The executive director had heard all she needed. It seemed clear to her that the agency could do more with parents. She then asked Lauren to form a small committee to explore what the agency could do to serve parents. She instructed Lauren to prepare a proposal with a few options for the executive team to consider. The executive director wanted Lauren to have the proposal ready to send to the executive team in six weeks. Lauren agreed to the plan. When the meeting ended, she walked back to her office wondering where to begin.

ENGAGEMENT

Relationships are the foundation of social work practice. Social workers must be able to create trusting and collaborative relationships. Deliberately using empathy and other interpersonal skills, social workers create an atmosphere where clients feel safe sharing relevant information needed to establish the parameters of their work together. Moving quickly, social workers guide the relationships to develop mutually agreeable goals and desired outcomes. Engagement begins before social workers even meet with clients. Social workers prepare for engagement by continuously reflecting on their professional development, expanding their knowledge of theory and practice methods, and remaining aware of their professional roles, boundaries, and the context of their practice.

As a competent social worker, Insoo Park needed to prepare for engagement with Mr. and Mrs. Carr before the hospital sent a referral for him to Senior Home Care. For instance, she needed to know the reasons clients were referred to the agency as well as the services available to help them. Preparing for engagement also required Insoo to arrive at work aware of her professional roles and boundaries. Whatever personal events and issues were going on outside work, Insoo must be ready to make her client's needs a priority. She must also come to work ready to demonstrate professional demeanor in her behavior, appearance, and communication.

When Insoo meets with Mr. and Mrs. Carr, she must quickly develop rapport and guide the conversation toward the purpose of their relationship. Being skilled in using empathy and other interpersonal skills, she must attend to the needs and concerns of the couple while recognizing the context of meeting with them in the hospital. Since the physician had scheduled Mr. Carr's discharge from the hospital the next day, Insoo has very little time to develop and implement an intervention plan with Mr. and Mrs. Carr. While validating their concerns, Insoo must help them prioritize their needs, agree on a short-term plan so Mr. Carr can go home, and then work together to provide the care he will need over the next several weeks.

Engagement is also important for Lauren Ainsworth, though in this case it is from a macro or community/organization perspective. As the supervisor of the behavioral counseling program, Lauren prepares for action with her staff, the members of the executive team, and the people she interacts with from other organizations that influence the work of Child Inclusion. She, too, must use her empathy and other interpersonal skills to develop partnerships that help the agency effectively serve clients. She also must create a work environment where everyone is clear about the purpose of the agency and contributes to desired outcomes.

Lauren demonstrated her ability to engage her colleagues in meaningful dialogue at the end of the executive team meeting. She started her comments by sharing her knowledge of effective behavioral counseling with children and families. She also relayed concerns from her staff so that the rest of the executive team could understand the issue. She then presented, in broad and tentative terms, the possibility of the agency doing more to include parents and legal guardians to improve their services. As she develops a small committee to examine possibilities and prepare a proposal, Lauren will need to identify the staff and bring them together around a shared purpose.

ASSESSMENT

Assessment, the second step in the generalist method, involves gathering information to make informed decisions with clients about how to proceed in practice. Social workers collect, organize, and interpret data about clients and the people involved in their lives, the situations they are dealing with, and the resources available to assist them. Assessment of clients usually focuses on identifying their strengths and limitations. On the one hand, social workers seek to understand the personal and environmental strengths that enable clients to function, experience hope, feel empowered, and cope with difficult circumstances. On the other hand, while social workers emphasize strengths, they also assess personal and environmental challenges.

The presenting situations or problems are also the focus of assessment. Social workers collect information about specific circumstances that bring clients to seek help in the first place. They also search for potential resources that can be used to develop mutually agreeable intervention goals and objectives. After collecting data about clients and their situations, social workers use that information to select an appropriate intervention strategy.

Before looking at the two case vignettes, there are two important points for students to remember about assessment. First, although social workers seek to gather as much information as possible, they sometimes have to select intervention strategies based on insufficient or incomplete information. Second, assessment is a continuous and ongoing process. When social workers use the generalist method in real practice situations, they begin collecting information before they even meet with clients (e.g., by reviewing client files or gathering information about the common problems faced by clients who come to the agency), continue collecting information as they implement intervention strategies, and collect more information as they evaluate the efficacy of the intervention strategies.

The purpose of Insoo meeting with Mr. and Mrs. Carr is to assess their needs and develop a plan to support them when Mr. Carr is discharged from the hospital. She needs to collect information about Mr. Carr, Mrs. Carr, the couple, their family, their friends, their sources of support, their finances, and their living environment.

Her emphasis will likely be on identifying the personal and environmental strengths they have that will help them cope during the recovery. Insoo also needs to identify potential challenges. Although she focuses on the people involved, Insoo also must collect data about the situation. For instance, she needs to acquire information about the recovery process for people receiving pacemakers. She also needs to assess the kinds of services usually required to help people recover at home. With data collected about Mr. and Mrs. Carr and what she learned about the situation, Insoo will talk with them to identify specific intervention goals and objectives to address their unique circumstances. By the time she leaves the hospital that evening, Insoo must select appropriate and mutually agreeable intervention strategies to help Mr. Carr go home the next day.

Assessment for Lauren Ainsworth involves collecting data from multiple sources. At a minimum, she needs information about colleagues, clients, and families served by the agency; clients and families receiving behavioral counseling services in general; and potential options for offering support. Lauren needs to assess who she should include on the committee. Some of the information she needs about colleagues could include their availability, their strengths, their knowledge of child and family needs, and their experience developing a proposal.

Once Lauren forms the committee, committee members will need to collect data about the current clients and their families. They probably need outcome data from current clients, information from parents and legal guardians about their satisfaction with the program, and the satisfaction of referring agencies. The committee may then want to collect data about what other programs are doing to include parents and legal guardians in behavior counseling. Of particular importance to the committee may be searching for ways to involve parents that seem supported by empirical evidence indicating positive outcomes.

INTERVENTION

Providing effective services that lead to positive outcomes starts with building trusting relationships and collecting information to develop intervention plans. Then social workers and clients (individuals, groups, families, organizations, or communities) work together to put the plan into action. Intervention plans involve social workers and clients using resources to achieve client goals. Social workers choose actions that empower client functioning. Then they monitor progress, resolve problems, make adjustments, and facilitate transitions and endings. Negotiating, mediating, and advocating for clients are also part of social work interventions.

Insoo Park initiates her plan with Mr. and Mrs. Carr as soon as she leaves the hospital. She has to make sure Mr. Carr has the necessary resources to recover in his home. For instance, Mr. Carr will likely need certain medical equipment and skilled nursing care for at least the first few days. Insoo may also have to negotiate and advocate with his insurance provider to make sure they cover what is needed. Beyond the initial services, Insoo will want to consider linking Mrs. Carr with someone who can teach her how to care for her husband over the next few weeks. She may also help encourage Mrs. Carr to engage family and friends to provide as much tangible support as possible. For instance, the couple may have friends or neighbors who can check in on Mr. Carr when she is at work. They may also have family members willing to help Mrs. Carr with household chores while she focuses on caring for her husband.

As Mr. Carr recovers, Insoo will monitor his progress. She will make sure that she balances providing him with needed services with empowering him to function on his own as much as possible. She will do the same for Mrs. Carr as well. As she develops confidence taking care of her husband, Insoo may adjust his intervention plan. She will also adjust the plan if they experience unexpected challenges or problems. When Mr. Carr begins feeling better, Insoo will facilitate transitions and endings. She may arrange for the removal of the medical equipment, refer Mr. Carr for additional support outside the home, and schedule follow-up visits with the couple.

Lauren Ainsworth and the committee she assembles will also initiate an intervention plan. The goal of the committee is to create a proposal exploring how the agency can involve parents and legal guardians in the treatment process. Lauren will need to assign tasks with members of the committee, monitor their progress, and facilitate group discussions when problems emerge. Moreover, as the committee works Lauren has to remember that the parents, children, referring agencies, executive director, and the rest of the executive team are all clients in this situation. She may have to negotiate, mediate, and advocate with the different client groups to balance providing the most effective services with meeting the needs of everyone involved. If, for example, the committee discovers a new treatment option that seems effective with parents but cost prohibitive for the agency to provide, Lauren may need to negotiate with the executive director to determine if the committee should include such an option in the proposal. It may be wiser for the committee to propose alternative options that are cost effective and feasible to implement, given the context of the agency.

EVALUATION

Competent social work practice should always involve implementation and evaluation of carefully planned interventions. Social workers plan for evaluation early and continue evaluating their practice throughout the four-step method. Even as social workers engage clients in trusting, collaborative relationships, they seek to develop mutually agreeable goals and outcomes. The goals and outcomes serve as benchmarks to monitor progress and examine the efficacy of the interventions. As social workers monitor progress, they can adjust intervention plans to improve outcomes with current clients.

They also can use the findings from an evaluation to improve their practice with future clients.

Evaluation with Mr. and Mrs. Carr will include Insoo analyzing the services throughout their professional relationship. Insoo needs to evaluate the initial intervention efforts used to get Mr. Carr home. For instance, she may examine whether all of the medical equipment ordered was ready for use when he arrived home. She also may examine whether the nursing staff and other support she recommended arrived on time and provided the needed services. As her work with Mr. and Mrs. Carr continues, Insoo may want to monitor how well the couple functions as the services provided by Senior Home Care become less extensive. When Mr. Carr has fully recovered, Insoo will want to evaluate his overall functioning, the functioning of the couple, and the level of satisfaction the couple experienced as clients of Senior Home Care. Following her work with Mr. Carr, she can use the findings to recommend changes at the agency. She can also reflect on what she learned from the findings to improve her practice as a social worker.

Improving services seems to be the broad goal of Lauren and the committee. Given the limited charge of the committee, however, it may be more appropriate for Lauren to evaluate the process and the task of the committee. As the committee collects information and discusses potential options, Lauren will want to evaluate how the committee is functioning. For instance, she may monitor how constructive and supportive the members of the committee are to one another. In the same way, she will need to evaluate the actual work produced by the committee members. On the one hand, she needs to make sure work is completed on time. On the other hand, she will want to evaluate the quality of the work that goes into developing the proposal. When the proposal is done and Lauren is ready to present it to the executive director and the rest of the executive team, she will evaluate her presentation of the material and their response. In the end, having a few viable options for the executive team to consider seems like a successful outcome in this situation.

SUMMARY

Social workers use the four-step generalist method as the foundation for almost every practice situation. Students choosing to pursue careers in social work will take other courses that focus on the nuances of using the four-step method with individuals, families, groups, organizations, and communities. Students continuing on for their MSW degree will learn to incorporate additional knowledge and methods for working in specific fields of practice.

Social work offers students a rewarding career with many options. In chapter 14 we explore some of the various fields of practice. Regardless of the specific setting or population, we want students to remember the commitment to the professional identity needed for competent practice. It is the synthesis of our professional identity—*why we do*—with our methods—*what we do*—that makes us social workers.

DISCUSSION QUESTIONS

Carefully read the case vignette, then practice using the four-step generalist method by answering the questions that follow.

CASE VIGNETTE 13.3. MARTIN PRESCOTT

Background

From an early age, Martin Prescott knew he would do something to serve others in need. He lived most of his childhood in Sudan and South Africa as the only child of parents who were Christian missionaries. When he was old enough to attend college, he completed a dual major in social work and religion. He accepted his first job as a case manager in a church that had a crisis intervention program. Two years later, the church paid for him to attend an MSW program in the evenings while he continued working. He eventually became the supervisor of the program.

The Context

Martin worked for a large church that had more than eight thousand members. In addition to offering worship services, Sunday school, and Bible study, the church provided many different outreach services to the community such as a food bank, clothing closet, marriage and family counseling, and a crisis intervention program. The crisis intervention program consisted of Martin, three staff members, and nine volunteers. The program provided emergency assistance for members of the church and the community. Emergency assistance included help with utility bills, coordinating needed construction, referral to other agencies, referrals to the church food bank or the clothing closet, help paying for medication, and assistance paying for public transportation.

Martin trained the volunteers to conduct crisis intervention interviews. He also managed the budget, created a report for the church leaders each quarter, and consulted with staff and volunteers on cases when needed. People coming in for assistance met with a volunteer for a fifty-minute interview. The volunteer then sat down with one of the three staff members to determine a plan of action. When emergency assistance involved costs of over $300, the staff members consulted Martin about the plan.

The Situation

Two days after a terrible storm, Martin received a phone call from a supervisor at the DSS. The supervisor explained that she instructed her staff to refer people affected by the storm to the crisis intervention program. She shared that at least fifty people had called for help during the past twenty-four hours and she expected more calls over the next few days. Within the hour, one of the volunteers interviewed a couple affected by the storm.

Steve and Lynn Mercer met with a volunteer seeking support after a tornado ripped through their home. As they took cover in the basement, the tornado snatched a large tree from the front lawn and whipped it through the downstairs of their home. The Mercers had lived in their home for thirty-three years, raised four children there, and had paid it off a few years ago. They explained to the volunteer that they were retired and living on a fixed income. They had very little savings and had all of their equity tied to their home. After the storm, they spent the night at a local hotel, but could not afford to stay there much longer. They shared with the volunteer that they had lost everything and did not know what to do next.

After talking with Steve and Lynn Mercer, the volunteer took their information to one of the staff members. As the volunteer reviewed the information, the staff member quickly realized she needed to involve Martin in the discussion. She explained to Martin that she was overwhelmed by the gravity of the devastation the couple had experienced and did not know how to begin helping them. She also shared her concern about trying to help other people who had been affected by the storm. Martin listened to her concern, then asked her to introduce him to the couple. As they walked down the hallway to the interview room, Martin wondered what to do or say next to help them. He also wondered what he should do to plan for other clients likely to seek help after the storm.

Step 1: Engagement

1. What additional information may have been helpful for Martin to have prior to meeting with Steve and Lynn Mercer?

2. What interpersonal skills does Martin need to utilize to establish rapport with the Mercers?

3. What topics might Martin have needed to research prior to meeting with the Mercers the first time?

Step 2: Assessment

4. What questions should Martin ask the Mercers when meeting them for the first time?

5. What do you suppose may be the intervention goals and objectives that may be agreeable to the Mercers and to Martin?

6. What preventive and restorative interventions might you offer to the Mercers if you were Martin?

Step 3: Intervention

7. What action steps would you take in Martin's position to achieve the Mercers' and the church's goals?

8. How might you negotiate, mediate, and advocate for the Mercers and other families affected by the storm?

9. How would you prepare the Mercers for the inevitable transitions that are about to occur in their lives? How would you prepare them for the termination of your work together?

Step 4: Evaluation

10. What would be your plan for monitoring your work with the Mercers and with the volunteers of the program?

11. How would you assess and evaluate the interventions that you would undertake?

12. How would you ensure that the results of your evaluation would inform future social work practice in similar circumstances?

CHAPTER FOURTEEN

The Fields of
Social Work Practice

Choosing a field of social work practice can be both exciting and overwhelming. Developing the knowledge, values, and skills for competent social work gives students many career options. Whether students continue in social work or pursue a different major, we conclude our introduction to the profession by providing a framework for exploring the various opportunities available.

OPPORTUNITY FOR FURTHER REFLECTION

In chapter 5, we provided students with questions to help them begin thinking about what they wanted to do in the profession. Now we encourage students to continue reflecting on the same questions as they consider where social workers practice.

- What types of people can you envision working with in practice?
- What size agency do you envision working with in practice?
- Can you envision working directly with clients?
- Can you envision working with individuals, groups, and/or families?

- Can you envision working with organizations and/or community members?

- How important is professional autonomy in your practice as a social worker?

- How important is structure in your practice as a social worker?

A FRAMEWORK FOR EXPLORING FIELDS OF PRACTICE

The options for competent social workers make it nearly impossible to list all of the potential ways to help people with an accredited social work degree. We believe creating a list does little to help students make informed decisions about what they may want to do in the profession. Instead, we seek to help students consider the primary factors that shape different practice situations. There are at least four broad factors to consider when describing social work practice: (1) the levels of practice, (2) the population(s) served, (3) the areas of practice, and (4) the settings for practice. Taken together, students can use the four factors to describe different fields and contemplate where they can envision working someday.

The Levels of Practice

Competent social workers with a foundation in generalist practice are versatile, helping professionals. Their training prepares them to be effective at the micro, mezzo, and macro levels of practice. Social workers engaged in *micro* practice deliver services directly to individuals, including couples and families. Social workers engaged in *macro* practice focus on changing larger systems, such as communities and organizations. Macro practice involves administration of programs where social workers focus on creating work environments that support effective practice at the micro level. Macro practice also involves policy practice activities such as lobbying, holding political office, or working as a policy analyst. *Mezzo* practice falls between micro and macro levels of practice. Social workers engaged in mezzo practice work primarily with groups, in either direct or indirect practice situations. In some cases, mezzo practice involves social workers providing direct services to a group of individual clients, couples, and/or families. In other instances, mezzo practice involves social workers interacting with groups to administer programs or improve communities and organizations.

Identifying the level of practice is a primary factor when describing a field of practice. The reality for most social workers, however, is that they take positions that may emphasize one level, but require work at the other levels as well. For instance, social workers providing direct services to children and families may realize that their agency needs to make a few changes to improve services. Recommending and implementing the changes will likely require social workers who are prepared to engage in mezzo and macro practice.

The Population(s) Served

The target population receiving services is another factor to consider when describing social work practice. Social work practice usually takes place in programs that serve one or more populations. Students can use the fourteen dimensions of diversity (see figure 11.1) to describe population groups and make a distinction between different fields of practice. For example, social workers may practice in agencies that serve young adults with small children, adult refugees, or adolescents with physical or emotional disabilities. As with levels of practice, social work positions may emphasize a certain population group but require social workers that are capable of engaging in practice with multiple populations to provide effective services. For instance, social workers providing counseling to adolescent girls may need to interact with parents, grandparents, teachers, and other helping professionals.

The Areas of Practice

Social workers use their knowledge, values, and skills to help clients address different types of problems. Although it is nearly impossible to list all of the reasons clients seek assistance, a broad system for classifying different areas of practice is helpful for introducing students to what social workers do. NASW identifies thirteen broad areas of practice (NASW, 2013): adolescent health; aging; behavioral health; bereavement/end-of-life care; children, youth, and families; clinical social work; diversity and equity; health; HIV/AIDS; international; peace and social justice; school social work; and violence. Other common areas for students to consider include child welfare, substance abuse and mental health, social work with persons with disabilities, forensic social work, social work with military families, social work with immigrants and refugees, and policy. Subspecialty areas of practice exist within each of the broad categories. The categories also tend to overlap. Furthermore, social workers may practice in positions that encompass more than one area of practice.

The Settings for Practice

Considering organizational and community context is also important when describing different fields of social work practice. As a case in point, social workers from two agencies can share similar job descriptions. The unique organizational cultures in each agency, however, can significantly influence the actual work that happens in each setting. For instance, the daily experiences of a social worker at a DCFS in a large metropolitan city will be quite different from the experiences of a social worker at a DCFS in a small rural community. In the same way, the daily experiences of a social worker providing substance abuse counseling to clients involuntarily committed to an in-patient hospital unit will be quite different from a social worker providing substance abuse counseling to clients seeking help in a private counseling practice.

There are several ways for students to describe different practice settings. Students can consider the type of organization, such as a hospital, a mental health center, a home health agency, a correctional facility, a school, a marriage and family clinic, a corporation, a children's home, a group home, or an assisted living center. They also can consider the size of the agency, the characteristics of the community where the agency is located, and whether the agency is for-profit, nonprofit, secular, or religiously affiliated. We encourage students to consider any factor that will help them understand and appreciate the context of different practice settings.

APPLYING THE FRAMEWORK FOR EXPLORING FIELDS OF PRACTICE

The case vignettes throughout the book provide students with the opportunity to describe different fields of practice. Consider the case vignettes from chapter 2, for instance. Recall that Ian Hawthorne (case vignette 2.1) is the mentorship coordinator for Alberta Children and Youth Services. Using the four factors, we might describe his practice as follows:

• Level of practice: The level of practice is primarily micro because he engages directly with youth and potential mentors. There is some mezzo and macro because he facilitates a monthly partnership meeting and serves as the liaison between the children and the agencies and business representatives.

• Population(s) served: Adolescents.

• Area of practice: Children and youth services in Alberta, as indicated by the name of the agency.

• Practice setting: Large government-supported social service agency located in Alberta Province.

Now consider the case of Sarah Ormsby (case vignette 2.2). Sarah is a social services director for a children's home in Tamil Nadu, India. Using the four factors, we might describe her practice as follows:

• Level of practice: Macro, because she spends most of her time planning and overseeing services provided to the children.

• Population(s) served: Children.

• Area of practice: Her area of practice could be described as international social work, administration, and child welfare (poverty).

• Practice setting: Residential Children's Home in the city of Tirunelveli, a large prosperous city in the region of Tamil Nadu, India.

Dustin Jordan (from case vignette 2.3) worked on a multidisciplinary team as a social worker in the homeless program at the VA Medical Center in Oklahoma City. We might describe his practice as follows:

• Level of practice: Micro, because he spends most of his time engaging in helping relationships with veterans who are homeless.

• Population(s) served: Adult veterans of military service.

• Area of practice: Military social work, poverty, homelessness.

• Practice setting: A large VA medical center; and other places he meets with veterans in the community, such as homeless shelters, food banks, parks, and so on.

Now we encourage students to use exercise 14.1 to explore the fields of practice for the other case vignettes.

Exercise 14.1. Exploring the Fields of Practice for the Case Vignettes

Case Vignette	Level of Practice	Population(s) Served	Area of Practice	Practice Setting
2.1. Ian Hawthorne	Micro (Mezzo and Macro)	Adolescents	Children and youth services	Large social service agency, government supported
2.2. Sarah Ormsby	Macro	Children	International, administration, child welfare, poverty	Residential children's home in Tamil Nadu, India
2.3. Dustin Jordan	Micro	Adult Veterans	Military, poverty, homelessness	Large VA medical center, homeless shelters, food banks, parks, etc.

Case Vignette	Level of Practice	Population(s) Served	Area of Practice	Practice Setting
3.1. Stacy Lynn				
3.2. Stan Harris				
3.3. Doris Lieberman				
4.1. Teresa Rogers				
4.2. Nicole Tanbaum				
4.3. Arnold Young				
5.1. Jeremy Williams				
5.2. Kristen Lancaster				
5.3. Courtney Whitt				
8.1. Camesha Talbert				
8.2. Jennifer Ibarra				

Case Vignette	Level of Practice	Population(s) Served	Area of Practice	Practice Setting
8.3. Cathy Jennings				
8.4. Jordan Zillner				
9.1. Violet Scott				
9.2. Dustin Sheldon				
9.3. Teresa Brown				
11.1. Nelson Huff				
11.2. Julie Shelton				
11.3. Cooper Fletcher				
13.1. Insoo Park				
13.2. Lauren Ainsworth				
13.3. Martin Prescott				

FINAL THOUGHTS

Finishing a course that gives an introduction to social work can be a special time for students. At this point, we suspect students have more clarity about whether a career in social work is what they want to pursue. Our intention all along was to provide students with a realistic account of social work as one of the most rewarding and challenging professions where our identity and purpose—*why we do*—always informs the methods of practice—*what we do*. We welcome students ready to make the commitment to become competent social workers. We also hope students choosing a different career path have a new appreciation for our profession.

DISCUSSION QUESTIONS

In this final set of discussion questions, we ask that you again engage in self-reflection as you think back on all that you have read and learned in this introduction to the field of social work.

1. Which aspects of the social work profession are particularly attractive to you?
2. Which aspects of the social work profession invoke discomfort for you?
3. What strengths do you possess that you think would be well suited to the social work profession?
4. What areas do you think you would need to improve on to be a competent social work practitioner?
5. How well do your personal values and beliefs mesh with the professional values and ethics of the social work profession as espoused in this text and in the NASW Code of Ethics?
6. If there are places where your personal values and beliefs seem to clash with social work values, principles, and ethics, how do

you plan to address those issues to ensure that you become a competent social work practitioner? For instance, you might discuss those issues with your instructor.

7. Is social work the career for you?

REFERENCE

The National Association of Social Workers (NASW). (2013). *Areas of practice*. Retrieved from http://www.socialworkers.org/practice/default.asp

Index

About the Authors

Michael E. Sherr, PhD, LCSW, is professor and department head of social work at the University of Tennessee Chattanooga. He also serves as a commissioner for the Commission on Education Policy for the Council on Social Work Education. Professor Sherr is an internationally recognized scholar with more than fifty publications, including two other books, on several areas of research and scholarship. In 2010, the University of Hong Kong awarded Professor Sherr the international Young Scholars Award for his research.

Johnny M. Jones, PhD, is assistant professor of social work at Baylor University. Previously on faculty at the University of South Carolina, he acted as interim director of The Center for Child and Family Studies, a research and training center within the College of Social Work. He is also former director of the South Carolina Professional Development Consortium, which includes all of the accredited social work programs in the state of South Carolina.